Stronger, Surer, Bolder

Stronger, Surer, Bolder

Ruth Nita Barrow

Social Change and International Development

Edited by

Eudine Barriteau

and

Alan Cobley

CENTRE FOR GENDER AND DEVELOPMENT STUDIES, CAVE HILL

and

UNIVERSITY OF THE WEST INDIES PRESS

Barbados • Jamaica • Trinidad and Tobago

University of the West Indies Press
1A Aqueduct Flats Mona
Kingston 7 Jamaica

05 04 03 02 01 5 4 3 2 1

CATALOGUING IN PUBLICATION DATA

Stronger, surer, bolder : Ruth Nita Barrow : social change and
international development / edited by Eudine Barriteau and Alan Cobley.
p. cm.
Includes bibliographical references.
ISBN 13: 978-976-640-101-6

1. Barrow, Nita, Dame. 2. Women in public life – Barbados. 3. Leadership in women – Barbados. 4. Women in development – Barbados. I. Barriteau, Eudine. II. Cobley, Alan.
III. Title: Dame Nita Barrow.

F2041.B316 S87 2001 972.981

Dedicated

to

honouring the memory

of Ruth Nita Barrow

1915–1995

and to the members of the

Barrow family, especially

Sybil Barrow

Contents

Part IV Citizen and State Diplomacy

Part V International Leadership, International Service

Tables

Foreword

Who was this woman, Ruth Nita Barrow, who so successfully and majestically strode the international, regional, and national stages with such confidence, dignity, and power? She could have been the woman whom Maya Angelou had in mind when she wrote:

> Women should be tough, tender, laugh as much as possible, and live long lives. The struggle for equality continues unabated, and the woman warrior who is armed with wit and courage will be among the first to celebrate victory. (Angelou 1994: 7)

Or, she could have been the person whom Pamela Mordecai had in mind when she wrote:

> And must I cede
> these expectations, Lord?
> I still think
> if my hand open wide enough
> it will catch the wind.
> (Mordecai 1989: 36)

Or, maybe she was the unpretentious, laughing, mother-figure portrayed by Kamau Brathwaite:

> since this was not yr style
> to be not ponderous or burdensome
> or overbearing proud even w/yr large, yr heavy, even w/yr Dame
>
> but to keep flowing w/the laughter, w/the water, like the silver blue
> unborrowed moonlight, like clear weather
> like the fantastic hats you sometimes wear
> like the patronal motherhood you bring this nation like kukoo.
> (Brathwaite 1996: 9)

Or, maybe she was none of those things, but simply a woman who was blessed with a multitude of gifts and talents, which she sought to use for the betterment of her fellow human being. The articles in this collection seek to reflect the wide range of issues that attracted her attention and dedicated action – the church, nursing and public health, women, youth, the environment, apartheid, adult education, the United Nations. Involvement in any one of these can, and frequently does, represent the entire career of a single individual. Yet this remarkable woman managed to combine all of them in her career and, in the process, to engineer significant changes to key institutions associated with every one of them. How did she do this? What perspectives did she bring to each of these issues? What elements shaped those perspectives? How did she manage her career? What can we learn from her?

The official biography by Woodie Blackman (1995) provides tantalizing glimpses into some of the answers. This collection attempts to take the analysis a step further by exploring the processes that an outstanding Caribbean woman has used to generate significant social change and bring a different world view to the development agenda of the region and, indeed, of the world. The collection is the first in a series intended to be part of an ongoing project entitled *Caribbean Women Catalysts for Change* being spearheaded by the Centre for Gender and Development Studies, University of the West Indies, Cave Hill, Barbados. The centre is an appropriate location for the genesis of such a project, embracing as it does the concepts of region, nation, women, gender all concepts with which Dame Nita empathized and that she fully embraced in her work. She brought to these concepts a kind of leadership that was always refreshing in its originality, encompassing in its reach and productive in its impact.

The United Nations Development Fund for Women (UNIFEM) is pleased to have been associated with this project at various stages of its formulation and implementation, not only because of the focus on Dame Nita, but also because the issue of leadership constitutes one of the key thematic areas of the UNIFEM programme framework. By applying the strategies of advocacy, the nurturing of partnerships, supporting pilot initiatives, extracting and sharing lessons gleaned from our experiences, UNIFEM has been moving towards the ideal of becoming a knowledge-based institution. Partnership with the Centre for Gender and Development Studies therefore allows us to move a little further along in the journey towards this ideal.

The rapidly changing social, economic, and political landscape of the global community, as it affects the regional, national, community and household levels, persuades us that a new kind of leadership is required. It is a leadership that begins with transformation at the individual level and leads to the redefinition of gender and power relations, in a process that fundamentally changes the structures, organizing principles, and operational practices of institutions and society. It is a leadership that is technically competent, politically aware, and culturally sensitive. It is also a leadership that has a passion for justice and that is concerned with caring, non-violence, the preservation of human dignity, and cooperation. It is a leadership that is grounded in the principles and values of genuine democracy. At UNIFEM we call it transformational leadership.

In the Caribbean, we recognize that there have been examples of such leadership in virtually all areas of endeavour throughout our history, but that perhaps it was never named. We also recognize that among such leaders are to be found many women whose contributions have gone unrecognized, unsung, unrewarded, and that even where their contribution has been acknowledged, it has not been documented. For this reason, UNIFEM welcomes the project and this inaugural collection as a step towards filling a critical unmet need for recognition and valuation of the contribution of Caribbean women to significant social change.

It is here that this collection can make a useful contribution. Each of the articles speaks to a different aspect of Dame Nita's concept and practice of leadership. Here was a woman who was a nurse, non-governmental organization activist, a tireless campaigner for the rights of women, the quintessential diplomat, and a lifelong friend. Most of all, here was a woman who was a wise and skilful leader whose deep spiritual strength and humanitarian principles enabled her to institute fundamental change to key institutions at the national, regional, and international levels. She did so, not only by virtue of her undoubted intellectual and organizational skills, but also by her ability to inject her own values and standards into the norms and values of the organizations with which she was associated. Her capacity to care and to enjoy people was the hallmark of her life, and these qualities came to characterize those organizations that experienced her leadership.

Was this unique to her or is it typical of good leaders? Was her leadership a gendered one or was it simply hers? The essays in this collection help to identify some basic principles that underpinned Dame Nita's approach to leadership. They tell stories of visioning the future; careful preparation and planning; positive action; lack of dogma; clarity of argument; insistence on communication; counselling; networking; respect for all views, cultures, and peoples; fostering of collaboration; and empowerment of others. Throughout, there is a sense of commitment to service, integrity and courage. But perhaps the most important principle that fuelled all of this was her commitment to the promotion of human rights of all persons, regardless of race, class, gender, or cultural difference. This was a powerful moral position that she acquired from an early age in her family and church. She firmly believed in a Supreme Being who is everywhere, not in any one religion or one church, and who provides guidance for everyone throughout our lives. She believed that without a rooting in some Being greater than ourselves, "we are almost rudderless". Thus, her adherence to the principle of universal human rights came primarily from her own personal creed for living.

Human rights also provides the framework for the many international instruments, conventions, declarations, and programmes of action to which the international community has committed in the quest for gender equality. One of the lessons that women have learnt is that their interests, needs, and rights are not automatically recognized or guaranteed simply because they are enshrined in various international instruments. Rather, they have to know them, articulate them, and learn how to protect them and what redress is available in case of denial or violation. Making such information available to women is a major contribution to the empowerment of women. Dame Nita understood this, and so empowerment was a standard item in her arsenal of leadership tools. She felt a need for greater numbers of women to agitate more effectively for greater involvement in decision making, in whatever area, and that more needed to be done to forge alliances with men in this quest. She herself never lost an opportunity to ensure male support for her own initiatives and their involvement in whatever success those initiatives produced. But she always made sure that she made the decisions. This apparently simple strategy worked very well for her and could presumably work just as well for women in decision-making positions today, although the circumstances may not be as receptive as in her day.

A final major question often asked with respect to Dame Nita's achievements is: How did she manage to succeed, particularly at the international level, at precisely the time when the boundaries between North and South were solidifying? We have already alluded to that part of the answer which rests with her own beliefs. But a role must be assigned to her upbringing – the era, the class, the socioeconomic context, the ideology of the times, her family ideals and traditions – all of which must have shaped her personality in a particular way. She was a single woman with no children, who presumably had the freedom and flexibility to follow her interests and ambitions, hone her skills, and maintain her personal contacts in a way that a married mother could not. But most of all, it was her awareness of her own self-worth, as described in a quotation cited by Kathleen Drayton in this collection, "You have to believe in yourself, but without arrogance . . . The security I am talking about comes from inside."

And so, while these essays address some of the critical issues that her stewardship exposed on a variety of levels, they also point to the importance of leadership, an area in which this region seems to be experiencing a crisis. In its report *Time for Action* (1992), the West Indies Commission, of which Dame Nita was the Patron, drew attention to what was described as "deep anxieties about the quality of governance", which it discovered during its visits and consultations. This in effect referred to a crisis in political leadership throughout the region. Similar crises may be found in other areas of regional life. One example is the women's movement of the region. Dame Nita was an ardent supporter of the advancement of women, which she described as "the most political of all issues". She saw clearly that all of the major social, political, and economic issues facing the international community could be more effectively understood and addressed if seen through the lens of women and gender. To this end, she avidly supported the initiatives of women's groups throughout the region, in particular the YWCA, but always stressed the need to recognize that women were not the only ones with problems in the society. Yet today, a male-inspired debate about the so-called marginalization of men has assumed significant proportions, fuelling a thinly veiled male backlash against the progress of women. This threatens to minimize the issues promoted by the women's movement and to undermine some of the real gains that women of this region have achieved over the past two or three decades. Somehow, the women's movement seems unable to respond vigorously to the challenge, reflecting, perhaps, a reversal of the ideals that Dame Nita embodied and a crisis in the leadership in an important area of social development in the region.

Other examples also exist, each simultaneously reflecting a reversal of an initiative, idea, or approach of hers and a crisis in the leadership of the relevant institution. Many of these examples represent not so much a rejection of enlightened change as a quest for power and strengthening of power bases.

They also represent a downplaying of, or perhaps an inability to recognize, the amount of nurturing that is required to ensure the maintenance of enterprising and reformative changes. They may also reflect an unwillingness to commit to long-term processes that require constant vigilance, time, and energy and that yield only slow incremental changes. Short-term quick fixes do tend to shore up power, whereas the longer-term processes may serve to dilute power.

Ultimately the question is: Power for what purpose? The essays in this collection demonstrate that Dame Nita was a leader, that she was not hesitant in using her power and authority to achieve organizational goals, but that she preferred to use her influence to empower others rather than to apply direct power. In the final analysis, her way turned out to be the greater power.

Joycelin Massiah
Regional Programme Director
UNIFEM Caribbean

Acknowledgments

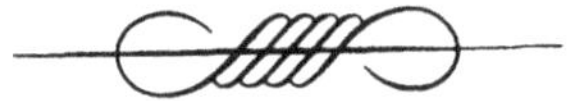

This book is the first major output of the project "Caribbean Women: Catalysts for Change", and its publication is due to the efforts of many women and men who gave generously of their time and energy to make it happen. It would be impossible to thank them all individually. However, we would like to express special thanks to a number of people who made special contributions to this endeavour. First, we would like to thank Connie Sutton, professor of anthropology at New York University who nurtured the idea of a study of the Caribbean women of Nita Barrow's generation who, she perceived, were making a disproportionately large contribution to international debates on women and development issues. How was it that women from such "tiny countries" could deliver such penetrating insights and possess such sweeping, global visions? It was in an effort to explore this seeming paradox that the original project was conceived.

Special mention must also be made of the members of the Women and Development Studies (WDS) group at the University of the West Indies, Cave Hill, Barbados, who were very receptive to and supportive of the project from the time it was first discussed in 1993. In fact, most of the members of the research team that was formed subsequently were drawn from the WDS group. The project also benefited greatly from the guidance of the overview committee, comprising Eudine Barriteau, Hilary Beckles and Joycelin Massiah. Alan Cobley played a key role as manager of the Dame Nita Barrow Project. Thanks also to the individual contributors to this volume, who made our task as editors a relatively easy one. The staff of the Centre for Gender and Development Studies as Cave Hill worked tirelessly over the long period required to take this project from research to publication. Our thanks go to Sharon Taylor, Karen Forde-Walcott, Rhonda Walcott, Elizabeth Wilson-Ciconte, Sherry Asgill, Veronica Jones, Jacqueline Morris, Carmen Hutchinson, Deborah Deane, and Olivia Birch for all their efforts.

In compiling the data on which this work was based, the research team was able to call upon many friends, colleagues, and acquaintances of Nita Barrow for interviews and advice. Among those who graciously granted formal interviews were Carmen Lusan, Carol Jacobs, Sir Kenneth Stuart, Ena Walters and Archbishop Ted Scott. Patricia Layne, secretary to Dame Nita Barrow during her time as governor general of Barbados, took our many phone calls and facilitated our access to Government House on numerous occasions with unfailing courtesy.

Finally, and most especially, we wish to place on record our most sincere thanks to Sybil Barrow and other members of the Barrow family for all their support, understanding, and encouragement as this work was taking shape.

Any failings or shortcomings that remain in this book after so extensive a collaborative effort are, of course, our own.

Abbreviations

ALECSO	Arab League Educational Cultural and Scientific Organization
ANC	African National Congress
BRNA	Barbados Registered Nurses Association
CANARI	Caribbean Natural Resources Institute
CARICOM	Caribbean Common Market, Caribbean Community
CDWA	Colonial Development and Welfare Act
CDWC	Colonial Development and Welfare Corporation
CGDS	Centre for Gender and Development Studies
CMC	Christian Medical Commission
CNO	Caribbean Nurses Organization
COWAN	Country Women Association of Nigeria
DAWN	Development Alternatives for Women of a New Era
EPG	(Commonwealth) Eminent Persons Group
FAO	Food and Agriculture Organization
GAD	Gender and Development
GDP	Gross domestic product
GNP	Gross national product
ICAE	International Council for Adult Education
ICPD	International Conference on Population and Development
IMF	International Monetary Fund
IWTC	International Women's Tribune Centre
JRNA	Jamaica Registered Nurses Association
KPH	Kingston Public Hospital
NCIH	National Council for International Health
NFLS	Nairobi Forward Looking Strategies
NGO	Non-governmental organization
ODA	Official Development Assistance
OECS	Organization of Eastern Caribbean States
PAC	Pan-Africanist Congress
PAHO	Pan American Health Organization

SIDS	Sustainable Development for Small Island States
UCHWI	University College Hospital of the West Indies
UNCED	United Nations Conference on Environment and Development
UNDP	United Nations Development Program
UNICEF	United Nations Children's Education Fund
UNIFEM	United Nations Development Fund for Women
USAID	United States Agency for International Development
UWI	University of the West Indies
WAD	Women and Development
WAND	Women and Development Unit
WCC	World Council of Churches
WDS	Women and Development Studies Group
WHO	World Health Organization
WICP	Women in the Caribbean Project
WID	Women in Development
WILPF	Women's International League for Peace and Freedom
WIWF	West Indian Welfare Fund
YWCA	Young Women's Christian Association

PART ONE

Introduction: Caribbean Women Creating Change

Chapter One

Before WID, Beyond GAD:
Caribbean Women Creating Change

[Eudine Barriteau]

Research on Third World women was mainly of external origin and had little effect on scholarship or on public policy but this is changing.

– Lucille Mathurin Mair

It is hoped however that these shared histories of our fore mothers and other forerunners can serve to open up the possibilities of the potential of Caribbean women to change their own lives and that of their people, in this way transforming the existing exploitative relations among human beings in Caribbean society.

– Rhoda Reddock

In January 1994 a research team assembled by the Centre for Gender and Development Studies at the University of the West Indies, Cave Hill campus, in Barbados, began a series of taped interviews with Dame Nita Barrow, then governor general of Barbados.[1] By the time of her death on 19 December 1995 the team had completed over forty hours of audio-taped interviews and had been allowed generous access to her personal and public papers spanning her sixty years of regional and international service.[2] The ten essays collected here are a product of that collaboration.

The extensive literature on women in the global South[3] is dominated by a focus on what is known as the Women in Development (WID) discourse.[4] To set this edited collection in proper context, therefore, and before discussing more fully its range and scope, it is necessary to begin by briefly reviewing the historical development of the WID discourse and to consider the growing critique of that discourse of which this collection is part.

A number of interrelated events generated the tendency to understand contemporary women's lives through the lens of the WID discourse. In 1970 Ester Boserup published *Women's Role in Economic Development*, which focused international attention on conditions affecting women's lives in the South. Boserup's work suggests that "many development projects rather than improving the lives of Third World women had deprived them of economic opportunities and status" (Parpart and Marchand 1995: 13). Boserup systematically delineated the sexual[5] division of labour that existed in agrarian economies and the disadvantages women experienced as a result. Although her work has been criticized for oversimplifying the nature of women's work and role, it constitutes a watershed by "focusing scholarly attention on the differential impact by gender on development and modernization strategies" (Rathgeber 1990: 490–95).

The second major factor contributing to the dominance of the WID focus on women's lives in the South is less well known but has been very influential. In 1973 the Percy Amendment to the US Foreign Assistance Act of 1961 advised that USAID programmes should be administered so as to:

> give particular attention to those programs, projects and activities which tend to integrate women into the economies of foreign countries thus improving their status and assisting the total development effort. (USAID 1978, also quoted in Charlton 1984: 202)

For developing countries, this meant that they might not qualify for development aid unless their governmental or bureaucratic structures included an office devoted to women in development. USAID's WID office was created and a growth industry of international, regional, and local WID experts and consultants was born.

In 1975 the United Nations held the First World Conference on Women in Mexico and, in 1976, the world body created the Voluntary Fund for Women which became the United Nations Development Fund for Women (UNIFEM) in 1985 (Karl 1995: 12). UNIFEM provides financial, technical, and cooperative support to develop and strengthen regional, international, and interorganizational programmes on women.

These changes do represent significant advances in countries grappling with issues of justice, social equity, and change. The combined effects of these pivotal developments generated women's bureaux, programmes with a focus on women and/or gender issues, and increased recognition by governments that they had not examined the human rights of women nor the adverse conditions under which the majority of women exist.

However, there have been unfortunate and perhaps unintended by-products of the international attention given to women and development in Southern countries. The cumulative effects of these occurrences contributed to producing a body of research and policies on women in "developing countries" which until recently excluded the contributions and perspectives of feminists from the South (Jayawardena 1986; Sen and Grown 1987; Wieringa 1990). The contributions of outstanding women who have acted as catalysts for change in the South have either been lost or obscured.

Feminists, WID practitioners, policy analysts and international development institutions have devised new conceptual frameworks, terminologies, strategies, and development approaches to examine, rethink, plan for, and critique women's lives in the South (Papanek 1977; World Bank 1979, 1989, 1990; Charlton 1984; Beneria and Sen 1981; Overholt et al. 1985; Sen and Grown 1987; Parpart 1989, 1993; Tinker 1990; Beckley 1989; Goetz 1988; Moser 1989, 1993; Rathgeber 1990; Momsen 1991; Marchand and Parpart 1995).[6]

This intensive focus defined the parameters of the WID approach. The early analysis examined the extent to which women had been excluded from models of economic development and devised strategies to ensure that subsequent development policy included women. The subsequent policy measures either devised new approaches for incorporating women into development or warn of the adverse impact of development as defined (Goetz 1988; Rathgeber 1990; Tinker and Bramsen 1976). This focus creates the idea that all the multiple issues and subjectivities of women's lives could be captured in the ideological, material, and chronological points of departure demarcated by Boserup's work, the Percy Amendment, and the UN initiatives.

This locus has reduced an understanding of women's lives to work and has spawned an extensive identification of women's work with subsistence or reproduction (Barriteau 1994). Boserup's study set the stage for filtering women's lives in the South through the lens of work, whether defined as production, reproduction, or subsistence. It was as if the only way to address the complex subjectivities of the life of the Third World woman was to examine how she interacted with the economy. It suggests that all the nuances, all the complexities, and the multiple experiences of women in the South could be contained in where women fit or do not fit in the ongoing permutations of the economistic development debate.[7]

From the perspective of feminist politics interested in developing transformative strategies, this approach minimizes the significance of the processes that Caribbean and other Southern women have used to deal with constantly mutating relations of domination. Methodologically, it obscures the extent to which women have become involved in other sectors of the public domain, are redefining their gender identities, while grappling with changing gender relations in the private. Despite the disproportionate focus on work, very little is known about women's experiences in occupations such as agricultural labourers, nursing, and administrative support staff. Women's increasing refusal to tolerate a range of acts of abuse and violence is inadequately examined under the WID approach.

The WID discourse has paid insufficient attention to the diverse ways women have acted and continue to act to spearhead social change in Southern societies. The WID focus constructs a Caribbean woman whose agency is suspect. It minimizes heterogeneity, difference, and diversity among women and in women's lives. The discourse sustains a false notion of homogeneity and victimhood that is not borne out by the complex and competing realities in the Caribbean (Barriteau 1994: 291; Mohammed 1994; Baksh-Sooden 1994).

Researching Caribbean Women as Catalysts for Change

In 1993 the Cave Hill campus unit of the Centre for Gender and Development Studies of the University of the West Indies, and the Women and Development Studies Group (WDS), conceptualized a research project, "Caribbean Women Catalysts for Change".[8] Lucille Mair notes that research on Third World women was mainly of external origin and had little effect on scholarship or on public policy, but she sees this situation as changing. This project is part of that change. The project is committed to documenting, analysing, and disseminating – at both the popular and academic level – the contributions of Caribbean women who influenced the altering of social and economic life within their societies. This publication builds on the database established by the WICP project and the publications produced from the inaugural seminars of the Women and Development Studies Project (Mohammed and Shepherd 1987; Leo-Rhynie, Bailey and Barrow 1997).

Geeta Chowdhry describes this perspective as "Third World Women's Feminism: the Empowerment Approach" (Chowdhry 1995: 36). Chowdhry drawing on Caroline Moser's earlier analysis states this perspective is influenced more by the feminist writings and grassroots organizations of "Third World women" and less on the research of "First World women" (Chowdhry 1995: 36; Moser 1991: 106).[9] Not withstanding the dissatisfaction with the hierarchies implied in the terms First and Third World women, the project provides the experiences of Caribbean women who have influenced change in our societies. Our goal is to examine and locate the activities of outstanding Caribbean women in six overlapping arenas of the contemporary public domain. These areas are:

- regional and international development
- politics and political participation
- women organizing and the women's movement
- trade unionism
- education
- agriculture and food production[10]

Our interest is in women who have broken new ground in these areas. CGDS has a responsibility to discover what these women have done. We need to understand and theorize the processes women use to alter conventional practices, subvert barriers to women's participation, and force societal changes that produce benefits for women as well as a more just society.

This volume of essays therefore originates in an explicit political project. We want to contribute to the growing literature that testifies that women in developing countries were working to transform their societies before the WID discourse discovered women in the South. In this project, we deliberately avoid filtering women's lives through the lens of women's engagement or contestations with economistic models of development. Instead, we focus on how women have sought to redefine social, economic, and political relations and in the process generate a different understanding of development.

Many feminists have attempted to broaden our understanding of women's lives in the South beyond a mapping on the development grid (Jayawardena 1986; Mernissi 1975; Mbiliniyi 1989; Mohanty, Russo and Torres 1991; Momsen 1993; Nzomo 1992, 1993; Wieringa 1995). In the Caribbean research by Erna Brodber (1986), Rhoda Reddock (1988, 1994); Joan French (1995) and Linnette Vassell (1995), among others, have helped to correct distortions and flesh out other realities about Caribbean women. We continue in that vein.

Nita Barrow and Regional and International Change

Ana Maria Brasileiro and Karen Judd described Nita Barrow as an enlightened leader who provided an important role model for other women (Brasileiro and Judd 1996: 8). In dedicating its publication, *Women's Leadership in a Changing World* to Barrow, UNIFEM remarked, "She taught us about the essential qualities of leadership that make transformation and empowerment possible" (Brasileiro 1996). A comprehensive biography of Nita Barrow by Francis Blackman was published in 1995. While it applauds the international recognition accorded, and the laudatory tributes that have been paid, to Nita Barrow, CGDS Cave Hill publishes this volume of essays for very different reasons.

In the initial meeting of the CGDS and the WDS group to discuss the first phase of the project, we selected Barrow as the woman whose public service would be documented and analysed in relation to influencing social change, and regional and international developments. Nita Barrow kept coming to the fore every time we discussed Caribbean women who have made extraordinary contributions regionally and internationally.

For example, Nita Barrow's involvement with women and leadership became international, well-publicized knowledge in 1985 when she convened the non-governmental organizations' meeting, Forum '85, held in conjunction with the UN World Conference to Review the Decade for Women in Nairobi, Kenya. Yet this was merely the latest stage in a career encompassing decades of development work with women, the character and results of which have never been properly analysed, documented, or disseminated. A synopsis of her developmental work includes:

- the development and institutionalization of advanced nursing education at the University of the West Indies

- pioneering primary and participatory health care in eighty-eight developing countries through the World Council of Churches and the World Health Organization
- Strengthening and advancing the mechanisms for the recognition of NGOs as equal partners at the United Nations
- using the church as an agent for social change
- advancing the scope, relevance and impact of citizen diplomacy as a member of the Eminent Persons Group (EPG) to South Africa[11]
- expanding and advancing the role of NGOs in international relations and international development

Arising from our interviews with Nita Barrow in 1995, there were many questions begging further exploration. How could a black woman from a Caribbean micro-state embark on such an international career, emerging at a time when racism, colonialism, and patriarchy imposed even more rigid boundaries on the daily existence of women and men in the South? What were the features of the colonial Caribbean political economy that propelled her forward or impeded her? How did she manipulate the intersections of race, class, and gender to ensure she was always the best candidate for the next path-breaking position? How did Nita Barrow use a deep commitment to a sense of West Indian sovereignty and a profound respect for indigenous practices to foster self-reliance and self-respect?

There is no question that Nita Barrow was an outstanding leader; but what motivations drove this woman? Why was she able to achieve the successes she did? She also met with failure at times in her career; what do we know of these failures and the reasons for them? In the majority of tributes paid to Nita Barrow since her death, there is a sense of awe, reverence, and even deification of this exceptional woman; but what were her political ambitions and how were they channelled? What are the lessons and strategies for women leaders, women's organizations, and Caribbean women and men?

Alan Cobley and I made no attempt to insist on a particular analytical or theoretical approach to examining the public life of Nita Barrow. We believe that to insist on a particular approach would introduce closure and would perhaps overshadow the different processes Barrow used in the organization and delivery of her public service. Instead, the coherence in these essays centre on this subject; how a Caribbean woman contributed to creating social change and shaping issues of development regionally and internationally.

Kathleen Drayton and Hilary Beckles explore the ideological, political, and social contexts that shaped early twentieth century Caribbean society and influenced Barrow's life. Many Caribbean women, including some who have been or are very active on issues affecting women's lives, are reluctant or have difficulty in describing themselves as feminists. The term has been exploited by the media and erroneously associated with only the sensationalized incidents of the Second Wave women's movement in North America and Europe. There are still other black women with a heightened consciousness of the oppressions black women experience but who prefer the term "womanist" created by Alice Walker, as constituting a fuller expression of black women's oppositional stance to sexism and exploitation. For those wary of the label, seeing only a derogatory, sensational, or exclusionary connotation, they either ignore or are unaware that feminism is a conscious, politicized commitment to exposing conditions and relations of domination in women's lives while actively seeking to change them.[12]

In chapter 2, Kathleen Drayton argues that although Nita Barrow never called herself a feminist, an analysis of her positions on many issues reveals a feminist consciousness. In chapter 4, Margaret Gill echoes this when she analyses Barrow's protest action at the Barbados General Hospital as indicative of a radical feminist consciousness. Drayton's assertions move away from the tendency to isolate individuals from the social context in which their ideas and agendas take shape. Drayton's premise is that only a woman who was driven by a belief in her own and women's equality could have accomplished so much in the context of a patriarchal, colonial, and at times racist, society.

Nita Barrow was undergoing basic nursing education at the Barbados General Hospital when the labour unrest and rebellions sweeping through the British Caribbean colonies in the 1930s descended upon Barbados. It was a period in which the traditional high unemployment in the colonies was exacerbated by the aftermath of the worldwide economic depression in the interwar years (Reddock 1988: 28). The intersections of racism and sexism in the class-bound, colonial Caribbean were palpable. There were very few jobs available to black women during that time. Colonial racist practices emphasized the hiring of fair-skinned or mulatto women in the few occupational outlets open to women in the private sector (Brodber 1986: 14). In the civil service and other sectors of the public space, institutionalized, patriarchal practices also meant a narrower range of occupations, less pay at the same level of employment, and severely constrained occupational mobility (Mayers 1995; French

1995; Henry-Wilson 1989). Amy Bailey, in giving the reasons for a women's conference in Jamaica in 1939, commented:

> We said, women should be inspectors of schools, they should be in universities, in the civil service; they should rise to be heads of departments. And all these things we brought to the attention of the public. (Brodber 1986: 9)

In chapter 3, Hilary Beckles dissects the social and political economy of this period to situate Nita Barrow's career in nursing. Beckles locates the latter at the intersection of the British government's reluctant acceptance of the need to improve public health and welfare in its neglected and now rebellious colonies, and Nita Barrow's determination and commitment to exploit one of the few career opportunities available to young, black, middle-class women.

As a significant source of skilled employment for working-class and lower-middle-class women, the political economy of nursing has not received adequate attention in terms of analysing women and work in the Caribbean. In fact, despite the extensive research performed on women and work in the Caribbean, none sought to problematize the experiences of women in nursing. In chapter 4, Margaret Gill examines social change and the politics of nursing during the period of Nita Barrow's active involvement in the nursing profession. Although she explores the role of Nita Barrow in nursing, Gill is careful not to assign to Barrow any singular, exclusive responsibility for improvements in the profession in the Caribbean. Her analysis assumes that Barrow could not have been a catalyst for change if nurses themselves were not, as a collective entity, ready and willing to bring about change.

In chapter 5, Sheila Stuart introduces a specific focus on the health areas to which Nita Barrow made significant contributions. Like Beckles, Stuart recognizes the limitations black women faced in colonial societies, but begins the process of documenting what Nita Barrow brought to the arena of health and development at the national/regional and global level. Both Gill and Staurt reinforce that Barrow's work in developing health care was devoted to consultation and participation and guided by a commitment to equity.

Janice Cumberbatch, in chapter 6, begins her analysis of Nita Barrow's involvement with environmental issues with a quotation from Barrow herself that immediately emphasizes one of the strategies she used most effectively in achieving her goals –*networking*. Numerous tributes following her death drew attention to her facility with this:

Nita
You have the greatest capacity for friendship of anyone we ever knew
We remember your very special black book of names and addresses
Held together with rubber bands and containing names of thousands of us
From literally every country in the world.
(Hall 1997)

Cumberbatch's analysis of Barrow's involvement with environmental issues underscores that Nita Barrow understood and practised the principles of communication as dialogue. In a quotation, Cumberbatch provides Barrow's philosophy on how to prevent stalled talks and non-action. Drawing on this philosophy Cumberbatch develops a blueprint for environmental management grounded in individual commitment and community involvement.

Barrow's involvement in international mediation began when she attended a World YWCA meeting and peace encounter in Lebanon in 1951. A concern with peacemaking and justice is a feature that characterizes her long tenure in the international community. In chapter 7, Alan Cobley contextualizes and analyses Barrow's contributions to the pioneering mission of the Commonwealth Eminent Persons Group to South Africa. Cobley argues that if Barrow had been nominated to satisfy the requirements of having a token woman, her ability to influence the process of mediation by filtering it through her "gendered experience" was not at all anticipated.

Cobley's work provides a comprehensive examination of Nita Barrow's contribution to this mission. He identifies and discusses the experience and insights that Barrow brought to the South African exercise in citizen diplomacy. His analysis forces us to consider two other issues from the perspective of gender: the underexplored role of women in international relations, especially international mediation and foreign policy, and women's leadership.

Women's work in the arena of international politics or foreign affairs is an area of Caribbean women's contributions that needs to be critically examined. Women have generally been ostracized from state centres of power and the agencies of foreign policy formation nearly everywhere (McGlen and Sarkees 1993: 2). In the postcolonial, independent Caribbean several women have been involved in international politics yet we do not have any assessments of their contributions.[13]

The years 1986 to 1990 marked the transition in Barrow's work from the global NGO community to the global political/governmental community. In

1986 she became Barbados' ambassador and permanent representative to the United Nations.

Marjorie Thorpe, a former ambassador to the United Nations on behalf of the Republic of Trinidad and Tobago, reveals a woman with a very politicized consciousness of how the international arena is dominated by a powerful handful of superpowers, often insensitive to the sovereign equality of micro-states. Nita Barrow's UN years provide clear insight into her political philosophy in ways her other areas of international service did not. She became a global leader in the international political arena and she accepted the responsibility of articulating the precarious positions of smaller powers among the world superpowers. As Marjorie Thorpe discloses, Barrow did not sidestep confronting the issues of racism, environmental degradation, and the vulnerability of small island states.

One of the goals of feminism is to transform the practices of power in the public domain. The phenomenon of leadership affords one of the more visible displays of the practices of power. Yet feminists harbour great ambivalence toward occupying positions of power and in exercising power (Pohlmann 1995). Max Weber refers to the structural power that comes from holding a formal, often hierarchical position in an organizational structure as "the power of office" (Ferguson 1984).

In chapter 9, Barriteau argues that Barrow harboured no ambivalence toward herself as a leader or her capacity to occupy positions of power and act decisively. Barriteau uses Nita Barrow's leadership of the World YWCA as a case study to explore the innovative leadership approach she brought to an international women's organization often perceived as traditional and conservative long after it had began to confront the complex issues of class and race. Using Barrow's experiences Barriteau indicates some observations to guide feminist leadership of non-governmental organizations.

In chapter 10, Budd Hall contributes an observation of Nita Barrow's influence on and leadership of the International Council for Adult Education (ICAE). During her eight-year tenure as president, he credits Barrow with strengthening the women's programme by building a network of women's activists working in the adult education movement and related organizations around the world. From Hall's comments, it is again apparent that Nita Barrow understood the dynamics of decisive leadership and was confident in her abilities to occupy and deploy institutional power.

Ultimately, Barrow's legacy to Caribbean women and men is a life of singular contributions in the public domain. Jeniphier Carnegie produces a selective curriculum vitae on Nita Barrow covering sixty years of service. This enables us to watch and chart the unfolding of a life dedicated to social change. What is immediately noticeable is how many of her international positions overlapped or ran concurrently.

These essays uncover many of the principles that brought Nita Barrow closer to the goals she set for herself and whatever organization she represented. The analyses reveal all these principles to be gender-neutral. What Nita Barrow accomplished can be achieved by other women and men willing to see these qualities not as grounded in a rigid understanding of appropriate female and male gender roles, but located in a conscious commitment to justice and equity. Her achievements underscore the critical significance of challenging fixed notions of gender identities so that a society can benefit from the contributions of all its citizens.

Ruth Nita Barrow was a very ambitious Caribbean woman, but she used the fruits of her ambition not for narrow individual gain, but for altering the processes of problem-solving and conflict resolution. A recurrent feature of her involvement in any endeavour was the continuous search for solutions. She understood and accepted that conflict would occur, but a major aspect of her legacy was finding a means of moving beyond what seemed like intractable problems. Her example teaches all students of social change and development that they must investigate the processes of problem solving if they are to rethink leadership models, organizational practices, and approaches to development in a meaningful way.

Notes

1. The project and research team comprised Eudine Barriteau, coordinator; Hilary Beckles; Alan Cobley, project manager; Janice Cumberbatch; Kathleen Drayton; Margaret Gill; Sheila Stuart; and Marjorie Thorpe.
2. Nita Barrow's papers are currently housed at the Centre for Gender and Development Studies of the University of the West Indies, Cave Hill. We await the formal handing over of the papers on the settlement of her estate, at which time the university will announce the establishment of the Dame Nita Barrow Women's Studies Collection.

3. I prefer the terms South and North to refer, respectively, to countries that were once colonized by European countries (and in the case of a minority, still are) and who were either force fed or willingly imbibed Westernization as development. By the North I mean the industrialized countries of the North Atlantic that were also former or current colonial powers. I find the terms "Third World", "developing", and "non-industrialized" problematic. I do not accept the embedded, pejorative connotations and hierarchical rankings they imply. However, I recognize that they are commonly used and will occasionally use them for variation.
4. Analytical approaches in this field have changed from its early formulation as Women in Development (WID), through Women and Development (WAD), to Gender and Development (GAD). However, beyond feminist critiques of this field what happens in women's bureaux throughout "developing countries" cannot be distinguished from the initial WID approach. For a clear delineation of the analytical distinctiveness of each approach see Eva Rathgeber (1990). For a critique of GAD strategies in the Commonwealth Caribbean, see Eudine Barriteau, *The Political Economy of Gender in the Twentieth Century Caribbean* (London and New York: Macmillan and St Martin's, 2001).
5. I prefer the use of "gendered" division of labour, but Boserup uses "sexual". Studies on the social relations of gender reveal that the divisions of labour that are supposed to originate in sexual/biological differences are in fact socially constructed and vary from society to society.
6. The literature in this field is very extensive. These citations are only a representative sample and are not intended to rank or slight any work by its exclusion.
7. I think the debate, criticisms, and alternative modelling are very necessary and should be continued. I am critical of the by-product that posits life in the South as women and work.
8. During the period in which women and development studies grew within the University of the West Indies, there have been two regional research projects on women in the Commonwealth Caribbean. The Women in the Caribbean Project (WICP) was the first multidisciplinary, regional project to explore the lives of Caribbean women. It contributed a two-volume collection of fourteen essays, numerous monographs, and established the benchline data on women in the contemporary Caribbean. An ongoing project, "Caribbean Women in Transition: A Research Programme on Women, Gender, and Caribbean Development", was formulated by the Women and Development Studies Groups. The Cave Hill project was conceived within the broad contexts of the latter's initiative to stimulate and coordinate research on the experiences and contributions of Caribbean women.
9. We make no attempt to reject the scholarly and analytical contributions of other feminists for a crude re-ordering of South over North. Instead, we want to add the work of Caribbean feminist scholars to the international body of feminist scholarship.

10. Caribbean and feminist historians are reclaiming women's past and forcing a reconceptualization of Caribbean historiography. Representative works include Mair 1974; Brereton 1988; Reddock 1984, 1994; Beckles 1988, 1989; Mohammed 1994; and Shepherd, Brereton and Bailey 1995.
11. For example, Dame Nita and the Commonwealth Eminent Persons Group's historic role as citizen diplomats preceded the activities of former US president Jimmy Carter by nearly ten years.
12. The means of exposing women's experiences of multiple relations of domination and the strategies to be employed to end these vary according to particular feminist orientations, analyses, practices, and visions. However, all feminists of whatever analytical or activist persuasion agree on the need for exposure and change of what is wrong for women. I deliberately avoid attaching feminist theoretical labels here because they emphasize analytical frameworks. Feminists agree that the organization of social life is unjust for women.
13. There are two women with historic links to the Women and Development Studies Programme and the Centre for Gender and Development Studies. They are Marjorie Thorpe, author of chapter 5 and former permanent representative and ambassador of the Republic of Trinidad and Tobago to the United Nations, and Lucille Mathurin Mair, former ambassador and permanent representative of Jamaica to the United Nations.

Part Two

A West Indian Consciousness, A Colonial Context

Chapter Two

A West Indian Feminist Consciousness

[Kathleen Drayton]

The meaning of the word "feminism" has changed over time although it has always involved the advocacy of equal rights for women. In recent times, a feminist is considered to be one who publicly acknowledges the oppression of women and is prepared to take conscious action to counter this oppression. "Feminism cannot be seen as a fixed ideology which developed in a particular country at a particular time. It is rather a form of consciousness and struggle of oppressed women throughout the world since their appropriation by men, ruling classes and patriarchal states" (Reddock 1984: 3–4).

Social conditions define the lives of women and consciousness is developed or learned from social experience. Our unique history, culture, and social organization have created the types of oppression and exploitation experienced by Caribbean women which have formed individual and collective consciousness and reality. This chapter was prompted by several conversations with Nita Barrow, as well as by statements found in some of her speeches and in the few notebooks that are available.[1] Barrow often talked of the social experiences that shaped her consciousness and contributed to her awareness of social injustice. Her comments and statements contribute to an understanding of how the feminist consciousness of this West Indian woman was formed. They also provide insight into how experience shapes consciousness and contributes to the development of the individual ideology that can influence the life's work of an individual.

Nita Barrow left her stamp on the twentieth century in which she lived and was one of the great West Indian women of this century. Her unassuming and open manner overlaid an impressive record of international achievement to improve the lives of women, and she was certainly one of the important international leaders of her time. In interviews, she identified the critical importance of experiences of her childhood and early upbringing, experiences in shaping her and this appeared in a 1993 speech:

> Bishop Barrow's deportation from St Croix created a single parent family, female headed household . . . It is as a result of this early conditioning . . . that I credit a deep and on-going interest in human rights, particularly the rights and interests of women. (Barrow 1993)

Barrow's reference is to her father's deportation from St Croix in the US Virgin Islands in 1922 for standing up for black workers' rights. Her mother, Mrs Ruth Barrow bought a house and remained in St Croix for four or five years longer with the Barrow children. While Barrow would only have been six years old in 1922 it is likely that the circumstances of her father's deportation would also have created early understandings of social discrimination and injustice.

When their mother decided to join their father in the United States, the children returned to Barbados in about 1926 to live with their maternal grandmother, Mrs Catherine O'Neal, who was also the mother of Charles Duncan O'Neal. Her grandmother was acknowledged by Barrow as another formative influence:

> My grandmother was very much a rebel herself. She had her own ideas. We didn't know it at the time, we just absorbed them. My grandmother raised us and she was quite an indomitable figure and she told us what to do – a very strict person . . . There were always standards which had to be observed. (Haniff 1988)

A third major influence in the shaping of Barrow's consciousness was her famous uncle, Dr Charles Duncan O'Neal, a socialist who became an elected member of the Barbados House of Assembly. He moved into his mother's house where he conducted his medical practice among the poor. It is likely that his work and ideas not only developed her understanding of injustice but contributed to her later understanding that health care was more than the treatment of sickness – it was itself part of the social and economic condition of the society. It can be argued that the experiences of her early years created a keen political awareness, although she never became directly involved in national party politics.

Barrow described the weekly correspondence that flowed between her parents in New York, herself, her siblings and Dr O'Neal in Barbados. She remembered the regular letter writing that she said he insisted on every Sunday. Unfortunately, this valuable correspondence was burned in 1942 by Barrow "in a clearing out of rubbish before I left for Trinidad for midwifery training".

Barrow entered her chosen profession – nursing – at a time when not only were the health professions firmly under the domination of men, but at a time when the hierarchical structures placed restrictions on the everyday lives of young nurses and used them as domestics. It was also a time when almost all senior positions in nursing in the West Indies were held by white expatriate women. As a young, black West Indian trainee nurse, Barrow would have experienced from her superiors, discrimination on grounds of sex, race, and class that would have taken no account of her social background. Her experiences as a nurse were obviously critical in shaping her awareness of women's oppression.

Barrow frequently referred to the organizations that were important in her life: nursing, the church, and the YWCA, "the organization, which after the church, has done so much for me" (Barrow 1973). As a young woman, Nita Barrow had recognized the importance of organizations, both in drawing together like-minded people with similar interests and goals and in creating the possibility for sustained collective effort to achieve goals. Her early involvement in organizations prepared her for later active leadership in the international struggle for human rights, which from 1976 had a major focus on gender.

Nita Barrow never called herself a feminist:

> I have not considered myself as a feminist leader. I have been a woman who by professional preparation as a nurse (mainly a woman's profession), involved in women's activities such as the YWCA locally, regionally and internationally [has] been involved in women's affairs. Through my church and the WCC's health care emphasis, seen the plight of women particularly in all parts of the world – naturally therefore issues and the concerns of women everywhere over the decade have been of primary interest. (Barrow 1985b)

Despite this assertion, an analysis of Nita Barrow's positions on many issues and her statements reveals a feminist consciousness. In an address made shortly after the successful meeting of non-governmental organizations known as Forum '85 (a meeting held in parallel with the third UN World Conference on Women in Nairobi in 1985, which was entitled the "World Conference to Review the Decade for Women"), Barrow referred to her perception of the oppression of women and to the care that must be taken in selecting strategies to counter the problem. She understood that just as women's oppression had taken different forms at different times and indifferent places, so the strategies and solutions used to address the problem would have to be varied: "There can be no one strategy – no simple alternative . . . although there are common roots to women's oppression and inequality, one woman's liberating truth can be another woman's destruction" (Barrow 1985a).

Feminists see gender as a central concept in the analysis of social phenomena and as essential to the removal of discrimination in society. They oppose the idea that women can simply be "integrated into development". Barrow very clearly shared this understanding. She recognized that the power structures themselves were discriminatory and thus simply to integrate women into the existing unjust structures would not remove discrimination. In 1986, when addressing the Committee of Experts that monitors the UN Convention on the Elimination of All Forms of Discrimination Against Women (CEDAW), she observed that while she supported "the full integration of women at all UN policy making levels, [she] hope[d] that this will not mean losing sight of *the real interest of women* . . ." (emphasis added). She added, "*the 'universal' similar experiences of women far outweigh their differences*" (Barrow 1986).

Another topic on which she frequently reflected and spoke was the difference in styles of participation and in styles of leadership between women and men. In one notebook we find, "Women's style of participation is different and therefore their difficulty in participating fully in institutions/organizations run by men" (Barbados n.d.b.). Elsewhere she said, "Male power is the power of domination, of confrontation. The power women generate is different from the popular concepts of what constitutes power from the masculine point of view. . . Do not let us hide behind supposed powerlessness – power by domination is not the only power" (Barrow 1984).

Barrow frequently spoke and wrote about her concern that women must be prepared for leadership, and in the statement below she sets out to identify the differences between male and female styles of leadership.

> The approach of the UN is essentially that of the male of the species, rational, cool and detached . . . (It) allows little regard for the essence of things; one which sidesteps and overlooks the sentimental and the emotional core of the human condition, and an approach which obscures the fact that we feel before we think, and that our most persistent activities flow not from what we think but from what we feel . . . I believe an understanding of our global problem demands first and always appreciation of the smallest manifestation, it demands an awareness that unless people are adequately fed and adequately housed they will turn on their immediate environment to survive. It is my conviction that women are better equipped to respond to and appreciate the smaller scale of problems, the level at which human feelings are engaged (Barrow 1983).

Barrow also always insisted that "collaboration and consensus", the preferred style used by women, was always superior to confrontation, which was the preferred style used by men (Barrow 1983, 1984, 1985a, 1985b, 1995f). After the failure of her campaign to become only the third woman president of the UN General Assembly in 1988, a position that rotates between world regions, Barrow felt that she had not received the same kind of commitment from her own Caribbean colleagues as that received by the successful Latin American candidate. However, her belief in the importance of consensus and collaboration was only strengthened by that experience, and it led her to institute regular monthly meetings of Caribbean diplomats at the United Natoions.

Barrow's own style of leadership involved empowering others or power-sharing. She argued that women must take initiatives and not be dependent, waiting for someone to tell them what to do. She insisted on integrity, honesty, and hard work in every organization and individual with which she worked and she sought to instil her own high values and standards into all the organizations she led. She was also very definite on the need for women to be what she called "passionately committed" to what they had undertaken. She herself never seemed concerned with acquiring power, privileges, or riches for herself.

She was already internationally well known as president of the World Council of Churches for the Caribbean region, as director of that organization's Christian Medical Council, as a president of the World YWCA, and as president of the International Council on Adult Education, before she undertook the task that brought her to the attention of the world's women and of all those people concerned with fundamental struggles for human rights. Nita Barrow was sixty-nine years old when she agreed to act as convener for the international NGO committee that organized Forum '85 as a parallel event to the World Conference to Review the Decade for Women in Nairobi, Kenya, in 1985. Forum '85 was perhaps the largest meeting of its type held anywhere in the world up to that time.

Barrow regarded the organization of this meeting as one of the greatest challenges of her life and it was certainly one where all who worked with her not only observed, but learned from her intellect, courage, initiative, and diplomatic skills. She started with a title but without funds, an office, a staff or even a clear mandate. She lived in a friend's home in New York (Dr Lucille Mair, UN ambassador for Jamaica) or travelled home to Barbados to save money, because she had been given neither a house nor any kind of housing provision. She used her contacts first to "borrow" office space and then requested volunteer support from the organizations represented on the NGO Forum Committee to keep the office running. With the help of these volunteers, proposals were written and funds raised, mainly to give support to initiatives of women's organizations worldwide that were eager to take part in Forum '85, and to help with travel costs for panellists and workshop leaders. For the final six months, Barrow had the assistance of a paid staff, including two programme coordinators and a secretary. However, she continued to personally handle most of the phone calls from women around the world, as well as coping with issues and concerns about Forum '85 raised by the leaders of the country which was to host the UN Conference.

During actual meetings, and when the conference started, Nita Barrow was available at all times to assist with problems and to settle crises between hostile groups that might have erupted in violence. At Forum '85 she made good use of the Peace Tent, an idea put forward by the Women's International League for Peace and Freedom (WILPF) and several other peace groups. When situations arose that seemed particularly hostile or that were developing rapidly into a crisis, Barrow would take the various parties to the Peace Tent, where they would talk through their issues and concerns.

The success of Forum '85 was a personal achievement for Nita Barrow. Her later appointments as ambassador and permanent representative of Barbados to the United Nations (1986–90) and as governor general of Barbados must have seemed restful after Forum '85.

Nita Barrow's feminist consciousness, developed in the Caribbean environments of St Croix and Barbados, shaped world affairs in the second half of the twentieth century at the highest political and diplomatic levels. She was well known and highly respected and admired for her contributions to the international struggle for peace, justice, and human rights. The work and achievements of this great catalyst of change need to be better known and appreciated, especially by the people of her own region.

Note

1. In 1995 Dame Nita Barrow gave a large collection of her papers and documents to the Centre for Gender and Development Studies, Cave Hill, University of the West Indies, The collection contains speeches and documents related to her public service, a large collection of letters written to her, photographs and one or two notebooks that she had kept. I had access to these. In 1985 I was a delegate to the Regional Hemispheric Meeting in Havana preceding Forum '85 and to the forum itself in Nairobi. I was privileged to see first hand Dame Nita's considerable intellect and diplomatic skills at work. Later, she described how Forum '85 came into being, and explained and analysed some of the events I had observed. In 1995 I had several conversations with Dame Nita on many subjects and two formal interviews when I made notes. The interview notes are "starred" with topics which were to be discussed further but her untimely death intervened.

CHAPTER THREE

Nursing Colonial Wounds:

Nita Barrow and Public Health Reform after the 1930s Workers' Revolution

[HILARY McD. BECKLES]

A recently published biography of Dame Nita Barrow confirmed what has long been conjectured about the 1930s workers revolt against colonial rule in the Caribbean: that the uprising had the immediate effect of restructuring imperial policy, advancing nationalist ideological processes, and enabling the privileged minority black middle class to seize an opportunity to advance its agenda of accessing professional careers. There was nothing particularly surprising about this social development. What was striking, however, was the alacrity with which the moderately propertied, formally educated, but racially oppressed minority moved to empower itself within the aftermath of Clement Payne's struggle for social justice for the poor. Before the ashes of the workers' violent assault upon colonialism had settled, it seemed, the middle-class professional revolution was well underway and had become a noticeable social feature (Blackman 1995; Hart 1993: 370–75; Post 1981; Munroe 1972: 36–45; Bolland 1988: 258–85).

The acceleration of the process of class formation was punctuated by specific imperial legislative moments, and propelled by a complex array of anticolonial tendencies that collectively illustrate the tensions of race and class within the white supremacy superstructure of colonial society. Seeking to situate Nita

Barrow, and her family, within the context of Clement Payne's Barbados, her biographer drew attention to the discourse of black and female marginalization within the shrinking labour market by specifically identifying its repressive race and gender relations. He emphasized the fact that women as a category were excluded from the mainstream of productive employment, but recognized that an educated black woman from an emerging respectable family might find employment as a stenographer clerk in the public service if she was willing to queue behind their historically privileged white and "coloured" sisters. He tells us, furthermore, that "the nursing profession, although it had not yet been designated as such, or elevated to that status, was attractive to many girls [of all races] who had completed primary school and would have done well in secondary school . . ." (Blackman 1995: 21; Momsen 1988: 141–60; Reddock 1993: 249–62).[1] Nita Barrow, on account of her lower middle-class status, was among this minority in 1935, two years before Clement Payne's intervention in the colony's politics.

The social circumstances of Barbadian – and indeed West Indian – workers were typical of those found throughout the British Empire one hundred years after the abolition of slavery. Constitutional reforms in the decades after the 1830s emancipation process did not open the franchise to workers in sufficient numbers for them to exercise any formal political authority. In addition, judicial and economic institutions were used by the planter-merchant elite to ensure their class subordination. When Nita Barrow entered the nursing service as a probationer in 1935, the majority of blacks in Barbados were still excluded from the political polls, for even with the reduced property requirement, voters were still required to have an annual income of £30 or more, and few artisans or agricultural workers earned £25 per annum.

The island in 1937, notes Mack (1967: 157), had been accustomed "for a hundred years to a social structure composed of a white upper class of plantation and sugar factory owners, appointed high government officials, and top professionals; a coloured middle class of lower professionals, shopkeepers, middle range government employees, and clerical and kindred workers; and a black lower class of craftsmen, peasant farmers, canefield hands, and other laborers". The nursing service was not a high profession, but was considered sufficiently prestigious to confer social respectability upon the white women who dominated its ranks.

The educational achievements of blacks in Barbados had exercised no significant effect on the general pattern of resource ownership and the broad parameters of social structures. The 1946 census showed that the island, unlike other colonies, had virtual universal literacy among adults; only 7.3 percent of the island's population over the age of ten years was listed as illiterate, the lowest in the British West Indies. Yet, the colony, according to Mack (1967), "had the reputation among West Indians of being the most prejudice-ridden island". That census listed only 15 percent of the labour force as skilled and professional, and 85 percent as poor, landless peasants and labourers.

Table 3.1 Population of Barbados by Race, 1946

Black	148,923
White	9,839
Mixed or Colored	33,828
East Indian	100
Syrian and Asiatic	7
Chinese	29
Not specified	74
Total	192,800

Source: Great Britain Colonial Office, *Digest of Colonial Statistics 36* (Jan.–Mar. 1958), 67.

With a population of some 148,923 blacks and 9,839 whites, "race was so closely associated with class position that they could usually be used as synonyms" (Mack 1967: 157). The significance of this social condition for blacks entering the nursing profession, and Nita Barrow's initial experiences, were enormous. Francis Blackman noted that the problems experienced had nothing to do with commitment to study or performance of duty. Most of these difficulties, he stated, were associated with "the attitudes on the part of the white Barbadian and English staff that any black person performing a service for a wage was, in effect, rendering servitude a remnant of the slave and master relationship of a period less than one hundred years past". "Injustice towards and humiliation of nurses and trainee nurses," he concluded, "were openly practised" (Blackman 1995: 22). This first generation of black women were knocking on the door of a profession reserved for white women since the slavery period. Creole white women perceived that they had the most to lose and were not willing to retreat on the issue. Trained nurses imported from England, who held the positions of authority, tended to see black probationers as labourers rather than colleagues and successors.

The workers' rebellion of 1937, then, was seeking in part to redress the institutional racism and class prejudices of the kind that confronted Nita Barrow's generation in quest of acquiring the qualification of nurse. The domination of the profession by English matrons was no different from that in other areas of public service. The contempt for black trainees, the closing of social ranks by local and English whites, and the general attempt at black exclusion by the establishment, typified the social culture that shaped other parts of colonial relations. The medical staff at the Barbados General Hospital, not surprisingly, was all white, non-resident and visiting (Blackman 1995: 26). All levels of the medical profession, then, reflected and supported the discriminatory relations of the empire. The workers' confrontation with the empire on the streets of Bridgetown, and other West Indian towns and villages, with sticks and stones targeted this specific industrial culture as part of the general mosaic of racist colonial domination (Post 1969: 374–90; Beckles 1990: 163–70; Reddock 1988; St Pierre 1978: 171–96; Richards 1987).

It was commonly understood, as a consequence, since black candidates were not openly welcome in large numbers to medical professions, that working-class communities would not be targeted for health care by public policy. The vital indices for the West Indies at that time indicated the extent of public health neglect. Infant mortality rates were generally high in all colonies although gradually declining; Barbados in 1946 had the highest rate (147) and Trinidad the lowest (75). The general death rates ranged from fifteen per thousand in Barbados to twelve per thousand in Trinidad and the Leewards; outside of British Guiana, Barbados also had one of the highest birth rates at twenty-nine per thousand (United Kingdom 1950: 52). While Barbados enjoyed a reputation for having the most developed political and judicial administration, mortality data showed it to be a hostile society for young black life. During the immediate postwar years, there was some amelioration of these conditions as shown by the following data for 1951, but the general picture remained structurally unchanged. Barbados continued to experience an infant mortality rate just under twice the level of the regional average. It was here that black women faced the greatest resistance to their entry into the nursing profession. Nita Barrow's survival and advance, then, reflected her considerable determination and commitment to the process of radical social change.

TABLE 3.2 VITAL STATISTICS OF THE BRITISH CARIBBEAN TERRITORIES, 1951

Territory	End of Year Population	Births	Deaths	Natural Increase	Birth Rates (per thousand)	Death Rates (per thousand)	Rates of Natural Increase (per thousand)	Infant Mortality Rates (per thousand) live births
Barbados	216,000	6,793	3,000	3,793	31.7	14.0	17.7	136.5
British Guiana	437,000	18,357	5,869	12,488	42.6	13.6	29.0	76.9
British Honduras	70,700	2,905	801	2,104	41.7	11.5	30.2	94.7
Jamaica	1,443,700	48,447	17,291	31,156	33.9	12.1	21.8	81.2
Antigua	46,900	1,733	605	1,128	37.5	13.1	23.5	76.7
Montserrat	13,600	436	177	259	32.1	13.0	19.1	126.1
St Kitts-Nevis	50,100	1,741	711	1,030	35.3	14.4	20.9	90.8
Virgin Islands	7,300	282	84	198	39.2	11.7	27.5	31.9
Trinidad	656,300	23,804	7,815	15,989	36.7	12.0	24.7	78.2
Dominica	54,900	1,891	870	1,021	34.8	16.0	18.8	130.1
Grenada	80,100	3,037	1,276	1,761	38,6	16.2	22.4	105.7
St Lucia	81,800	2,892	1,389	1,503	35.7	17.2	18.5	134.2
St Vincent	70,100	2,911	983	1,928	42.3	14.3	28.0	100.3
Total Region	3,228,500	115,229	40,871	74,358	36.1	12.8	23.3	86.8

Source: *Development and Welfare in the West Indies, Comptrollers Report 1952*, Colonial Office, 1953.

Barbados' display of the highest infant mortality rates in the region, furthermore, stood as testimony of the deep poverty that characterized the lives of the labouring classes in the Bridgetown slums and rural villages. Government indifference, or helplessness, with respect to the proliferation of urban slums resulted in the creation of an environment within which poor families became accustomed to burying their infant victims at faster rates than their West Indian counterparts. Black women's forced entry into the public health business through the nursing service, and the workers' revolt in 1937, therefore, were intricately bound by the intransigent colonial culture and the popular search for the kind of governance that promoted social care and held the public accountable.

The interconnectiveness of Nita Barrow's private and public spheres helped to illuminate a torn and tortured West Indian world that seemed in its social and ideological composition much more homogenous then than now. Revolts spread through the colonies like a windswept canefire – driving south from

St Kitts into St Vincent, Trinidad, Barbados, Guiana, before turning north like September hurricanes towards Jamaica in 1938. Arthur Lewis, the young on-the-spot West Indian intellectual, argued that the working classes were determined to confront social and economic injustices in all forms, and were expressing a blunt refusal to accept any further the suffocating, debilitating racist nature of colonial governance (Lewis 1939; Browne 1939). In the decade after 1937, Nita Barrow's career in public health nursing also swept through the West Indian colonies, and was symbolic of the intentions that informed the aggressive democratization process released by the workers' revolution.

As was often the case in such circumstances, the British Empire struck back with the establishment and field deployment of a Royal Commission of Inquiry. The records of such discourses show that the more prestigious the commission, the greater the perceived threat to the empire (United Kingdom 1945; Johnson 1977, 1978). In this instance, the West Indies signalled the onset of endemic forms of anti-imperial protest, but no one had clear reason to believe that the mass politics of these micro-colonies could send such disturbing shivers down the spine of the imperial structure. It is true that the revolts against slavery one hundred years earlier had located the islands at the centre of a global political and philosophical debate, and that the postslavery rebellions of peasants and landless labourers had created the contexts within which Marcus Garvey effectively mobilized the black "wretched of the Earth" in a pan-African struggle for freedom and justice. But it was unexpected that the entire archipelago of poverty and misery could find the spiritual and intellectual resolve to stand up all at once in defiance of colonial domination. The seemingly unrelenting economic depression of the capitalist industrial economies also generated its own worker agitation, and cannot be discounted as a significant contributory factor to what was in fact an age of revolutionary nationalism within the colonized world.

The Royal Commission was a high-powered one – including prominent politicians, distinguished economic advisors, labour union officials, and chaired by the respected Lord Moyne. It carried out an extensive investigation of social and economic conditions in the region during 1938–1939; it held public hearings, examined the records of colonial governments, and sought to hear the many voices of West Indian communities. Its task was to evaluate the life experiences of colonial subjects and account for the causes of the workers' rebellion in order to formulate appropriate and feasible remedial recommendations for the imperial government.

A summary of the commission's report was published in February 1940. The full report appeared in 1945. Its recommendations were clear. The British Empire was in trouble, and the West Indian part of it could be saved in the short term only if major transformations were to take place in the social lives of the majority. The report noted that the social services in the area were quite inadequate for the needs of the population, and that none of the colonies could provide from its own resources the funds that would be necessary to put these services on a proper footing, and foster development in general. The main recommendations of the commission to meet this situation were that there should be established a West Indian Welfare Fund (WIWF), to be financed by an annual grant of £1,000,000 from the UK exchequer for a period of twenty years; and that there should be set up to administer it a special organization under the charge of a comptroller, who should be assisted by a number of expert advisors.

The commissioners recognized that the imperial government had no good reason to be critical of these recommendations. The social and material oppression of the labouring poor had already been detailed in the 1897 Royal Commission on the Sugar Industry (Richardson 1992). The special objects of the welfare fund, then, would be to finance schemes for the general improvement of education, health services, slum clearance and housing, land settlement, and social welfare facilities. The comptroller was required to keep the social problems of the West Indies constantly under review and to collaborate with the local governments in the preparation of long-term programmes of social reform. In addition, and with respect to the financial administration of "development" grants for the empire as a whole, the British Parliament enacted in July 1940 the Colonial Development and Welfare Act (CDWA) which provided that the sum of £5,000,000 should be made available annually from UK funds for social and economic development in the empire for a period of ten years ending on the 31 March 1951; with an additional £500,000 a year for the same period for research (United Kingdom 1947: 1–5; 1950: 5–6; Stolberg 1989: 143).

Claus Stolberg's argument that the CDWA of 1940 was conceived and designed only to "touch up" the worst eyesores produced by the economic and social deficiencies of British colonialism in the worst-case scenario of the West Indies is consistent with the assertions and thinking of West Indian political nationalists of the 1940s. Stolberg is also on firm ground with the statement that an important consideration behind the promotion of this British social welfare and public health policy response was awareness of the ideological objection to European colonialism in the hemisphere that had long informed United States politics (Stolberg 1989: 153). Colonial Office officials and West Indian labour leaders were aware that £1,000,000 was woefully inadequate and that at least £10,000,000 annually was needed to develop any meaningful programme.

Public relations successes rather than social and economic development were paramount on the agenda of the Colonial Office. Gerald Clauson, economic planner in the Colonial Office, admitted the political rather than development aspect of the 1940 legislation when he stated that "there have been two motives behind this proposal; the one a desire to avert possible trouble in certain colonies, where disturbances are feared . . .; the other a desire to impress this country and the world at large with our consciousness of our duties as a great Colonial Power" (Public Record Office 1939). Constantine (1984: 249) added to these objectives "the need to woo neutral opinion by demonstrating a constructive colonial policy, and the need to prepare for postwar criticism of Britain's role as a colonial power".

The conceptual and financial limitations and drawbacks of the 1940 CDWA were fully exposed by Caribbean critics, and the Colonial Office in 1945 responded with two significant legislative developments. The first was the passing of a new CDWA, which greatly increased the fund and provided for more flexibility in its administration. The new act made available a total sum of £120,000,000, not by annual vote, but over the period of ten years ending on 31 March 1956. The second significant development in 1945 was the decision of the secretary of state to inform each colony of the amount of assistance it could expect to receive for the ten-year period of the act (United Kingdom 1947: 3). The British West Indies was to receive £15,000,000 for the ten years, in addition to the sums spent up to March 1946 under the 1940 act. Of the £2,500,000 spent under the 1940 act, £1,800,000 went to the West Indies, and £1,500,000 of this to Jamaica, the colony perceived as having the "most serious unrest" (United Kingdom 1947: 3; Stolberg 1989: 155).

Within the British Empire, the West Indies colonies were undoubtedly favoured for "development aid" under the new legislative arrangements. The per capita receipts in the West Indies under the 1940 act was 14 shillings compared with 5 pence for all other colonial subjects. The proximity of the islands to the United States and Canada was certainly a majority consideration here. Britain was in fact paying for its political embarrassment in the American

TABLE 3.3 FUNDS AVAILABLE TO WEST INDIAN COLONIES UNDER THE CDWA, 1945

Colony	Funds (£)
Barbados	800,000
British Guiana	2,500,000
British Honduras	600,000
Jamaica	6,500,000
Leeward Islands	1,200,000
Trinidad and Tobago	1,200,000
Windward Islands	1,850,000
West Indies General (Bahamas)	850,000
Total	15,000,000

Source: Development and Welfare in the West Indies, 1945–46, Colonial Office Report 1947, p. 4.

sphere of geopolitical influence. It started by recognizing that the general health and sanitary conditions of the region, thanks to worker protests, constituted an open wound that required considerable nursing, although with an inexpensive aid programme. Africa was virtually ignored, and India was considered too far gone with respect to the politics of welfare reform pacification.

TABLE 3.4 POPULATION ESTIMATES FOR THE WEST INDIES (IN THOUSANDS)

Colony	1896	1921	1936	1946
Jamaica	695	858	1,139	1,296
Trinidad and Tobago	248	367	448	558
British Guiana	279	298	333	376
Barbados	186	166	188	192
Windwards	146	162	210	252
Leewards	131	122	140	109
British Honduras	34	45	56	59
Total	1,719	2,018	2,514	2,843

Source: Development and Welfare in the West Indies, 1945–46, Colonial Office Report 1947, p. 55.

The immediate postwar comptroller for development and welfare in the West Indies, Sir John MacPherson, understood the magnitude of the reform process and stated explicitly that "no permanent advance in the public health of these colonies can be secured unless staff fully trained in preventative medicine" could be built up and secured. This staff, he noted, should work towards the establishment of a "solid foundation of improved environmental hygiene – that is to say, improved domestic and commercial sanitation, improved water supplies and better housing" (United Kingdom 1947: 19). The Development and Welfare Organization was set up to achieve these objectives with greater focus on preventive – as opposed to clinical – medicine.

During 1945–1946, research was funded and reports submitted on a number of problems in the area of preventable diseases and special matters directly affecting public health, such as the containment of leprosy and tuberculosis, human nutrition, and international quarantine procedures. The operations and work of the Yellow Fever Control Unit in British Guiana, the Malaria Research Units of British Guiana, Trinidad, Jamaica, the Windwards and Leewards, and the Caribbean Medical Centre for the Control of Venereal Diseases were hampered by the chronic shortage of trained nurses in the region. In 1942–1943 a scheme was put in place under the guidance of the London County Council hospitals to receive seventy-two West Indian nurses over a period of four years for four-year training courses. The cost was estimated at £26,250. The first twenty-seven nurses were already in England when the war ended in 1945. MacPherson considered this initiative a mere beginning and reported the need for a considerably expanded programme.

The provision of training facilities for nurses was arranged by the appointment of sister tutors in the various colonies, and by sending selected nurses to the United Kingdom. Sister nurses were appointed between 1943 and 1945 in Barbados, Guiana, Antigua, and Trinidad. The grant for the appointment of a sister tutor in Jamaica was approved but was not filled because of difficulties experienced in finding a suitable candidate. The twenty-seven nurses from Barbados, British Guiana, British Honduras, Dominica, Grenada, Montserrat, St Kitts, St Vincent, and Trinidad, assigned to London hospitals were expected to return home on completing their four-year programme and take up duties in public hospitals and rural clinics. In October 1946, a delegation from the United Kingdom. consisting of persons nominated by the General Nursing Council and the Royal College of Nursing arrived in the West Indies to examine the situation, and to make recommendations with respect to the deployment of nurses graduating from the London Hospital programmes (United Kingdom 1947: 100–102).

The nursing delegation was also expected to make recommendations with respect to the training of nurses in their West Indian environment. Reports of racism daily experienced by black nurses in England, in addition to the difficulties experienced by the London County Council in securing their placements in hospitals, resided at the core of a need for an urgent policy shift to train nurses at home. While West Indian nurses were aware that their racial experiences in postwar England paralleled those of other blacks, direct responsibility of the Colonial Office for their professional training set them officially apart from their compatriots in the transport, manufacturing, and auxiliary service sectors. The delegation completed its visits to all territories by April 1947, and submitted a report that covered all aspects of training and the principles that should be applied to raise the local standards of nursing in the various territories. In several of the larger colonies, modifications of the training curriculum were immediately introduced on the basis of their recommendations, and new legislation relating to the organization of the profession drafted.

A critical decision taken by the Colonial Office from the delegation's report was that the Royal College of Nursing should arrange a one-year course of training in ward sister duties for select senior nurses who had received their basic training in the West Indies. This recommendation was supportive of the position set out by the Moyne Commission whose report stated:

> We are impressed by the fact that very few West Indian nurses hold senior positions in nursing services. We consider it a real grievance which should be remedied as soon as possible. The present training of nurses in small hospitals and their accommodation and conditions of service are . . . unsatisfactory. It would be far better to have a few good training centres in large hospitals with adequate residential quarters. Above all, a good type of sister tutorship should be appointed and a training syllabus of lectures and practical work suitable to the health conditions of these colonies should be carefully arranged at each centre. (Blackman 1995: 37)

Fifteen nurses from various territories were selected for this training course, the cost of which was borne by a Colonial Development and Welfare Scheme. In addition, the Trinidad government sent six nurses at its own expense for the ward sisters course and two for a postgraduate course in district nursing. Three members of Queen Elizabeth's Colonial Nursing Service were sent for courses of training in hospital administration and health sister duties under the scheme.

With respect to the organization of the profession nurses' homes were built in Trinidad at the Colonial Hospital, Port of Spain, and the hospital at San Fernando, which were the nurses' training schools for the colony. The facilities for training and residency in Barbados were improved by the opening, in 1948, of a Maternity Training Hospital, which was funded by a grant of £24,000 from the Development and Welfare Fund. It was also expected that these facilities would provide part of the staff of qualified nurses required for the University College Hospital under construction in Jamaica.

Meanwhile, the first group of nurses granted scholarships for training in general nursing and midwifery in the United Kingdom were completing their basic training. In some cases, nurses applied for permission to take post-diploma experience or additional courses of postgraduate instruction. In 1949, fifteen locally trained nurses who were selected for the postgraduate training in ward sister duties in the United Kingdom were reportedly "acquitting themselves with credit" (United Kingdom 1952: 58). During 1950, grants under the West Indies Training Scheme were given to seven nurses and two technicians for courses of instruction at the Caribbean Medical Centre in Trinidad in the techniques of treatment and control of venereal diseases. Within the context of these advances, the American-based Rockefeller Foundation, active in the field of West Indian public health care since 1943, expanded its programme to facilitate training on a West Indian basis for public health nurses and sanitary inspectors. The Public Health Training Station in Jamaica was supported in part by the Rockefeller Foundation (United Kingdom 1952: 59).

Nita Barrow's professional benefit from these developments constitutes critical reference points. After completing five years of training in Barbados under the auspices of the Colonial Development and Welfare Project, she took the opportunity of Rockefeller funding to enter the University of Toronto School of Nursing in 1943 to pursue a one-year course in public health – the target area of specialization by the Colonial Office. The expected result of this career path was that she would take up employment with the Colonial Development and Welfare Project. Instead, she accepted another year's Rockefeller funding to pursue further studies in public health, after which she travelled to Jamaica to participate in the Colonial Development and Welfare-funded public health nurse training programme organized by the West Indies School of Public Health. The position she occupied in the programme in 1945 was assistant instructress. The following year she was given responsibility for the training of public health nurses as well as for part of the training of public health inspectors (Blackman 1995: 37–38). The school provided extensive training for public health nurses and sanitary inspectors up to 1951. During this period, grants under the West Indies Training Scheme were provided to enable ten nurses and eleven sanitary inspectors from various territories, other than Jamaica, to take the nine-month course given at the school. In addition, territories sent students, at the cost of local colony funds, for basic, and in some cases advanced, courses (United Kingdom 1952: 59).

In March and April of 1951 the chief nursing officer of the Colonial Office, Florence Udell, OBE, visited the West Indies to obtain firsthand information on the stage of development of the nursing and hospital services, and the facilities for and standard of training in the region, the recruitment and staffing requirements, with particular reference to the placing of West Indian nurses who were receiving training in the United Kingdom under Development and Welfare scholarships. A conference on medical services was arranged in Barbados to coincide with Udell's visit to discuss general colonial nursing policy and its application to the West Indies. Of special concern was the objective of achieving recognition of West Indian qualifications by the General Nursing Council of England and Wales (United Kingdom 1952: 51).

It was also agreed by conferees that officials of the General Nursing Council would make periodic inspections of West Indian training schools and that facilities for postgraduate training in the United Kingdom would be expanded. Furthermore, that there should be enactment of nurses' registration ordinances and creation of statutory nurses' councils and the formation of professional nurses' associations. The conference endorsed a recommendation that, when unification of the government medical services was projected, this should also include unification of nursing services. The proceedings and recommendations of the conference were circulated to governments and were recognized as a seminal departure for the progressive improvement of the status and standards of the nursing services in the region.

Conference recommendations were endorsed by all governments, and one important development was that the nurses' training school of the University College Hospital would be organized on a basis from the outset to meet the requirements of the General Nursing Council. Grants for training in the United Kingdom were made subsequently from Development and Welfare funds only for special post-registration courses and those leading to the sister tutor's qualification on other teaching diplomas or certificates. During 1951

Table 3.5 Allocation of Training Grants, 1952

Territories	Number of New Course	Total Allocation
Barbados	3	1,603
British Guiana	8	2,037
British Honduras	5	1,415
Jamaica	7	3,706
Leewards	12	3,765
Trinidad and Tobago	6	2,357
Dominica	7	1,095
St Lucia	6	1,462
St Vincent	4	1,319
Grenada	3	639
Total	61	19,398

Source: Development and Welfare in the West Indies, 1952, Colonial Office Report 1953, p. 88.

and 1952, several such grants were made under the West Indies Training Schemes, and one was made for special instruction in the nursing aspects of the radium technique. Public health nursing accounted for the largest number of the new courses in 1952, with twenty-two out of sixty-one. Some 60 percent of these new courses were arranged for training in the West Indies, which was in line with colonial policy to conduct as many courses as possible in the region.

These efforts, however, were of a minimalist nature in comparison with the magnitude of the health care problem within West Indian societies. Stolberg's conclusion that the Colonial Development and Welfare acts, and policy initiatives that emerged from them, were no more than "symbolic gestures aimed at the world outside of the empire", and designed to have a "pacifying effect within the West Indies", provides an accurate framework of analysis. It was not a coincidence, he argues, that the West Indies, described by W.M. Macmillan in 1935 as "on the whole ahead of Africa, where the medical services are so inadequately staffed", was chosen as the first region to receive the new programme's benefits. It was part of the wider strategy to "pacify the United States' anticolonial opinion and neutralize the growing interest of the USA in the region" (Stolberg 1989: 157; Macmillan 1935: 123).

The training and deployment of nurses and other public health officials as a result did very little in the way of alleviating the root cause of the poverty and malnutrition that was endemic among the majority of West Indians. Altogether, £1,273,061 was made available between 1946 and 1950 for medical, public health, and sanitation projects from a total budget of £10,793,781. Twice as much went to projects in agriculture, and marginally more to programmes in (1) water supplies, drainage and irrigation, (2) education, and (3) transport and communication. The single greatest investment in agriculture and veterinary science reinforced the plantation bias of the economy and signalled commitment to agriculture and the planter elite as the principal local development agencies. There were no surprises in this regard. Colonialism was designed in the Caribbean to consolidate productive resources and the institutions of assets management in the hand of local and imperial white elites. The dependency of the landless poor, who constituted some 80 percent of the population, upon seasonal employment on the depressed sugar industry, resided at the core of the subsistence crisis that typified black life.

TABLE 3.6 FUNDS MADE AVAILABLE FOR DEVELOPMENT AND WELFARE, 1946–1950 (£)

Colony	Public Health and Sanitation	Total for Colony	Expenditure as % of Total
Barbados	18,837	640,001	2.9
British Guiana	56,286	1,761,188	3.2
British Honduras	37,102	764,412	4.9
Jamaica	532,457	4,010,696	13.3
Cayman Islands	22,486	41,132	54.7
Turks and Caicos	1,815	55,216	3.3
Antigua	10,756	257,656	4.2
St Kitts-Nevis	47,752	133,004	35.9
Montserrat	15,752	54,766	28.5
Virgin Islands	8,390	465,974	1.8
Dominica	39,260	432,765	7.5
Grenada	19,002	279,855	6.8
St Lucia	45,387	646,587	7.0
St Vincent	39,151	262,412	14.9

Source: Development and Welfare in the West Indies, 1950, Colonial Office Report 1951, p. 10.

Table 3.7 Infant Mortality Rates in the West Indies, 1950 and 1952

Colony	1950	1952
St Lucia	104	–
British Honduras	120	–
Barbados	140	136
British Guiana	77	76.9
Leewards	78	–
Jamaica	–	81.2
Trinidad	–	78.2

Source: Development and Welfare in the West Indies, 1952, Colonial Office Report 1953, pp. 85–86.

The high infant mortality rates throughout the region directly relate, for example, to the degree of landlessness among the poor. The crisis of subsistence was deepest in Barbados where historically the greatest alienation of the workers from ownership of the land was most extreme. This relationship was recognized by officials administering the Colonial Development and Welfare Fund. Several attempts at funding land settlement policies were initiated, but all fell short of what would constitute a viable land reform programme. Colonial officials recognized that as had long been the case, the infant mortality for Barbados was the highest.

The health problems of the Barbadian poor were aggravated by the fact that the colony was the most densely populated; the implications of the success of any land settlement scheme were negative from the outset. Demographic pressure on economic resources in Barbados continued to mount as reductions in infant mortality after the war accounted for noticeable increases in population. The region as a whole showed significant levels of natural increase. Between 1948 and 1952, the annual rate of increase was 2.4 percent and it was projected that by 1970 the region's population, in the absence of significant emigration outlets, would double. Increasing levels of poverty were expected, given the inflexibility of resource ownership and usage patterns and officials of the Colonial Development and Welfare Fund were not optimistic that their programmes would have any significant impact on the severe health care and infant mortality crises. In fact, the comptroller for development and welfare,

Table 3.8 Population Density in the West Indies, 1948

Colony	Population/Square Mile
Barbados	1,221
Windwards	326
Trinidad and Tobago	304
Jamaica	292
Leewards	258
British Honduras	7.5
British Guiana	4.5

Source: Development and Welfare in the West Indies, 1947–1949, Colonial Office Report 1950, p. 109.

Sir John MacPherson, noted in his report for 1945–1946, that "in nutrition, the most important aspect of school health in the West Indies, it may be said that there is a little light in the sky but the dawn has not yet broken" (United Kingdom 1947: 89).

From the outset, public health nurses emphasized that the insanitary conditions of West Indian urban slums were a principal contribution to ill-health and high mortality. Housing surveys conducted in the postwar years revealed the very high proportion of unhealthy living conditions in towns. Officials of

Table 3.9 Annual Natural Increase of Population

Colony	1921–25	1951
Barbados	300	3,800
British Guiana	1,200	12,500
British Honduras	600	2,100
Jamaica	11,500	31,200
Leewards	600	2,600
Trinidad	4,300	16,000
Windwards	3,300	6,200
Total	21,800	74,300

Source: *Development and Welfare in the West Indies, 1952*, Colonial Office Report 1951, p. 86.

TABLE 3.10 HOUSING CONDITIONS OF WEST INDIAN URBAN SLUMS

Town	Number of Dwellings Surveyed	Percent Recommended (less than 40 sq ft per person)	Percent Structurally Unfit and Beyond Repair	Percent New Dwellings Required to Cure Slum
Bridgetown	1,030	20	42	44
Georgetown	7,994	28	40	85
Belize	1,270	28	8	14
St Johns	697	55	45	48
Basseterre	573	35	9	20
Castries	2,521	19	30	36
Kingstown	346	25	45	50
Roseau	1,501	37	54	57

Source: *Development and Welfare in the West Indies, 1945–46*, Colonial Office Report 1947, p. 112.

the Development and Welfare project concluded that "the standard of sanitation in urban housing is deplorably low. It consists often of a standpipe in the street shared by several families, and a bucket latrine, also frequently shared" (United Kingdom 1947: 112).

While it was recognized that drastic action was needed with respect to slum clearance and resettlement in order to remove or minimize the threat to public health, officials realized that the funding made available by Colonial Development and Welfare was woefully inadequate. For example, in the first provisional draft of the development plan of the Leeward Islands, it was found possible to include only £42,000 for housing over the ten years from 1946 to1955. Yet the cost of clearing one of the worst urban slums in Basseterre, and rehousing a total of 187 families was estimated at £40,000.

Under these conditions, West Indian subjects of the British Empire had no reason to expect to live to a ripe old age. While life expectancy increased gradually in the years between the wars, West Indians could not expect to reach their sixtieth birthday. Life in the colonies for most subjects was short, malnourished and unhealthy. Public health nurses and other officials were sent forth into such communities across the West Indies as emissaries of the empire with plasters for the small sores and bandages for the big ones.

TABLE 3.11 LIFE EXPECTANCY IN THE WEST INDIES (YEARS)

Colony	1920–22		1945–47	
	M	F	M	F
Jamaica	35.89	38.20	51.25	54.58
Trinidad and Tobago	37.59	40.11	52.98	56.03
British Guiana	33.5	35.8	49.32	52.05
Barbados	–	–	49.17	52.94
Leewards	–	–	49.53	54.76
British Honduras	–	–	44.99	48.97

Source: Development and Welfare in the West Indies, 1949, Colonial Office Report 1950, p. 57.

The Government of the United States spoke about the health menace to the south, and implicated Britain as responsible for the ugly diseases and early deaths that resulted. The working classes, in general, did not see the issue so clearly in this way. They knew that their material poverty, landlessness, and lack of political rights had more to do with the privileges of local elites than with the policies of imperial governments – although they knew of, and understood, the historical alliance between the two.

Yet, despite the British primary concern with the politics of the empire, advances were made with respect to the development of policy and public infrastructure to deal with the historically neglected issue of public health. The establishment of the Colonial Development and Welfare initiative, which called into being the extensive training of health care officials, represented a break from the tradition of the plantation, vestries, and almshouses as agencies for dealing with public health. In this sense, public health policies and initiatives constituted the frontier on which the British sought to modernize on the cheap, its extensive empire.

The open wounds of colonization were there for all to see when the postslavery dispensation took shape during the 1850s and 1860s. As is so often the case, these wounds of social neglect and negation had to erupt into open bloodshed before imperialists act with any meaningful humanitarian concern. Progress, once again, was found in the aftermath of a path of material destruction and the social display of anger and hatred by the dispossessed and alienated.

The workers' revolt of 1937, then, opened vistas for a new dialectical interaction between various segments of the colonized population. The professionalization of public health care was welcomed by the working people in so far as it is constituted the acquisition of badly needed skills. The differential availability of health care services across the social structure, however, reinforced their view that colonial professionalization inevitably results in the setting of market rates way beyond their own financial parameters.

Nita Barrow understood and engaged all of these moments and processes within which West Indian public health care emerged and evolved. While in many ways she was a product of colonial policy with respect to the establishment of a democratic nursing culture, Nita Barrow had the special talent of turning the imperial sword into a native ploughshare by building social bridges that created powerful alliances for human liberation. Her imagination and ideological postures were never confined by the thinking and policy initiatives of the Colonial Office. She was a rebel who knew how to make the best of available resources in the search for strategic advances.

It is also true that Nita Barrow never acquired a reputation for using the political technique of frontal assault, but it could always be assured that somehow she would emerge on the progressive side of discourses in support of agendas of popular empowerment. The wounds that she nursed were those of her own people seeking release from colonial entrapment. She knew that black people's pathological condition was one that produced what Frantz Fanon described as "pain all over". In her attempts to alleviate this condition, Nita Barrow inflicted her own telling wounds on the colonial order, and offered to many throughout the colonized world the kind of nursing hand never envisaged by the Colonial Development and Welfare Project.

Note

1. For a discussion of women's work and politics, see Vassell 1993; Momsen 1988: 141–60; Reddock 1993.

Part Three

The Politics of Health, Nursing, and Networking

CHAPTER FOUR

Nursing Politics and Social Change in the Caribbean:
The Nita Barrow Years

[MARGARET D. GILL]

INTRODUCTION

The period from 1935 to 1969, when Nita Barrow was directly active in nursing, is also associated – as Hilary Beckles has shown in the chapter 3 – with some of the greatest changes in the profession in the Caribbean. Nursing care became less associated with physical hard labour and an unending, frequently unsuccessful, fight against disease. Needed material and technical supports and benefits were introduced and conditions considerably improved. Caribbean nurses were able to establish full careers extending to supervisory and management levels within the profession. They had been debarred from attaining these positions under colonialism, since British, Canadian, or Australian nurses were brought in by the Colonial Office to fill the top nursing posts. Nursing education developed into an independent pedagogical programme from the apprenticeship system it had been historically. In short, the legitimacy of the Caribbean nurse as an integral and dynamic part of health administration was established, and their status considerably enhanced.

It might be tempting to ascribe these changes in nursing to the generally rapid growth of technology and modern science that has occurred throughout this century. There can be no doubt that rapid advances in external material and social forces, particularly in the post–World War II period, impacted greatly on local nursing conditions. Within the context of nursing history, war itself had earlier provided the fertile circumstances that produced the narrative of the nurse as "saving angel". The legends of Florence Nightingale and, closer to home, Mary Seacole from Jamaica were born out of their escapades in bringing ease and comfort to wounded soldiers during the Crimean War in 1854. The advanced technologies of modern warfare, including the development of biological and chemical agents of war, provided the means to inflict grave bodily abuses on larger numbers of people simultaneously. These, along with concomitant social and health problems, significantly increased the demand for nursing care. War, ironically, continued in this century to provide an opportunity for nurses to achieve prominence internationally.

Apart from these demand-driven improvements in nursing, major leaps in medicine and other natural sciences that occurred during the period under study undoubtedly impacted significantly on nursing. The health sector benefitted from internal advances in mechanical and pharmacological technology. Dr Ena Walters (1995), looking at nursing from the late eighteenth century to the late twentieth century, argues: "the discovery of the sulphonamides, and later, the wonder drug penicillin, brought about revolutionary changes in health care delivery". Computer applications improved medical diagnostics, lab analysis, and patient surveillance; developments in germ theory led to the application of more efficient antisepsis techniques. Health care was also influenced by spin-offs as the space programmes of the United States and the former Soviet Union emerged. Collateral developments from these programmes significantly boosted the level of technology utilized in microbiological analysis, patient surveillance, as well as expanded and enhanced pharmacology and, thus, the management of disease. In addition, rapid advances in the human sciences of sociology, psychology, and economics facilitated clearer ideas of the cultural dimensions of health and disease.

These changes profoundly affected nursing as they reoriented the way the body, health and sickness, and hence health care, were conceptualized. Using science, doctors strengthened their authority over the body. If, as Poovey argues, nineteenth century medicine "privileged the patient's own experience of the body over any abstract theories the doctor might possess", the opposite is true of this century, even as early as the 1930s (Poovey 1988). In this century, science and technology have more often than not been the primary responses to physical and even social pathologies, as more has come to be known about how the body functions (dysfunctions).

Tied as the Caribbean was to the various imperial centres, these changes internationally had great local impact. However, it must not be ignored that the reflections, actions, visions and perseverance of Caribbean nurses themselves, collectively, and also of some outstanding individuals, carry significant weight in explaining changes in the profession in the period examined.

This chapter describes and analyses the inputs in the development of nursing in the Caribbean over the thirty-four years between 1935 and 1969 by the highly acclaimed Nita Barrow, whose contributions in many ways and on many occasions provided the catalyst that moved the profession forward. While dedicated to exploring the role of this outstanding individual, however, my analysis assumes that Barrow's role could have been catalytic only insofar as nurses perceived themselves as a collective, ready for and willing to bring about change.

The chapter also analyses how the system of gender relations and general social and political turmoil acted on the profession itself, how nurses used their developing capacity for impacting on the process of change that Caribbean society underwent during this period, and what all this meant for the individual nurse.

Nursing Conditions and the Social Context

Research in women's studies since the 1970s in the Caribbean has shown that women made significant and ofttimes central contributions to the development of the region from early settlement and onwards.[1] However, in health care, as in many other spheres of economic and social life, these contributions are generally unrecognized. In 1935, when the eighteen-year-old Nita Barrow's career started in the profession of nursing, women as a group, and even more so black women who formed the majority, were marginalized, exploited, and subordinated in the society. Few opportunities for secondary education were open to them, even where parents thought it useful to educate female children beyond the barest minimum (Cole 1982). Census data located them mainly in the sectors of agriculture, where they held the most menial jobs as unskilled labour, in small-scale agricultural distribution as hucksters, and in domestic and other personal service areas such as dressmaking (Massiah 1993). Although relatively small in absolute terms compared to the previously mentioned occupations, increasing numbers of black women were working as teachers and nurses. However, in the government service, they were discriminated against in favour of men, and in favour of white women in commerce and banking. Primarily as a consequence of the history of slavery when all able-bodied black women worked, Caribbean women exhibited high levels of labour force participation. At the same time, their earnings were low and generally below men's; certainly in agriculture this was the case where, by law, minimum pay rates were specified by sex.

A similarly low occupational status attended the position of black women in the system of health care, as we shall see. Their opportunities to advance within the sector were circumscribed; they were barred from decision-making processes; and their pay bore little relation to the efforts extended or the contributions made. Nevertheless, as one of the few professions available for women to map out careers, however limited at the time, nursing was to become a space where women could gain recognition for the offering of public service as well as improve their collective conditions. As a consequence, and in support of a similar conclusion drawn by Mary Poovey in her analysis of Florence Nightingale, nursing offered some resistance to male domination. As Poovey argues, Nightingale's conceptualization of nursing as an independent profession which motivated the changes she was able to achieve, "ultimately challenged the basis of medical men's power – the right to define who was a patient in need of health care" (Poovey 1988). Caribbean nurses brought a similar challenge to the administration of health care during the period of this study.

Nita Barrow and many of her counterparts in nursing and nursing leadership came to recognize the role and value of their profession to Caribbean development and, despite the limitations they faced, acted to emancipate the profession to enable it to undertake that role. Further, they came to this view despite perceptions to the contrary held by the general public as well as by doctors and other health care administrators. As Barrow herself said in response to a question about the perception of the public about nursing in 1935:

> The public thought nursing was just above being a domestic. It was not seen as a profession. We were not self-directed. In the halls of academia nursing was not included. (Barrow 1995b)

Her philosophy, which she explained quickly grew out of her experiences in nursing, came to be that, "Women must be perceived as an integral part of planning at the policy level" (Barrow 1995b). Several factors came to be responsible for the attitudes to their profession taken by Nita Barrow and other nurses who challenged the status quo. The most critical of these, which is explored below, are the combination of frustrating and oppressive conditions of nursing and the popular spread of liberal ideology, the growth of the local middle class, and the pursuit of opportunities for employment by members of this class.

Dr Ena Walters, a former matron of Barbados' general hospital, the Queen Elizabeth Hospital, recently published the first history of nursing in Barbados containing useful historical statistical data.[2] In it, she records the dismal public health conditions existing in the country in the 1920s and 1930s. Morbidity and mortality rates were very high due to the prevalence of a large number of serious communicable diseases. Epidemics of typhoid, yellow fever, smallpox, malaria, and diarrhoeal diseases were common. The infant mortality rate was high, ranging between 217 and 222 per 1,000 live births, and this was more often than not the result of preventable diseases like neonatal tetanus, enteritis, prematurity, diarrhoea, congenital debility, and congenital syphilis (Walters 1995).

Walters attributes these gloomy public health statistics to poor social conditions and widespread poverty as a result of gross unemployment. Even among those fortunate to get employment, pay for the majority of the working population, who were mainly black and mixed race, was very low and incapable of moving them above the poverty line. This group also lacked political power in formal government structures. At the time, only the privileged land-owning class, those with an annual income of £50, or a university graduate could vote or be elected to parliament. The reports of the Moyne Commission following the labour disturbances of the mid to late 1930s throughout the region recorded similar conditions in other Caribbean countries.

With the level of technology at the time being very basic in the circumstances described above, nursing care was very labour intensive. The application of available and improvised pharmacological treatments, feeding, observing, lifting and tending of patients with severe prolonged illnesses were normal challenges to the nurse. In addition, nurses on probation had to sweep and dust the wards, and keep all patient utensils clean, from bedpans and urinals to food service items (Walters 1995).

The existing structures, benefits, and supports of nursing in 1935 hardly compensated for the level of energy and commitment expected of the nurse. The norm for hours worked per week was in excess of sixty hours, and vacation was at the exigencies of the service. For the first time, nurses were immunized against typhoid fever despite their exposure to the many opportunistic diseases encountered in their daily round. Pay was very low, ranging from $4.32 for a probationer of one to two years of service, to $10 for a nurse with five years of experience (Blackman 1995). Local nurses were unable to reach the level of sister or matron because these posts were filled by British, Canadian, or in some instances, Australian nurses sent out by the Colonial Office.

The epistemological framework that guided nursing in Barbados in 1935 derived from a racist, patriarchal, class-based philosophy that was rooted in colonial notions of exclusion and difference. The very concept of health itself was defined in an exclusionary and limited way as the treatment of disease, and the targets of public health meant poor sick labourers, the indigent, and the aged. Nurses, recruited from the black population, were held in low regard, as were the patients they resembled and treated. Historically, women undertaking nursing functions for those who were enslaved or otherwise disenfranchised had been recruited from among the slave population. Quakeresses and "Methodist ladies" from among the privileged classes also nursed the sick as an extension of the concept of Christian care during slavery. With the opening of hospitals, when the function of "nurse" became an occupational category, the majority of nurses still came from among the poorly educated working-class population. This was a function of the local history of the profession, its continued lack of education requirements governing selection of candidates, and its ad hoc and limited view of nurse education as skills learned under a system of apprenticeship.[3] In carrying out their function of treatment of the sick, nurses were expected to be identified with their patients in an ethic of service, sacrifice, and obedience to superiors (meaning doctors, who were males, and white, expatriate sisters and matrons).

This ideal of the nurse as dedicated care giver pursuing a calling was upheld in the life of Florence Nightingale, who is said to have given up all privileges to answer the "call". However meagre and problematic nursing education in the Caribbean was during the period under consideration, it did not fail to immerse all nurse probationers in narratives of the life and activities of the legendary "lady with lamp" (Barrow 1995b). According to the Nightingale ethic, the rule of the nurse's life was devotion, and selfless service and obedience to her superiors. This ideal was not unlike that promoted in the larger society. The authoritarian patriarchal structure of Barbadian and Caribbean society determined that the general populace was incapable of decision making. Hence, the responsibility of the people in terms of their own health care lay with reporting when ill to the few existing health care facilities available, where doctors would then treat them for ailments that the doctors diagnosed with little input from or questioning by the patient. No doubt, as anecdotal evidence suggests, resistence to this lack of consultation led many sick people to resort to their own health practices rather than engage the medical service.

Nurses, in turn, shared in this general infantalization of the population, which left them no significant decision-making power in the health care setting. Not the least significant expression of this was the requirement that they sleep in open dormitories under strict regimes of times on and off duty, and even sometimes of how time in residence was spent.[4] Doctors, on the other hand, at this time still only men and still mainly expatriates out of England from the Colonial Office, enjoyed living arrangements that confirmed their status as adults. On wards, they made the only diagnoses, determined whether a hospital stay was indicated, prescribed the kind of nursing care they deemed necessary and supervised nurses in carrying out their instructions. What little formal training nurses received, doctors also provided.

In 1935, there seemed little departure from the historic notion of nursing as a religious duty.[5] What did not survive history was the value placed on nursing, and this expressed itself materially in the considerable financial differences between the pay of nurses and that of doctors.[6] The doctor was not only universally regarded as practicing a prestigious profession; he was commensurately recognized and rewarded socially and economically. In 1935 in Barbados, the pay schedules shown in Table 4.1 obtained in the hospital (Blackman 1995).

The wide differential in pay, not only between doctors and nurses but also between doctors and the top nursing posts of matron and sister, expressed the status accorded doctors. About the attitudes of doctors toward nurses, Dame Nita (1995b) recounts: "Nurses were handmaidens to doctors. On a ward round, the senior nurse had to give the doctor information and *actually be there to carry water to wash the doctor's hands*" (emphasis added).

Another significant element is revealed by statistics. Although sharing in the subjugation of all nurses, nurse leaders enjoyed considerably different conditions of service than their local colleagues. In addition to receiving between

TABLE 4.1 HOSPITAL PAY SCHEDULE (BARBADOS), 1935

Profession	Monthly Salary
Probationer (1–2 years of service)	$4.32
Nurse-in-training (3–4 years of service)	5.76
Nurse (5 years of service)	10.00
Sister	70.00
Matron	100.00
House Surgeon	130.00

Source: Blackman 1995.

seven and ten times greater levels of pay, matrons and sisters had the privilege of individual living quarters. Furthermore, perhaps in an effort to raise their own status vis-à-vis doctors as well as to declare their status as expatriates, nurse leaders adopted authoritarian, patronizing attitudes towards their local subordinates. Local nurses, who up until the 1950s could only reach the grade of staff nurse or charge nurse, could be suspended, fined, or deprived of leave by nurse leaders for breaches of discipline or could be subjected to high-handed treatment by these leaders. In a keynote address to the Sixth Biennial Conference of the Caribbean Nurses Organization in 1968 Barrow (1968) described the quality of the relationship between nurse and matron or sister thus: "Senior personnel . . . had somewhat of the right of 'Queens', and let us be honest, exercised this right." Blackman (1995: 24–26) cites a few of the more glaring instances. There was, for example, the withholding, at the matron's pleasure, of Certificates of Nursing from local nurses who had successfully completed their five years of training. Barrow herself suffered this treatment and joined with a group of her colleagues in 1940 to request of the hospital directors that they be granted their rightfully earned certificates. The matron and sister had failed to grant them upon request by the group of nurses, responding instead with the question as to why the nurses needed them. The response by Barrow and the other nurses that they wanted them because they had earned them did not satisfy the nurse leaders, as such requests were previously not made or expected – even if in principle they were legitimate. Nurses were expected to await the hospital administration's pleasure. In another case, the matron refused to grant the certificate to a duly qualified nurse who wanted it to enable her to take a job offer at another health facility. The matter, as in the previously mentioned case, was only resolved after the hospital's board of directors and trustees became involved and eventually ordered the granting of certification.[7]

It was not unknown for sisters to lock subordinates who were going on night duty later that night into their dormitories after noon for an enforced rest. Nurse leaders also ensured the enforcement of such arcane rules as fining nurses for breakage of any hospital equipment they worked with or used, including plates or cups. Barrow recounts the incident where she was charged along with several nurses for plates broken during one month in the nurses' living quarters. She said that not only had she not broken any plates, the amount being deducted from each nurse's pay was disproportionately large. She recalled that she then took a plate outside and dropped a stone on it, declaring that if she was to be charged for something she had not done, she was now going to set that right. "This is my plate for which I have been already charged which I have just broken!" she told astonished colleagues (Barrow 1995b; Blackman 1995: 25). Several others promptly followed her example.

Eventually, the state was forced to acknowledge these discrepancies in status between nurses and their supervisors. The Halliman Commission of 1950, called in response to widespread discontent among nurses, recorded in its evidence the problematic situation of "imported officials whose work and conditions of service . . . rendered them as somewhat superior beings, apart from the general body of nurses" (Walters 1995). It is somewhat curious that the commissioners did not comment on the even wider distance between conditions of doctors and those of nurses, but this was a measure of their ideological blindness.

Evidently, nurse leaders shared in an imperial narrative of dominance and difference with respect to the local nurses which enabled the former to mask the real relations to the hospital administration which they held in common with these other nurses in the health care system. However, the increasing presence of local (and sometimes black) male doctors, and the conditions of superiority such as Barrow described that doctors enjoyed over all nurses, presented expatriate nurse leaders with ideological contradictions. These contradictions arose where narratives of ethnicity or race came into conflict with narratives of patriarchy. For example, nurse leaders, although playing the role of handmaiden, would also have been exposed to the liberal and liberating aspects of Florence Nightingale's thought. Nightingale sought reform in hospital administration in order to put nurses in charge of nursing services and nursing training, taking these functions away from doctors. Nurse leaders no doubt saw the advantages that these changes would bring to nursing as a profession. At the same time, they recognized that large numbers of their ranks were educationally unfit for the kind of autonomy such changes would imply. In addition, promotion of reforms would jeopardize the privileged status that expatriate nurse leaders enjoyed.

The outworking of these contradictions was expressed in the willingness of some expatriate sisters and matrons to form alliances with local nurses when the latter started to replace them in the 1950s. In Barrow's case, for example, several expatriate nurses gave the advice and help that enabled her to make important career moves. These instances included training at the University of Toronto, taking up the post of instructress at the Caribbean School of Public Health, becoming principal nursing officer in Jamaica, and joining the Pan American Health Organization as leader of the management team in the research of Caribbean nursing education. These alliances between expatriate and local nurses also came to operate at the institutional level with nursing organizations of developed countries providing advice and technical support to Caribbean nurses in the formation of local and regional nurses organizations.

Struggles and Strategies

Nurses in the 1930s were struggling to bring about material and ideological changes and the historic circumstances of the period seemed most favourable to produce them. After nearly two decades of working in a collective situation, which included spending much of the time not actually working but being together socially because of dormitory living, nurses had started to build a strong consciousness of themselves as a group. The fact of the historically strong workforce participation of women in the Caribbean meant that the domestic ideal of the home-bound woman offered little resistance to nurses' consciousness of themselves as workers, in a period when workers generally were becoming more conscious of themselves as an industrial political force. The fact that nurses' collective conditions had changed very little over the years provided the grounds for unrest. In addition to this, several other stimulants to change emerged.

Increasingly, women of the middle classes with better education, experience of easier lifestyles, and social connections were being attracted to the profession. Perhaps, as in England, the mythology of Florence Nightingale and the circulation of popular British fictional texts starring middle-class women who found adventure and romance in nursing lured young, educated, relatively well-off and well-connected women to the profession locally. In any event, with the opportunities for the education of women increasing, the need for areas of work for this emerging group led many to pursue nursing. As Barrow explained, she saw herself faced with two choices, becoming a teacher or becoming a nurse:

> You wouldn't see women who looked like us [black skinned] working in the banks or stores in town. Teaching or nursing were the main, if not the only jobs women of my background faced. (Barrow 1995b)

In fact, she spent a term as a student teacher but thought her temperament was not suited for that job and thus turned to nursing.

The arrival of the bright, strong-willed Nita Barrow proved to be a significant event in the history of nursing in the Caribbean, not least because of the family background from which she came, as Drayton explains in chapter 2. Her father was an university-trained Anglican priest who worked in several countries of the Caribbean; he was noted for his strong sermons against the inequities in Caribbean societies and his agitation on behalf of the poor. The family also included an uncle, Duncan O'Neal, a doctor, who in 1924 founded the first popular political party in Barbados, the Democratic League, which campaigned for adult suffrage at a time when income and educational qualifications precluded the majority of the people from political participation. Barrow's paternal and maternal genealogy included lawyers, doctors, senior civil servants, a head teacher, and a trade unionist (Hugh Springer). This cousin, lawyer Hugh Springer, played a key role in the formation of the Barbados Workers Union, the first trade union in the country. He was later knighted and ultimately became governor general of Barbados. Nita Barrow's brother, Errol, became a lawyer and founder of the Democratic Labour Party, and as Barbados' first prime minister led the country into independence in 1966.

When Nita Barrow entered nursing in 1935 at the age of eighteen years, the labour riots which were to shake the foundations of Caribbean society were in the making. As Beckles shows in chapter 3, Barbados was to experience its share of the popular uprisings that spread through the entire region between

1935 and 1938. The masses faced severe hardships in this post-depression era due to intolerable levels of unemployment and generally low levels of national production, exacerbated by the inequities of income distribution. The uprisings therefore underscored popular demands for a greater share of economic resources, freedom from oppression, and ownership and self-determination in respect of countries over which colonialism still held rule.

Within the profession of nursing itself, agitation had also been emerging for changes to exploitative and oppressive working conditions. Nurses were becoming very vocal about their grievances as they rebelled against the poor diets, the long hours and low salaries, the arbitrary and oppressive discipline, and the idea of dormitory living. Nurse leaders, finding themselves with numerous instances of insubordination and resignations as nurses migrated overseas, also appealed for change. And this agitation did achieve some success. A post of chief nurse was introduced to supervise on the wards; nurses were removed from the hospital dormitories and housed in the Nightingale Home where they were able to have more individual privacy and live more comfortably; meals improved, and fines and suspensions for breaches of discipline were abolished. Two other changes also occurred that laid the foundation that led to the later transformation of nursing.

In 1926, the Public Health Commission responding to growing demands among nurses, had recommended among other things improvement in the training of public health nurses, midwives, and other nursing staff, and the institution of an act for regulating the practice of midwifery. Five years later, those recommendations had still not been implemented. Nurses forced this situation to a head with their continued insurgencies (Barrow 1995) and two fundamental changes were made: in 1931, the post of sister tutor with responsibility for training of nurses was created; and in 1932, the Nurses and Midwives Registration Act was passed, which provided for a nursing council for the registration, discipline, and training of nurses and midwives.

By regularizing and controlling entry into nursing, not only midwifery, in addition to formalizing the training of nurses, these two institutional responses did much to purchase the professional image being sought by nurses. A definite identity for nurses separate from that of doctors was thereby facilitated and this went far in helping nurses in their demand that others take them less for granted. It enabled them to start to view their services less as some religious imperative and more as a specialist craft. The ad hoc feature of nurse training was now removed and this set the stage not only for nurses to view certification as an entitlement, as Barrow and her colleagues did when they demanded their certificates, but also gave them a foundation to challenge the limiting of their professional advancement only to the level of charge nurse. If basic training could be recognized then the case for advanced training could be made, which would make it that much more difficult for authorities to justify going outside the country to recruit sisters and matrons. Previously, as Barrow (1968) identifies: "The nurse . . . was not given the preparation to rise to the decision-making group within her profession. She was not given the preparation for thinking but simply for doing . . . . The formalization of nursing as a profession contained in the 1931 and 1932 actions would lay the groundwork for nurses to change this."

Another benefit of this state recognition was the facilitation of the formation of a private professional body by nurses. Nurses realized early on that they could enhance their professional image and their conditions by such a move, and by 1936 had established the Barbados Registered Nurses Association (BRNA). It is significant that the young Nita Barrow became a student member of an early executive of this body. The BRNA from its outset established itself as an organization that both looked inward to the advancement of its membership, as well as outward to serve the community. Two programmes it promoted were the free donation of the services of members to the community (Barrow 1995b), and its arrangement with the colonial hospital of Port of Spain, Trinidad, for the provision of advanced training in midwifery to some of its members (Walters 1995: 18). Barrow herself came to benefit from this training when she was forced to resign from the Barbados General Hospital. Nurses went on to build the status of the BRNA, the first of its kind in the Commonwealth Caribbean, by having it incorporated by an act of Parliament in 1943. Ten years later, the body was granted associate membership in the International Council of Nurses and achieved full membership of that body in 1957.

The provision of autonomous nursing training under the control of nurses and the establishment of a nurses registration board also enhanced the status of nurses vis-à-vis doctors. A feature by which men in the "professions" (particularly doctors and lawyers) distinguished themselves from other workers, the process of registration could now be claimed by nurses as well. Previously, both doctors and nurses cared for the sick, but the marker of registration that distinguished them from each other also facilitated the definition of nurses as adjuncts to the self-identified doctors. This form of territorial demarcation and definition was traditionally accepted by all concerned, including nurses. As Poovey argues, "Nursing was from its earliest modern organization a profession that proudly claimed a supportive, subordinate relationship to its male counterpart" (Poovey 1988: 166). By contrast, state recognition of the craft of nursing, and by extension the exclusion of non-certified practitioners through registration, was an explicit signifier of the devolution of some of the power of definition and control within the health care system away from doctors. It marked the transformation of the health system from a two-tiered power structure to one with three distinct factions headed by three separate authorities:

1. Hospital administrator for lay staff and services
2. Medical head for medical services
3. Matron for nursing services and nurse training

Although the medical head continued to wield significant power, he no longer had responsibility for the training, allocation, and evaluation of nursing resources in the hospital. Given the criticality of nursing functions in a hospital and the literal outnumbering of doctors by nurses, the loss, in particular, of allocative power over nursing personnel was a significant loss of power in hospital and therapeutic management by doctors. This paved the way for further consolidation of status by nurses in their encroachment into an area long held as the preserve of doctors and scientific men – the area of research. It is in these areas of training, and research in particular, that the most significant inputs were made by Nurse Nita Barrow.

A Leading Caribbean Nurse

It is against this background that the subsequent contributions of Nita Barrow must be seen. Both at home, in the social circles that were mobilizing to bring political and economic change in the country, and at work, where representational and transformative politics were evolving, Nita Barrow was being influenced to develop a political consciousness of her work. She recognized the political soundness of nurses joining together in a professional body. As a student member of the early executive of the BRNA, through discussion and exposure, she began to formulate ideas about how nursing should be transformed. Some of these ideas led to the severing of her links with the Barbados General Hospital.

It is instructive to recall how that specific separation came about. It was the normal practice that nurses would get one weekend off per month, and on one particular weekend Barrow was preparing to take her assigned leave. However, just hours before she was to leave and without prior notice, the English matron summoned her and informed her that her leave was cancelled. Barrow protested both the highhandedness of the action and the loss of her weekend. As she stated strongly in our interview, "I tried not to let my personal life get subsumed by the hospital" (Barrow 1995b).

Barrow's defence of her personal life was a remarkable attitude of resistance given that, up to that time, nurses were still expected to live in communal residences and observe restrictive rules regarding use of time. However, she felt sufficiently strong about the principles involved to proceed on leave regardless of the consequences. She called her uncle Hugh Springer, with whom she was now living since the death of her mother, and asked his opinion. At this time he was involved in steering the emergence of the Barbados Workers Union, Barbados' first trade union, and was facing some of the same issues presented by his niece with respect to the working-class members and potential members of the union. After ascertaining that she had made previous arrangements in regard to her shift, he encouraged her to "rebel"; and if the matron still insisted, to resign and come home. Barrow promptly took his advice and made her case to the matron. The latter proved intractable. Barrow therefore resigned and then went into private practice for a short while before going to Trinidad to do further training in midwifery. It was while she was there that a former sister who had supervised her, a Canadian, Mrs Stoute, encouraged her to seek further training at the University of Toronto where Mrs Stoute herself had been trained under a Rockefeller Fellowship. Barrow had never considered the possibility of this before, but nevertheless wrote to an uncle who made contacts which eventually led to her selection for one of the fellowships.

Barrow's action in resisting the unfair treatment by the matron was not, as we have seen, the first time she had participated in protest action, and it can be read in two ways. First of all, it was indicative of a radical feminist consciousness for the time. With the ideology of nursing still such that nurses had to resign if they got married, her insistence on preserving a separate personal life at the same time that she committed herself to a career (at that time, she was nurse in charge of surgery) was remarkable. On a more pragmatic level, Barrow's actions and the subsequent events point to the growing opportunities and power of the economic and political class to which she belonged. This class was increasing its ability to mobilize resources. It must be recalled that this period marked one of the significant phases of migration from the Caribbean to England and, to a much lesser degree, Canada. This migration was primarily of Caribbean males who went to work for the British transport and mail services. However, because of the pressures of the world wars on the supply of nurses, England, the United States and Canada were sending matrons to tour Africa, Asia, and the West Indies to recruit nurses. A population of West Indians who had emigrated to fill this and other needs, was beginning to build a presence in those countries. Thus, although the Rockefeller Foundation had up until this time funded only nurses out of Latin America in this region, Barrow's candidacy could secure notice despite the minuscule size and still dependent state of her country.

This training proved pivotal, both in Nita Barrow's life and for nursing in the region. It enhanced her orientation towards viewing nursing from a regional perspective and it outfitted her for location in a key health area at the time. She had analysed that public health nursing was an area of great need in the Caribbean and selected to study that area when she went off to do her year of study at the University of Toronto. Her choice both of field of study and of university was well timed and perspicacious. The focus of national and regional politics at the time, as a consequence of popular agitation, was social engineering towards increasing the quantity of goods and services and income in the countries. Nationalist leaders had started to wake up to the fact that this required raising the dismal living standards of the population if they were to become the industrial force envisaged.

The Moyne Commission of 1938, created to examine the circumstances that gave rise to the 1930s' labour riots, underscored a critical finding of the 1926 Public Health Commission. There was a great need for improvement in public health to reduce the prevalence of preventable disease and the high mortality and morbidity rates. Barrow recalled that in discussion with other Barbadian nurses they often remarked that as long as "Cat's Castle" existed – a slum area in urban Bridgetown – nurses would always be assured of jobs. Nurses on their own initiative had already started to mobilize to try to address this concern. As we have already seen, one of the earliest programmes of the BRNA was the free donation of the services of some of its members in community health care for one month, in rotation, throughout the year.

As Beckles shows in chapter 3, faced with the findings of the Moyne Commission in the late 1930s, the Colonial Office in London was forced to recognize that it needed to improve on the existing poor living conditions in the Caribbean if it wanted to avoid a repeat of the disturbances seen in the region between 1935 and 1938. It therefore passed the Colonial Development and Welfare Act (CDWA) 1940 and established the Colonial Development and Welfare Corporation (CDWC). Impressed with Barrow's competence and her extracurricular work in the Nurses Association, the CDWC committed itself to employing her on her return from her year of training at the University of Toronto. However, this was not to be.

Barrow's selection of the University of Toronto was fortuitous on several grounds. First, as Blackman notes, the University of Toronto School of Nursing was building a reputation of excellence for its innovative programmes of nurse training. It was one of the few schools in North America that recognized certification for basic nurse training done outside of Canada. It offered one programme which combined liberal arts with post-basic nursing for an undergraduate degree. It offered another, which Barrow took, which qualified post-basic students for leadership positions in nursing. This school therefore honed Barrow's leadership attributes, evidence of which had been clear for quite some time.

Second, experiences at the University of Toronto enabled Barrow to start to view herself as a nurse trainer. Contacts made at the university also consolidated her orientation towards regional nursing. Blackman (1995) notes that Barrow came to the notice of the Adviser on Nurse Training to the Rockefeller Foundation, Ms Tennant, who was impressed when she heard Barrow deliver a speech at a university gathering on public health services and the training of nurses in Barbados. Ms Tennant encouraged her not to return for the job at the CDWC but to apply for a second fellowship to undertake the programme combining the teaching of nursing and nursing education. Although highly unusual, a fellowship was granted to Nita Barrow for another year. On the advice of Ms Tennant, she was able to use part of it to conduct a month's field work in Jamaica. Not surprisingly, the Rockefeller Foundation offered her, on completion of her studies, the post of assistant nursing instructress at the Public Health Training School in Jamaica, which it was funding in a novel form of technical assistance for the time.

This move put Barrow in a position to advance her own ideas about the need to professionalize the nursing service. It also put her in a position to influence the direction in which mass health care in the Caribbean would move, which would continue to consolidate the power of nurses in health care delivery. Barrow's conceptualization of nursing was marked by her experience of the 1931 and 1932 changes to nursing in Barbados, but she felt that more fundamental change was needed. She declared in one speech: "Nurses had to be seen as practitioners of nursing rather than as servants of an institution" (Barrow 1968: 14). Nurse leaders still had difficulty claiming the power offered by the 1932 Nursing and Midwives Registration Act, as they continued having to fit training activities around the flow of regular ward duty. It was critical, Barrow felt, for nurse training to be an activity with its own integrity if nurse leaders were to be integrated into decision making at the highest level. For her, the basic problems had to do with separating the need for training from provision of low-cost service on the wards and providing training to the nurse as a continuous process throughout her career.

Barrow argued, further, that there were strong connections between the health status of the masses of the population and the training preparation of nurses. She believed that nurses could be a decisive force in spreading beliefs about cleanliness, good sanitation, and efficient bedside care among the poor. She argued: "To set standards [of good public health] you had to revolutionize nursing education." This principle was grounded in the concept of preventative health care, which would be emphasized more strongly in the 1950s (Walters 1995: 20). Evidence collected by the Moyne Commission had supported the need for significant changes in the local basic and post-basic training of nurses, expansion of scholarships for advanced training, the registration of midwives and the formation of nursing boards (Blackman 1995: 37). However, these changes had been slow in coming, hamstrung no doubt by the lack of continuity characteristic of the colonial recruitment policy for nurse leaders, and its built-in demotivation for advanced training among local nurses. With the Moyne Commission mandate for training and her own agenda for the profession, Barrow set about to help transform nurse training. A key area was curriculum development. The syllabus for nurse training was generally still very basic, including only anatomy and physiology, hygiene, and theory and practice of nursing. By 1953, this had been expanded to include the following: "bacteriology, pharmacology, dietetics, medicine, surgery, gynaecology [and] paediatrics" (Barrow 1995b).

In addition to preparation in practical knowledge areas, however, Barrow had another role for nursing education:

> If the nurse's academic preparation makes her sensitive to people and their needs, including respect for them as people, this is an asset. If the preparation increases her sense of professionalisation and self-worth to the extent that anyone lesser prepared is considered 'not competent', then it is of negative value. (Barrow n.d.a.)

Barrow's opportunity to implement her ideas while in Jamaica was increased by the unexpected expansion of her role as assistant nursing instructress upon her arrival in Jamaica. She arrived to find that the nursing instructress, a Canadian whose assistant she was expected to be, had left the day before! Barrow therefore had to immediately assume the role of instructress, which included, in addition to the training of nurses, the responsibility for delivering aspects of the training of public health inspectors.

Barrow's preparation of public health workers during the next five years, in the classroom and in practical working sessions in the community – promoted, if not pioneered, the model that subsequently came to be advocated by the World Health Organization as the best means for improving mass health. This model stresses participatory care. It emphasized that members of the community are to be seen as equal partners with health workers, and that their experiences and knowledge should be recognized and respected in order to bring about real health care change. This view, even if not universally articulated, was implied in the preventive programme of health education in which nurses were engaged in the 1950s. Walters records that in Barbados, along with the health clinics which were beginning to be established:

> Nurses immediately launched a massive Health Education Programme which was carried out mainly at night in order to have access to the greatest number of people . . . There was individual teaching, group discussion, group teaching, films, posters and leaflets. (Walters 1995: 20)

As a philosophical approach which has yet to make a serious impact, Nita Barrow's practise of this approach in 1946 was revolutionary.

A significant example of her use of this approach was displayed when Barrow and a group of public health nurses were to undertake an immunization programme among a community of Rastafari in the Spanish Town, St Jago district of Jamaica. Barrow's initial action was to send emissaries to explain the objectives of the programme and to ask the permission of the community for the team to enter and conduct the immunizations. Rastafari was still an emerging group in the country but had sufficiently established itself as significantly different in appearance, aspirations, religious beliefs, and practices that they were being rejected by other non-Rastafari communities. Barrow was known to express the view to her students and colleagues that the ostracism of Rastafari was "a lot of foolishness" (Blackman 1995: 41).

Admittedly, Barrow could have been motivated by pragmatic security concerns in requesting permission to enter the community. An outcast group could reasonably be expected to be less than welcoming to representatives of "Babylon", as the establishment was known among Rastafari. However, Nita Barrow and her team would have been coming with the weight of official requirement and hence of official sanction. Rastafari, on the other hand, had not yet sufficiently consolidated, neither in terms of numbers nor social legitimacy, to recognize themselves or be recognized as an interest group strong enough to resist official imperatives. Disregarding the community's opinion therefore, might have made the job of Nita Barrow and her team more difficult, but probably would not have precluded its implementation. Not only allowing but seeking that opinion as if the community mattered won Barrow and the team compliance plus appreciation for the respect shown. This was expressed in gifts of food provisions and much-needed firewood. Francis Blackman quotes Barrow as saying: "I learnt much about the local culture from the people. *I could not just walk in and start immunizing. I had to learn what social behaviour was acceptable*" (Blackman 1995:42).

Monica Baly, analysing social change and attitudes to care, cites as problematic the gap that has been created between the patient and the medical elite within a twentieth century culture which views life from conception to death as an illness (Baly 1995). This gap and perception, she argues, more or less guarantees the continuous need for the medical elite and thus disempowers the ordinary citizen. Unfortunately, this problem continues to be a feature of the Caribbean nursing environment. However, Nita Barrow and other enlightened nurses such as those conducting the public health education programmes in Barbados in the 1950s were evidently inclined to stretch the national conception of self-direction on the front of politics and political franchise to its logical limits in health care.

The value of this approach rests in its recognition that people are more than the targets of development, but that they should be central to and participate in any plan for change.[8] However, while this might be described as a feature of Barrow's praxis and a few others like her, its general implementation continues to be a problem. It can be argued that development in the Caribbean up to now may be characterized by three features: institution strengthening, product diversification, and market diversification. In essence, this is a process focused on economic growth. The feature of human development, where the well-being and self-direction of people are at the centre of plans for change, rather than an assumed effect of those plans, is less present in development planning (Gill and Massiah 1986).

Barrow's stay in Jamaica for just under twenty years saw her bringing this value of self-determination to bear repeatedly. Her next opportunity came when she took up the job as sister tutor at the Kingston Public Hospital (KPH) in 1951. The new appointment came after a year's study of a sister tutor's course in Edinburgh and Ireland. That programme had included a six-week study tour of European institutions that gave her further exposure to the provision of advanced training in public health and in the administration of nursing schools. At the KPH she joined three other sister tutors to implement the idea of promoting the integrity of nurse training as a legitimate activity expected of nurses along with their ward work. Barrow's concern was for nursing education to be perceived as a discipline rather than as the accumulation of a set of skills, and so she worked with the other sister tutors to formalize the allocation of blocks of time for an educational programme to be implemented, and to standardize that training for all trainee nurses in the country.

The efficacy of this approach was validated when officials decided to have the nurses recruited for the new teaching hospital, the University College Hospital of the West Indies (UCHWI), trained at the KPH. This connection with the new regional university (established in 1948 with its first faculty in medicine) created more legitimacy for nurse training as well as cemented Barrow's status as an innovator and a regional administrator. This was confirmed when she was offered the appointment as matron of the University College Hospital in 1954, the second person to hold this post and the first West Indian to do so. Here again, she proved equal to the task. Sir John Golding, writing about the UCHWI, speaks thus of those formative years of the institution: "The overall aim was to make the new University College Hospital the standard for the whole region so that everyone would know what patient care really meant" (Golding 1994: 4).

Golding describes the attitude being fostered among nurses thus:

> The attitude of nurses to their patients and the contribution to patient care was modelled on the idea of respect for the patient as a person and concern for them as individuals – not as

disease entities . . . Patients were called by their names – Miss, Mrs or Mr as a prefix – they were never to be regarded as a case, bed number or diagnosis. (Golding 1994: 4)

In addition to promoting this idea Barrow was also fostering nurses' conceptions of themselves as an interest group – not only nationally, but also regionally.

Out of the consciousness and growth generated by the experience of being in the Barbados Registered Nurses Association, Barrow became a driving force behind the formation of a similar body in Jamaica in 1952 – the Jamaica Registered Nurses Association (JRNA). In an unpublished article entitled "Notes on Nursing", she writes about the need for an association of Jamaican nurses "to ensure the rights and responsibilities of nurses and nursing". She recalls that several meetings were held at her house as she and several colleagues planned the launching of this milestone in nursing history in Jamaica. Because of her initiatives in its formation, Barrow's Jamaican colleagues voted her the first president of the JRNA. As a consequence of this involvement, she had input in Jamaica's subsequent establishment of a Nurses Council and Nurses Registration legislation, two institutional responses that played critical roles in nursing in Barbados.[9]

In 1956, just two short years after she was appointed matron, Barrow was given another opportunity to cut new ground. On the advice of Florence Udell, a Colonial Office chief nursing officer, she was offered the newly created position of principle nursing officer of Jamaica. She started almost immediately to make sweeping changes (Blackman 1995: 48–52). She persuaded Jamaican prime minister Norman Manley to increase the budget for nursing services from J$1 million to ten times that amount by her second year in the job. She then restructured the Public Health Division, differentiating its functions more adequately, consequently improving career possibilities for staff of this division who could now aspire to management positions within their division. She raised the entrance qualification for nurse training from a primary school-leaving certificate to the secondary school-leaving Cambridge School Certificate, renamed trainees as student nurses, and started the rationalization of the basic curriculum to promote standardization of basic nurse training across the country. Barrow was also instrumental in getting a substantial increase in the number of community health centres, facilitating the organization of public health care on a parish basis throughout the island.

By the late 1950s, the concept of a national nurses organization had spread rapidly to many of the territories of the Caribbean. In fact, nurses had started to entertain the idea of a regional organization. Such a body, the Caribbean Nurses Organization (CNO), was formed in 1957 on the initiative of Mavis Harney, at that time president of the Antigua Nurses Organization. The objectives of the body were for the most part focused on improving nursing services for the betterment of Caribbean people, through exchange and interaction. However, two of those objectives stand out:

- to promote understanding and friendship between nurses in all parts of the Caribbean, and in neighbouring islands and countries
- to consider, follow through, and work on projects and/or surveys that will lead to better health care for the people of the Caribbean

Significantly, the CNO predates the federal experiment between several Caribbean countries by a year. The first objective identified not only speaks to the fact that nurses were helping to foster that spirit of integration promoted at the level of national politics, but it demonstrated a definition of Caribbean, unique for the time, which was inclusive of the non-English-speaking countries of the region. The second objective here identified sparked the interest of the new federal government once it came on board and led to the first Regional Nursing Conference, convened by the federal government in 1959. This conference became pivotal in Nita Barrow's life because it sparked off her involvement in the World Health Organization through its Pan American Health Organization (PAHO/WHO) office.

The Regional Nursing Conference, held to examine nursing standards in the Caribbean, made the recommendation that PAHO/WHO be approached to assist the region with a survey of nursing schools. The concern of nurse leaders and educators was to introduce basic standards of training and thereby facilitate accreditation of nurse training in the region. PAHO agreed to fund the project to survey the twenty-three schools existing at the time, and offered the role of leading the research to Nita Barrow. Together with a Canadian consultant she had identified who had done her doctoral dissertation on nursing education systems in Canada, Barrow designed the survey and set about conducting it. In chapter 5, Sheila Stuart discusses the PAHO project and its outcomes in detail; however, two points of particular note are the methodology of the visits and the conduct of the three seminars that formed part of the project. In our interview Barrow (1995b) remarked that "the countries had to own the survey" if the planners hoped to have the necessary follow-up, which could only happen at the national level once the survey was over. As a consequence of this objective a detailed consultative process was put in place.

A board of review consisting of the senior nursing officer from each participating country was set up and a seminar held with them to orient them on and to discuss the criteria of evaluation. During the visits, Barrow, accompanied by a senior nurse from another country, would interview nurse educators, Ministry of Health representatives, matrons of hospitals, nurses' organizations representatives, and representatives of different health services. Before leaving a country, the survey team would present a report of its findings to a meeting of these same persons. Two other regional seminars were held: one to review the overall findings of the survey, and the other of nursing educators to plan basic nursing education programmes and discuss curriculum development (PAHO 1968).

Remarkable too was the methodology used during the seminars. The process facilitated changes in the programme throughout the seminars to meet the needs of participants. Individual consultations were also arranged between the project directors and participants at the latter's requests. In this way, a process that was complex to begin and that had the potential for becoming problematic was made easier.[10] Out of the research and project seminars, several key changes emerged. The Regional Council of Nursing with responsibility for accrediting nursing schools in the Caribbean was formed; curriculum changes were made in many of the schools; the teaching process was updated; and training in nursing administration and nursing education was initiated. Talks were also begun on the provision of an Advanced Nursing Education Unit to deliver advanced training at the University of the West Indies. Barrow remained with PAHO until 1969, providing technical assistance to governments in the region on nursing policies, after which she left to take up the appointment of assistant director of medical services at the World Council of Churches.

Conclusion

Histories of Caribbean development usually identify the nationalist struggle, conveniently placed in the 1930s, with the struggles of men for political self-determination and wider distribution of social resources such as jobs, income, and education. The imagery of this process usually describes the exchange of one set of (white) men for another set of (black) men, although the discourse purports to be inclusive of the struggles of all Caribbean peoples against colonial domination. And this presentation of the issue is not limited to the interpretations of history by men. For example, in explaining the factors responsible for the low social prestige of nurses in Latin America, de Monterrossa, Lange and Chompre state that "Nurses as a social group have limited or no participation in social and political movements" (de Monterrossa, Lange and Chompre 1990: 221). However, a careful analysis of nursing history would reveal that nurses, as well as being outstanding individuals, did contribute significantly in their struggles to the social and political movements and thus to the overall democratization and development of Caribbean countries. If the development and strengthening of a middle class is taken as demonstrative of the success of the goal of widening the distribution of resources in the society, a clear concern of the shapers of Caribbean independence, then the struggles of nurses can be counted as an important factor in the achievement of this goal in many Caribbean countries.

Health policies that are now taken for granted, such as the establishment of community health centres and public health education campaigns, were the result of direct efforts on the part of nursing personnel. Sometimes they were initiators of these policies, such as in the case of Nita Barrow, but certainly they played key roles as implementers in the development of the health sector and in the improvement of conditions of employment for workers in the sector. The struggles of nurses to be self-determining cannot be separated from the quest of Caribbean societies for political self-determination. An examination of the life of Caribbean nurses can offer much scope for understanding how Caribbean countries function and how issues of gender, race, and class influence change in our society.

Notes

1. See Mair 1974; Gill and Massiah 1986; Beckles 1989.
2. Walters 1995.
3. The only criteria for selecting nurse probationers were age and size; the latter relating apparently to the presumed level of physical hard labour involved (Walters 1995: 5).
4. In his biography of Dame Nita, Francis Blackman records that whether on duty or not all nurses had to be on hospital premises by 9:00 p.m; furthermore, nurses on night duty were expected to be on the premises by 12:00 noon and be in their dormitories "resting" until they went on duty (Blackman 1995: 24).

5. Histories of nursing locate its origins in religion. Gertrude Swaby, a prominent Jamaican nurse, locates this origin under Christianity in the command to "love thy neighbour". Swaby (n.d.) notes that the care of the sick, the poor and the aged (historically linked) was considered a religious rather than a social duty in the Caribbean and was historically performed by religious functionaries.
6. It is widely known that in Western societies women were once the society's acknowledged healers. They were particularly the ones who assisted in childbirth, hence the term "midwife". Male usurpation of the role of female medics, or witches as they were then known, led to the association of witchcraft with evil and the separation of medical from nursing functions.
7. As Blackman argues, the hospital board was also slowly being changed as more non-white members were added and colour prejudices and oppression could no more be openly supported over reasonable positions (1995: 29).
8. Since the mid-1970s this point has been made repeatedly in "women in development" and feminist literature analysing the development of so-called Third World societies.
9. Blackman records that "with the strong support of the growing Jamaica Nurses Association, legislation requiring registration of nurses, including those in private practice and those employed by private companies, was introduced. With the support of ministers of health, the cooperation of the chief Medical Officer . . . and the General Nursing Council a unity of service was created which produced a stability and sense of well-being previously unknown" (1995: 51).
10. Blackman records that respondents during the survey, finding themselves for the first time able to unburden their minds on the issues raised to other West Indian colleagues, unburdened not only information but also petty jealousies, animosities and suspicions (1995: 58).

Chapter Five

The Smell of Sweet Apples

[Sheila Stuart]

Introduction

The professional growth and development of women within the Caribbean is very rarely planned, and career choices tend to be rather limited and limiting. As Beckles and Gill have shown in chapters 3 and 4, this limitation was even more pronounced in the 1930s. In those years, the young Nita Barrow was faced with a choice between only two possible careers: nursing or teaching.

Barrow chose nursing, but from the beginning she refused to allow her life chances to be limited by that choice. She struggled against all odds to become one of the region's most outstanding public figures. As part of the colonial and postcolonial Caribbean social and political order, she understood very clearly the problems and needs of these societies, which were juxtaposed against the dynamics of class, colour, race, and gender. Thus, nursing became her personal lodestar, leading to an illustrious career in health at the national, regional and international levels.

This chapter explores the contribution of Nita Barrow to the field of health at national, regional, and international levels. In this exploration, I place this contribution within a historical, political, and social context. In terms of structure, the first half of this chapter focuses on a number of specific health areas in which she worked at the national level in Barbados, at the regional level in Jamaica, and with the Pan American Health Organization as a consultant.

Barrow's contributions to health in the areas of public health and primary health care are discussed in an effort to assess her role in developments in these areas at the regional and international levels. The final section of the chapter focuses on Barrow's advocacy and her role in health and development at the global level.

Health and Development at the National and Regional Level

There is no doubt that good health plays an important role in the life of any community. There is indeed an integral relationship between health and social and economic development. It is therefore also true that "properly organized and delivered health services are basic to the achievement of economic and social goals set for a nation" (Barbados n.d.a.).

At the dawn of the twentieth century, the quality of life of the individual and the community in Caribbean societies was very poor, resulting in frequent epidemics of smallpox, typhoid fever, yellow fever, dysentery, and other diseases directly associated with poor housing and living conditions. As Beckles and Gill have shown in chapters 3 and 4, that Barbados, the home of Nita Barrow, was no exception. In describing the health situation of the region at that time, Barrow recalled:

> Some communicable diseases which were associated with poor sanitation, for example, typhoid fever – the vomiting sickness of Jamaica – were all then very much a part of the scene. When I trained at the Barbados General, whole wards were set aside for typhoid. We used to say, you could smell typhoid, because it *smelled like sweet apples*. (Barrow 1995c)

The major health problems facing Barbados and the region at that time included a high infant mortality rate and a high incidence of communicable diseases. Given such a scenario, health policies were designed that placed much emphasis on "a preventative rather than a curative approach":

> . . . on the grounds that if certain diseases could be prevented . . . then more suffering can be eliminated and large sums saved by establishing the services necessary to prevent disease, than by allowing people to become ill and providing aid and treatment for them. (Barbados n.d.a.)

As Beckles reveals in chapter 3, within the prevailing climate of social and political change that was sweeping the region in the 1930s and early 1940s, the colonial authorities deemed it both necessary and expedient to provide some of the basic social services. In Barbados, for example, the area of public health policy became the major focus of attention, wherein government began to introduce measures to expand water facilities by increasing the number of standpipes and public baths. Increased emphasis was also placed on the updating and reorganization of medical and public health services, which led to initiatives by health services and medical personnel to improve the quality of life of the population through health promotion activities.

It was against this background that Nita Barrow's pioneering work in health began to flourish. During these early years, there was a sanitation service which took care of the environment, housing and food services, all of that came under the umbrella of public health, which Barrow defined as "The preventative aspect of health care" (Barrow 1995c). This encompassed a broad spectrum of activities relative to the maintenance of good health. According to her, this development was "new to the Caribbean until the mid-forties and then it began to grow" (Barrow 1995c).

Another critical aspect of the public health approach to improving the quality of life in the Caribbean region was that of community participation. Dame Nita saw the education and motivation of the community to maintain certain minimum standards of sanitation as the key to the improvement and maintenance of health and well-being. According to her, public health differed from primary care:

> Primary care dealt not only with prevention of disease but with people taking care of the first aid measures. For example, if a child is vomiting, the mother should not have to wait to take it to the doctor, but instead she would be taught how to prepare a simple prescription – a fluid which you can give that takes care of that. In public health she would wait to go to the clinic to the nursing advisor. If the child, falls and has a cut or wound, you don't have to wait to go to the general hospital, the mother in a primary health care concept is taught, or someone within the community is taught how they can take care of that. And it is trying to prevent complications whilst taking care of the measures immediately any individual in the community can give. (Barrow 1995c)

Given the scope of public health, it therefore must be carried out at a number of levels and by a variety of personnel and institutions because "public health care emphasizes the education of people as to the prevention of disease". (Barrow 1995c)

Maternal and Child Health

Maternal and child health was one of the major health problems facing Barbados and the Caribbean region. During Barrow's early career in nursing, for example, the antenatal services for mothers were not as effective as they could have been, "and therefore you had women dying of the complications of childbirth, [or] dying of things such as toxaemia of pregnancy, a pre-complication to childbirth." As Barrow stated, diphtheria, malnutrition, and gastroenteritis were all killers of children during that time (Barrow 1995c).

Maternal and child health became one of the pivots of the public health policies because mothers and children were deemed the two most vulnerable groups. The provision of health care services was designed around these two groups and included programmes such as the inoculation of infants and schoolchildren against the various infectious and communicable diseases prevalent at the time.

There was also much concern about the quality of life of the population, which was directly linked to the lack of adequate provision of nutritional needs, a situation that had its roots in the prevailing socioeconomic conditions of the Caribbean societies. This was one of the critical factors impacting the quality of child health. Barrow lauded the work of stalwarts such as Dr Frank Ramsey in Barbados, who established the National Nutrition Centre in the 1960s. The strategy devised by the Nutrition Centre emphasized and promoted the use of local resources such as the use of local foods that would provide children with much needed nutrients, taking into consideration the economic circumstances of the majority of the population at the time.

One very successful programme that Barrow highlighted was the backyard gardening project in the 1970s a project that encouraged mothers to grow in containers "things like spinach, which were easy to grow and which added to the child's nutrition" (Barrow 1995c). The underlying premise of this strategy was that most childhood diseases are preventable by adequate nutrition and good hygienic care. This called for continuous public health teaching.

One of the tragedies of this period was that most mothers were being encouraged to bottle-feed their babies. This became a very attractive lifestyle option, but a devastating health problem in terms of child health in the region:

> We had gone off breast feeding and we were doing all the bottle feeding, and you know we had quite a campaign in the 70s in Europe – the famous Nestle bottle babies . . . and we got a surge in the developing world away from breast feeding because all the companies did, was

to target Third World countries with their formulas and unfortunately the medical and nursing profession all fell for it and they were all giving away the one tin of formula and the mothers in hospitals were being told it is easier to feed their babies by this method. (Barrow 1995c)

The problem with the extensive use of infant formula was that breast milk is an important source of nourishment for babies. Breast milk also provides babies with their first course of immunization, and thereby protects them against many childhood infections such as diarrhoea, coughs, colds, and other common illnesses. Also, families were often not in a position to afford sufficient supplies of milk powder or infant formula or were not educated in the need to properly sterilize teats and feeding bottles.

Managing Health Care in the Region

As Gill reveals in chapter 4, Barrow's pioneering role in the development of public health in the Caribbean began to take shape when, as a trained nurse, she moved from Barbados to Jamaica in 1945 to take up the position of assistant nursing instructor at the School of Public Health. (The establishment of the school is discussed by Beckles in chapter 3.) As a health educator at the regional level, Barrow's concern with health care moved beyond the national level in Barbados to embrace health care concerns within the wider Commonwealth Caribbean. She therefore had to focus on the delivery of health care to populations that differed qualitatively as well as quantitatively. Their needs were as varied as their countries, characterized by differences in demography, geography, physical facilities, communications, equipment, and administrative infrastructure (Anglin-Brown 1994)

As an educator, Barrow had responsibility for ensuring that efficient use was made of available national and regional resources, given the limited financial resources and the constraints of operating within the differences described above. She was acutely aware of the need at that time in the history of the Caribbean, when the region was going through the throes of economic and political transformation, for "home-grown" health professionals to assist with the development process.

Traditionally, governments assumed responsibility for sanitation measures, working conditions as well as the health care of high-priority groups such as mothers and children. As Barrow (1995c) recalled, "even under slavery poor law institutions provided health care for slaves" because one of the major problems affecting the supply of slaves was the high infant mortality rate of children. And because slaves were an economic asset, measures were introduced that gave greater care to pregnant slaves, as well as to reducing the high infant mortality.

In Barbados, for example, there was a system of local government where the vestries, located in each of the eleven parishes, were responsible for providing health care. This system of local government replicated the English model of administration and was premised on the concept of bringing the government closer to the people, thereby promoting a sense of citizenship and responsibility. Adequate financing of health care was therefore critical, because this determined the delivery of services. No major changes were made in this basic model of health care in the region over the years. Therefore, the government's health policies were devised to extend the coverage to a wider population by expanding the existing system. This expansion of services necessitated an increase in spending on health services. As Barrow stated, in the Caribbean generally:

> Most governments' substantial budgets were being spent on health care. When I have compared those with other countries, the Caribbean Governments on the whole, contributed immeasurably to their health budgets. I think Barbados was 12 percent at one stage. On the whole, the Caribbean Governments provided free health care to the majority of their people, you know it is only today that we talk about health insurance schemes and so on, and so health care was dependent on government expenditure and like . . . education, health had a much higher profile in most of their budgets than you find in many developing countries. (Barrow 1995c)

Given the scarce resources within the region, the main thrust of health policies was to focus on the integration of the preventative with curative health services as a means of improving the efficiency of institutional and non-institutional health care, a strategy that Barrow promoted through her teaching of public health nurses. The preparation of public health nurses and sanitary inspectors, now called public health inspectors, was seen as a cost-effective strategy "because they were the ones in whom the whole concept of preventive care was based" (Barrow 1995c).

Prior to the 1940s, administrative positions for women in the health sector were not very common, particularly for Caribbean women. The transition from teaching to administration was therefore a milestone achievement in the career of Nita Barrow, who became the first Caribbean matron at the University College Hospital of the West Indies (UCHWI). There she helped to establish the nursing education faculty.

The University College of the West Indies and the Medical Faculty had been incorporated only five years prior to Barrow's appointment as matron and was responsible for professional training of nursing and medical personnel. The university became a major player in the social and economic development and change in the region, particularly in the field of health development.

Barrow's appointment as matron was regarded as a major triumph for the Caribbean and black West Indians, and a giant step for women of the region. The position of matron was a prestigious one, a position that commanded a good measure of power and authority. According to Blackman (1995), this "was an achievement and a signal that West Indians had come of age". As matron, Barrow was responsible for a staff of ten, all of whom were British:

> To have a West Indian in charge of an institution where the first line of subordinate staff were white and British as well as West Indian was new not only for the Caribbean but throughout the so-called non-white segments of the British Empire. (Blackman 1995: 46)

As a regional health administrator, Barrow had to keep abreast of trends in demographics, and technological as well as social and economic changes which impacted on health care. At UCHWI she was well-placed to be fully aware of these trends, thus enabling her to implement training programmes that responded to community needs.

Through her role as matron at UCHWI, and her involvement in the health programmes of the University of the West Indies, Nita Barrow had a direct role in identifying critical factors that impact on health, particularly in the areas of health management and administration, and the education of health personnel. She had responsibility for ensuring that Caribbean nationals were educated to a standard that would enable them to take on leadership and decision-making roles:

> One of the reasons for stressing training at the local level, apart from the economic costs, was the fact that nurses who left the region for further training often did not return, and their services were therefore lost. One could also impute some political motive in this strategy, since it represented a move towards the preparation of Caribbean nationals to take on the role of self-management and development, given the impetus towards political independence in the region at that time. (Barrow 1995c)

Barrow's involvement in this prestigious regional institution brought her recognition in many areas. It also brought her into contact with many people who would later achieve excellence at the regional and international levels.

Many of the leaders in the field of health today are products of the programmes she helped to establish at the UCHWI. She also developed many significant professional relationships with colleagues, for example, the Revd Dr Philip Potter, who later became president of the World Council of Churches and who would help to propel her career into the international health arena.

Some two years after assuming the position of matron at UCHWI, Nita Barrow's professional career was taken a step further when she took up the position of Jamaica's first principal nursing officer. The creation of this position enhanced the development of nursing services and public health in Jamaica. As principal nursing officer, Barrow's responsibility was now much greater than it had been as matron at UCHWI.

In this new role, Barrow had responsibility for a staff of over three thousand spread around the country. One of her major objectives was the creation of a more integrated and efficient nursing service. This necessitated the revision of management structures and procedures, supervision and training, and financing and budgetary controls. Because there was no model existing elsewhere to build upon, Barrow drew on her management skills and ability to conceptualize and be innovative.

The integration of nursing services as well as her attempts to improve the status and roles of nursing personnel were perhaps her more difficult tasks, because she encountered significant opposition from the medical fraternity. Despite the opposition and the desire on the part of the medical officer to maintain the status quo, she was not deterred. Her determination resulted in the improvement of the self-image and professional status of nursing personnel.

Barrow's experience in the administration of health services in Jamaica presented her with many challenges, all of which she directly confronted. Her efforts to provide health services to the entire Jamaican population required that substantial funds be allocated for infrastructural development and administrative costs. Barrow proceeded to prepare a budget that was ten times greater than the J$1 million previously allocated for nursing services. She was allowed to defend her budget at the Estimates Committee presided over by, the then prime minister and minister of finance, Norman Manley. Her ability to present and defend her proposed programmes resulted in acceptance of the budget, which enabled her to implement projects such as the building of health centres at the parochial level and improved training for nursing personnel (Blackman 1995).

It was Barrow's determination, her ability to manage competently, together with her growing wealth of experience, that set her apart as one of the region's leading female nurses. It was also responsible for propelling her professional career to new heights.

Pan American Health Organization

In chapter 4 Margaret Gill reveals how Barrow's transition from national to regional and international figure occurred in the late 1950s and early 1960s. Suffice to say here that in 1964, when the Pan American Health Organization of the World Health Organization (PAHO/WHO), was looking for a project leader to "undertake a survey to review standards of training schools for nurses", Nita Barrow was the obvious choice. Barrow's twenty-five years of experience of nursing at local and national levels in Barbados and Jamaica had prepared her to move on to a new stage in her career.

As nursing advisor/consultant to PAHO/WHO, she was specifically responsible for assessing nursing education and nursing service resources in the Commonwealth Caribbean. This covered territories from Belize to Guyana, from Trinidad to Jamaica, including all the islands of the Bahamas and the Eastern Caribbean. The survey was intended not only to assess the twenty-three schools of nursing in the region but also included the development of plans that would:

> Seek to improve nursing education throughout the region, which entailed an examination of the nursing services to see what was required in the preparation of nurses to meet the needs of those services, which included not only general nursing but public health and what we call clinical nursing services, and psychiatric nursing. The (Metropolitan) countries had psychiatric nursing, so it was felt that we should have it, and of course the key was . . . to prepare nurses for adequate health care in public health. (Barrow 1995c)

The survey was originally designed to conduct research to assess training needs and make recommendations for improvements during a period of three years. In reality, it extended over a period of eight years. As Barrow indicated, the PAHO/WHO was very good about trying to meet all identified needs. This often involved liaising with health personnel to implement training programmes at the local level. For example, several training programmes were mounted in Barbados for senior nursing personnel who needed to be prepared so that they could supervise more adequately. To assist with this training, a local team of nursing appraisers would be identified and selected. "Barbados, for instance, prepared nurses at the Ward Sister level, and the Sister responsible for this training was Ms Marie Matthews. She was part of the training team, with others being brought in from time to time" (Barrow 1995c). Other activities included teaching in the schools of nursing in those territories. The need for auxiliary personnel to relieve nurses on duty was one of the needs which was recognized and recommended as a result of the study. Training was therefore implemented to prepare what were called the nursing assistants:

> We could not wait for the one year programme which eventually grew at the University and so there were short term teaching programmes being carried out in some territories. But at the same time, there was a need to sensitize Governments, administrators and the University to the need. (Barrow 1995c)

Training seminars were also held every year for the first three years in different territories for nursing administrators, teachers, doctors, ministries of health, and university personnel. These seminars were followed by a series of meetings that brought together important officials in the region's health sector, such as the regional head of PAHO, health planners, and others who were more directly involved in the implementation of the recommendations emanating from the survey.

As a result of the PAHO survey, considerable changes were made to the schools of nursing, particularly in the areas of curriculum development, supervision and training, and teaching staff assigned to the schools. In addition, some twenty-six educational activities, in which over five hundred nurses were involved, were cosponsored during this period by PAHO/WHO in collaboration with the governments of the Caribbean. The survey also led to the establishment of a regional nursing body.

Another outstanding policy proposal during Barrow's tenure at the University of the West Indies and PAHO concerned the post-basic preparation of senior personnel. This led to the establishment of the Advanced Nursing Unit at the university. It required the governments contributing to the university to make a significant commitment:

> Although it was behind the scenes work, it was us in PAHO who had to get that commitment because no government wanted to go ahead. Then we got the endorsement of the medical faculty and that was a major policy in postgraduate education.

> We got several of the countries which did not have general nursing councils to put those in place and in addition we got a regional nursing body which then began the coordinating, advisory body to the Ministers of Health which again were instituted during that period. (Barrow 1995c)

Nita Barrow was also instrumental in obtaining governmental cooperation in allocating bigger budgets for and improvements in training schools, which at that time were considered major policy and financial decisions.

However, it is important to understand that policies are not formulated in a vacuum, but emerge within the context of the political economy of a given time (Ward 1987). The period of the 1950s and 1960s was a period of great political transformation in the Caribbean, and Barrow's pivotal position as former matron of the University College Hospital in Jamaica and consultant with PAHO brought her in direct contact with policy makers. This meant that Barrow was in a position to assist in agenda setting, decision making and policy implementation. Equally important was her position in terms of key conditions such as class, occupation, family background, and political orientation. Combined with her own training and character, these aided her access to the channels of power and decision making.

Health and Development at the International Level

Christian Medical Commission

Health is inextricably linked with social and economic development and therefore depends more on meeting social needs than on the provision of medical services. No one understood this better than Nita Barrow, whose concept of health was that of the community taking responsibility for the delivery and maintenance of health care. According to Potter (1995), Barrow had a vision of health that was refreshingly new as "she saw health as a function and goal of the entire community". The approach to health adopted by Barrow could be considered as egalitarian because she believed that access to health care should be available to everyone. In fact, her approach was to demystify medical care because her concern was not only with the provision of services but also with the removal of barriers to their utilization. It was this *vision* which propelled her to embark on yet another phase in her personal and professional life.

In 1968, at the invitation of Revd Dr Potter, she assisted the World Council of Churches in establishing the Christian Medical Commission (CMC), which had as its goal the promotion of community health care through the churches. Three years later Barrow became a leading member of the CMC serving as associate director and later as director. This period of her career transformed her into a truly international figure, as her responsibilities included advising church-affiliated health institutions worldwide on developments in health care.

The CMC regarded itself as a consultative, enabling body to church health services and church-related individuals and groups around the world engaged in many facets of health care. The CMC occasionally performed the role of broker to assist in securing funds, but it was not itself a funding agency. Relationships in the field were initiated by individuals and groups who approached the CMC, rather than the other way around.

The key to the CMC's relationship with its constituency in the field was its efforts to encourage people's participation in identifying their health needs, and in planning, implementing, and evaluating their own and their communities' health care. The CMC was instrumental in bringing about the formation of some eighteen National Coordinating Agencies for church-related health services, and separate Protestant and Roman Catholic national agencies in a further four countries during Nita Barrow's term in office.

The CMC policy of strengthening programmes of community involvement in health development with its concentration on both participation and local level care was not accidental because it was based on experiences straight from the field. Barrow, in her role as senior administrator of the CMC, had travelled to numerous countries in Asia, Africa and Latin America where she witnessed first-hand the community-based health care programmes that offered an alternative to the elaborate physical infrastructure of more formal health services. For example, in 1979, she visited the community health project at Kaimosi, Lugulu, in Kenya. This was initiated by Dr Miriam Were of the Community Health Department of the University of Nairobi and the Anglican diocese of Maseno South Rural Development Programme. Aspects of community participation observed during the visit included (1) the building of latrines and baths; (2) child welfare clinics and daycare centres; and (3) school nutrition programmes.

According to Barrow, one of the adages underlying the CMC concept of health care was the old Chinese one:

> If you give a man a fish, you feed him for a day; if you teach him to fish, you feed him for the rest of his life and the idea is if you teach people how to take care of their own health. It can be a political dynamite, because when people learn to take care of their own health, they also learn other things about their own ability to cope and therefore you always have be aware that sometimes you may run into political problems if a group gets really enthusiastic about wanting change. (Barrow 1995c)

Barrow stressed that development had more to do with improving the human condition through the efficient use of resources, rather than with the adoption of elaborate macro-economic structures. This concept of building self-reliance rather than dependency was the foundation on which her work was built. Despite its limited financial and human resources, the CMC under Barrow did much to get health to the people through their worldwide network of church-affiliated organizations. The focus on preventative health care was a constant throughout her career, as was her commitment to recognizing and valuing the contributions and abilities of communities to improve their own health care rather than imposing foreign values and methods.

Alternative Forms of Health Care for the Underserved

From her early days as a nurse in the Caribbean, Nita Barrow had been exposed to the complexity of factors that led to ill health in communities, and the influences that impacted on individual decision-making relative to seeking health care. But it was through her travels to countries in the major regions of the world as a commissioner of the CMC that Barrow learned more about *underserved* populations, which she describes as "those people who may consider themselves outside the watershed – the catchment area of health care" (Barrow 1995c). In some countries, for example:

> It is because of geography where health care was delivered by people from outside, like the churches, and this is how the Christian Medical Commission became involved. They would often congregate in areas around towns where there were populations because the interest was not only in health care but it was proselytization, that is, spreading the gospel. In some countries, for example, they would have a number of hospitals of varying sizes around an urban area and then 200 miles, 100 miles, or 50 miles away there would be no health care

facility with trained personnel, therefore there would have a watershed of a large number of people who had no health care as we know it, neither in the field of preventative medicine, public health nor in institutional care. (Barrow 1995c)

Populations can be underserved for a variety of reasons, for example, a lack of personnel, a lack of facilities, and, equally important, the inability of the community to pay for health services. Underserved populations were found in all corners of the world, including the United States: "They have some of the biggest underserved populations right in their big cities, such as Chicago and New York" (Barrow 1995c). This ironic situation Barrow attributed to the cost dynamics of the health systems in the United States where it is not the lack of health facilities, "it is the cost that puts it outside the gate" of the majority of the population.

According to Barrow, these underserved communities sought to develop their own systems, but would often need assistance in terms of organization, management, and conceptualizing their activities to enable them to better achieve their goals. The philosophy of the CMC was such that when they discovered health care at this level of operation, they would be careful not to assume that the needs of a community could be met by the introduction of medical services. Rather, the strategy would be to identify the needs of the underserved population. As Barrow stated, "it was often found that the need was simply for the facilities to be upgraded or for their own personnel to be given some additional training and not simply bringing in people from outside who leave again" (Barrow 1995c). She also stressed that it was always critical to work from the bottom up rather than from the top down:

There may be a problem where a group is suffering from a lack of water, well there is no sense talking to them about nutrition when they haven't got water to grow the crops, to feed the chickens and to feed the children. So you start with identification of the need of the community, and the community itself works with you on meeting that need. (Barrow 1995c)

Reproductive Health

During Barrow's first years in Geneva reproductive health was one of the major areas she pursued. According to her, reproductive health was one of those areas around which medical care revolved during the 1960s and 1970s. The shift from a focus on maternal and child health to embrace all facets of reproductive health represented a significant achievement in terms of addressing the issue of population. The new orientation focused attention on the social, economic, and cultural factors that contributed to high fertility, poor maternal and child health, and the spread of sexually transmitted diseases.

In 1974, Barrow led the CMC delegation to the first UN International Conference on Population and Development in Bucharest. At this meeting,

> The battle was not with the Churches, but mainly with governments who did not see reproductive health as an important health matter. But by that time, it was the era of development, and all the agencies giving 'development aid' to many of the new developing countries of Africa and Asia realized that part of their problem was the huge populations with yearly massive increases which meant that their aid couldn't go very far when there was an unlimited number of people entering the population every year. (Barrow 1995c)

It was in this context and environment that reproductive health became a major platform. In terms of historical context, Barrow understood the root causes, characteristics, and consequences of unprecedented population growth in the developing world. As always, her first point of reference was the Caribbean, where overpopulation had been the root cause of many of the social and economic ills and where in Barbados this had led to widespread migration in search of employment and a better quality of life.

According to Barrow, Barbados was considered one of the more progressive territories in that it was recognized early that a programme of fertility regulation was needed. The establishment of the family planning unit, which was a private organization, owed its success to people like Sir Randall Phillips and Lady Adams who pushed the reproductive health programme in Barbados in the same way that Jamaica's programme was pushed by Mrs Beth Jacobs. Barrow was very aware that the family planning programme was not popular with some governments because of opposition from some churches which were against it. But in Barbados, and from its inception, it received much needed support from the government:

> It would have been mass suicide to have gone on reproducing as we were. I think that one of the platforms that Barbados could speak on, is the question or rather the statement, that when you increase peoples' education, you give them opportunities in employment and professional development [and] that this is one of the best ways to reproductive control that you could have. (Barrow 1995c)

In 1995 Barrow noted there had been a shift away from the former concentration on contraception and fertility regulation to a focus on health as it relates to reproduction. Further, there had been some recognition of the fact that female morbidity and mortality was linked to a woman's reproductive system. Conditions such as breast and cervical cancer were major killers of women. One of the most effective methods of combating these diseases would be "to alert the women to the need for early vigilance. The question is how do we educate women to do the early tests that would save them from the extreme cases of cervical and breast cancer?" (Barrow 1995c).

In more recent years, reproductive health has been further threatened by the emergence of new diseases linked to sexual activity (for example, HIV/AIDS, and the continual spread of new strains of sexually transmitted diseases). There continues to be a need to develop new ways of empowering individuals and communities to deal with sexuality and health conditions. Women's sexuality has been, and continues to be, at the forefront of the fight against women's attempts to control their fertility, thereby improving their reproductive health; and as Dame Nita observed "it is a myth to believe that by giving women control of their bodies that they will become promiscuous" (Barrow 1995c; WHO 1994).

Traditional Medicine

Another major accomplishment of Nita Barrow during her tenure at the CMC was the endorsement of traditional medicine[1] and healing as a component of health care. This achievement was significant because it came at a time when the very mention of traditional medicine evoked cries of "witch doctor" and "obeah". But Barrow was more concerned about the uncritical imposition of Western medical systems of health in societies that already had their own traditional methods of healing, than with the negative associations. The CMC's focus on traditional methods of healing was seen as one way of endorsing and supporting existing health actions at the community level.

Despite the fact that traditional medicine was viewed with suspicion by the medical profession, one of the objectives of the CMC was to bring traditional medicine into its own by enabling medical doctors and non-practitioners to recognize the strengths and the weaknesses in it. Therefore CMC sponsored a number of regional meetings in various regions of the world, which brought together Western-trained doctors and traditional healers and community leaders (pastors of the churches, teachers, and government personnel):

At the African regional meeting, held in Botswana, one of the participants was a Western trained doctor. He was the only doctor we could get from South Africa at that time . . . he was a white doctor who was working in a mission hospital . . . when he came to the meeting and heard that there were traditional healers he said to us – do you expect me to sit down with witch doctors – because right away that was his concept. One of the keynote speakers at that conference was a Ghanaian, Dr Nartey, who was a chemist and whose father was in the British Army and had been a traditional healer for years. He delivered a very powerful address on the role of traditional versus Western medicine. At the end of the address, this South African doctor came up to me and said 'what a powerful speaker', and I said, 'and he is the president of 250,000 traditional healers in Ghana, as well as running a very big hospital'. (Barrow 1995c)

The CMC also commissioned a book on traditional medicine which was written by a Finnish theologian who went to Tanzania to teach in a seminary. While there, he found that the most powerful man was a *Meru*, who was a traditional healer. The Finnish theologian apprenticed himself to the *Meru* for two years:

He went out with him as he gathered the herbs and the bark and the leaves. His wife in Finland was a botanist, and he would send back the things to her, [and] she would do the drawings and get the botanical names and so when it came time for publication – we paid for that publication. The book gives some idea of what I call, a Western writings about the subject, taken from the perspective of a well prepared man, not a doctor himself, but one who went into the study of it, in-depth. (Barrow 1995c)

The Relationship between CMC and WHO

During Barrow's tenure as director of the CMC of the World Council of Churches, a close working relationship developed between the staff of the CMC and the staff of the WHO, both of which were situated in Geneva, Switzerland. Barrow headed the CMC's team that formed part of the official joint standing committee between these two organizations. This partnership between the CMC and WHO led to the International Conference on Primary Health Care at Alma-Ata, Russia. This conference produced a statement on "Health for All by the Year 2000", which according to the Revd Dr Potter (general secretary of the World Council of Churches for the Caribbean) was one of the "greatest of the many contributions she made" (Potter 1995: 19).

One of the policy objectives of the CMC was to promote innovative approaches to health care consistent with its understanding of health and healing for the maximum benefit of individuals, families, and communities especially the deprived. This work was disseminated through a newsletter called *Contact*. According to its editorial policy, *Contact* dealt with "varied aspects of the Christian community's involvement in health, and sought to report topical, innovative and courageous approaches to the promotion of health and integrated development".

It was this policy and the programme activities of the CMC that intrigued the director general of WHO, Dr Karsten Mahler, who, shortly after assuming office, saw *Contact* and invited the staff of CMC to meet with the staff of WHO to brief them on the work of the CMC and "we always say six of us went to talk to thirty-two heads of departments" (Barrow 1995c). It was as a result of that initial consultation, that a long-standing relationship was established between the two institutions. What became evident was that the "WHO was spending money but the CMC were getting health to the people. Dr Mahler proposed that an official joint standing committee be set up between the two organizations which Nita Barrow chaired" (Barrow 1995c). According to Philip Potter the imbalance between the small staff of the CMC compared to the twelve hundred staff of the WHO prompted her to remark, "I feel like David confronted by Goliath" (Potter 1995).

As chair of the standing committee, Barrow was strategically placed to guide and direct health policies at the international level:

> The concept of Alma-Ata grew out of the work of this committee and Dr Mahler co-opted the assistance of UNICEF, who at the time was quite excited about it too, and the Government of the USSR provided the venue. The conference of Alma-Ata was held in September 1978, [and] brought together all the governments of the world you could think of because Dr Mahler's idea was to spread the concept of primary health care because as you can imagine the medical profession was the most vocal against anything that eroded what they considered as theirs . . . on health care and the fact that we were saying that people who were living in areas where they had never seen a doctor or nurse, that they had developed ways of coping with disease. (Barrow 1995c)

Dr Mahler, who was regarded as one of the outstanding personalities in international health and development at the time, proposed that members of the communities involved in this process, as well as the people who were practising it, be brought together to engage in dialogue about the most appropriate method of cooperation between these groups in terms of meeting their needs and sharing health care. The basic premise of this collaboration was not focused on

> getting rid of nurses and doctors but you were saying that in addition, to the health professionals there was [a] need to prepare a level of worker whose role would be to help people to identify health needs. The major stumbling block however, was perceived to be one of acceptance of this strategy and a commitment from all parties involved to the whole concept. (Barrow 1995c)

The Primary Health Care Strategy

The concept of primary health care as an equity-oriented health and development strategy became the leading health policy in national and international health care. An integral component of the concept was its emphasis on the full participation of individuals and families in planning and decision making relative to their own health care. The root of the concept of primary health care is community involvement, requiring people to become involved in their own health care. In addition, the concept is based on the cooperation of all sectors of society with a concern for health. It also embraces and gives recognition to local cultures and traditions by making use of local resources, and which together contribute to minimizing the cost of health care. The cornerstones of primary health care are therefore based on self-reliance, equity, community participation and intersectoral collaboration.

One of the central concerns in primary care is the prevention of disease and disability, which requires that medical professionals provide curative care. It requires that individuals and families be educated on healthy lifestyles, and communities be educated on protective and supportive health measures. The primary health care strategy also requires nurses to undertake tasks and responsibilities formerly performed only by doctors, including the examination of patients, treatment and identification of sources of health problems, and prevention of major diseases.

It was not that the concept was a new one, because local communities, particularly those without access to health facilities, had for centuries adopted a proactive role in taking responsibility for their health. However, the endorsement of the concept of community involvement in health care by a leading UN institution thereby legitimized a process that was previously neglected.

Through its affirmation of indigenous methods of health care, the CMC brought about a profound change in the processes of conceptualizing health care.

It is especially noteworthy that the primary health care strategy also indirectly targeted women, the major providers and consumers of health care, but whose responsibility to family limits not only their free time but also their access to health facilities. The strategy opened up channels for participation by women, so that their special needs could be met. Women's traditional role as health care providers within the family and the community was therefore validated.

It is important to understand Barrow's catalytic role in the introduction of this concept to the international community. It could be argued that without her input into the proceedings of the joint CMC/WHO standing committee, and without her vision, the outcome may have been totally different. Barrow, for example, headed the delegation of the CMC to the Alma-Ata conference where the world community, represented by some 168 countries, endorsed the principle of global health equity and where primary health care was declared to be the key to achieving the goal of "Health for All by the Year 2000". The main feature of this goal was its comprehensiveness, with health being regarded as one of the major components of each community's well-being. One year after the conference, the WHO encouraged its member governments to define and implement strategies for attaining this goal. The WHO promoted the objectives and initiatives of primary health care within its internal programmes and with its member governments and articulated a historic consensus on the world goal of "Health for All by the Year 2000". By 1980, some twenty-four governments had formulated and presented national strategies of primary health care as the foundation of the development of their health systems (PAHO 1980). Member governments agreed that the principal social goals in the coming decades should be "the attainment by all citizens of the world by the year 2000 of a level of health that will permit them to lead a socially and economically productive life" (PAHO 1980).

The Caribbean Community (CARICOM) convened a regional conference in 1980, with the assistance of PAHO/WHO, UNICEF and the Commonwealth Secretariat. This allowed Caribbean countries to further review the concepts and implications of their application of the primary health care strategy, which was subsequently endorsed by individual governments. Primary health care, along with complementary strategies, were endorsed as the key to achieving this goal as part of overall development and in the spirit of social justice.

Alma-Ata was therefore an event of international significance because the slogan "Health for All" became watchwords of international health programmes, where the concept of equity was also established. Although Alma-Ata has had its critics, it has found a lasting place in the history of health care policies.

Health and Development at the Global Level

Nita Barrow's retirement from the CMC marked yet another new phase in her career in public health. She maintained her links with the WHO, serving as health consultant. She contributed to many WHO policy statements through participation in WHO decision-making conferences and meetings. She was considered one of the world's leading authorities on public health and health education and was called upon to serve on a number of WHO health commissions. Two such commissions on which she served were the Global Commission on AIDS, which was part of the WHO Global Programme on AIDS, and the WHO Global Commission on Women's Health. This association reflected the high regard that the WHO held for her work by maintaining their links long after her career had indirectly removed her from the health field.

Barrow was also involved for many years with the National Council for International Health (NCIH), serving on the international jury for the Hunger Project's Africa Prize for Leadership. In 1995, the NCIH presented Nita Barrow with its International Health Leadership Award, for her pioneering and visionary work in the field.

Health Problems Today

Speaking in 1995, Nita Barrow identified a number of health problems that have confronted the global community within recent years and that, despite major accomplishments in health, continue to impact social and economic development:

> I don't have to tell you that if anything stands out it is AIDS: And the other thing is that you have a number of the sexually transmitted diseases which for a time with vigorous attention from WHO and others had subsided but unfortunately they are recurring more and I don't know that Governments' are in tune with the trends. (Barrow 1995c)

For Barrow, the problem was compounded because, whilst many diseases had been virtually eradicated through immunization programmes, a number of the diseases of poverty (such as malnutrition and the gastrointestinal diseases) remained and had even made a comeback in some countries. For example, she lamented the fact that the world had been declared almost malaria free, yet malaria was re-emerging as a major killer.

As Barrow pointed out, some of these diseases are not readily identified by modern health professionals. When tuberculosis reappeared in the United States, health officials did not recognize it because the disease had not occurred for such a long time. Similarly, Jamaica had an outbreak of typhoid fever in 1994 in an area where there had been a terrible outbreak twenty years before and where a new hospital had been built:

> They told me [that] when it recurred, most people did not recognize it because they hadn't had typhoid for so long. There were one or two carriers left in the area, who still carried the typhoid bacillus, . . . of course a perfectly healthy person can be a carrier . . . and the person could have passed it on through cooking or something and it took them a little while to realize that an outbreak had occurred. (Barrow 1995c)

According to Barrow, the major problem in locating and identifying the carrier was the fact that the younger medical professionals who had not dealt with typhoid before could not diagnose it. "A young medical colleague told me that this was her first typhoid case, she said that it was only after one of the older persons had identified it that she recognized *the smell of sweet apples*" (Barrow 1995c).

> I think the worrying thing for some health professionals is the fact that the diseases that are recurring are those that have become resistant to the drugs which treated them, like antibiotics. We are therefore faced with having to look for new ways of treatment. (Barrow 1995c)

The global movement of people was also seen by Barrow as a major factor in the spread of diseases worldwide. For example, she noted that the world has been declared "smallpox free, but we only have to have one case of smallpox in the Amazon and with the way people are travelling, we get a re-infestation that a hundred years ago was impossible." All of this has been militating against the achievement of the goal of "Health for All by the Year 2000":

> Not unless we find an answer to AIDS, not unless we find a way to reverse the trend of . . . communicable diseases to recur, like malaria and tuberculosis, as long as we have pockets of these chronic diseases, with global travel, re-infestation of people will always occur. (Barrow 1995c)

Barrow was convinced that education was the most critical factor in the promotion of healthy lifestyles, particularly in relation to combating the HIV/AIDS crisis:

> I think we speak of the role of education and we tend to be very flip about it. We say it as though it is just a word – education. What we are really saying is that people have to be equally aware of their own responsibility. (Barrow 1995c)

In Nita Barrow's view, one of the shortcomings is in the preparation of Caribbean children to deal with their sexuality. She felt that this stemmed from the fact that most parents are not prepared to talk about sex education because nobody had prepared them to do so. In her view, parents do not feel adequate to answer the questions because of the way they were brought up. This inability of parents to adequately inform their children about the biological and physical changes related to the onset of puberty and related topics hampered their ability to manage their adult life. She suggested that one measure to overcome this difficulty in parenting skills is to routinely include family life education as part of the socialization process in the home. She advised that parents should use opportunities that inevitably present themselves:

> Anytime a child asks a question, they should never be shut up. Parents and other adults should give them an answer. Children often ask where do babies come from, and people tell them about the stork and this and the other. You only have to give the child an answer that is two sentences long, satisfies them and gives them the truth. And then later on, as they grow older, you give them the facts, because there is no doubt that children learn from their peer groups and they often learn the wrong things. (Barrow 1995c)

There was also a need to introduce what Barrow called, "a simultaneous educational programme", that is, "talking to children at all levels and at the same time getting adults to be aware of their responsibility to learn how they teach their children. Most of the time they and other people shy away from the subject" (Barrow 1995c).

Barrow also highlighted the inherent contradictions prevalent in society as a factor which impacted on attitudes and behaviour patterns. For example, one of the biggest problems was the total lack of censorship of home videos:

> There is no use trying to give constructive teaching and nobody tries to control the kind of X-rated movies and other video products that are brought into the region, and of course with the growth of [satellite] dishes there is unlimited and uncensored access to the X-rated channels. (Barrow 1995c)

She was critical of "this business of putting children down in front of the television and leaving them" because, as she recognized, young children become adept at manipulating this situation and therefore become exposed to negative education.

Barrow was aware of the escalation of a number of global trends, particularly the global economic crisis with its social and political consequences and its special impact on health and development. It has challenged the optimism of the primary health care strategy, and she realized that the goal of health for all by the year 2000 would not be achieved. Whilst the costs of health care have continued to rise, public-sector health budgets have decreased due to structural adjustment programmes (Barriteau 1996a). The demands for AIDS programmes and the increase in chronic non-communicable diseases have meant that governments with limited budgets have reallocated funding. She argued that the ability of the public sector to sustain health services had become severely constrained and as a result, there was a growing trend towards "fees for services", resulting in inequities in access to services. In Barrow's view, the cost of health care was one of the major problems today.

Despite these modern trends, Barrow was very positive regarding developments in the Caribbean, which she recognized had become more sophisticated with higher technical inputs. She stressed the commitment of Caribbean governments to provide health services. Citing Barbados as the health care system with which she had most experience, she stated:

> In Barbados we still provide a level of free health care which gives the average person access to emergency and other services. The person may decide they don't want to go on a public ward so if they go to a private ward they have to pay for it but basically if you go to emergency or to the outpatients you can get it. There are some places where that is not possible. In Barbados we have the polyclinics which have been set up around the country. Anyone can walk in and get health care. I don't think there is any means [of] testing and that at least is a

first line of care. You would not find that kind of health care in the community in the United States, in the sense of being able to go in and get to see doctors certain days of the week. (Barrow 1995c)

Within an environment where the provision of health care becomes constrained because of a lack of resources the challenge will be to provide health services to the population in an equitable manner. The growing trend toward private care (where the costs are controlled by those persons who deliver the health care) means that in the long term large sections of the population will be deprived of much needed health care.

Conclusion

From what could be described as the foundation years of her career, Nita Barrow displayed a concept of health that embraced the key elements of education and community. She regarded health care as more than a medical concern; rather, she considered it a "a political force intended to free individuals from the liabilities of nature and direct their energies toward social and economic development". Ideologically, she believed that the well-being of the individual was critical to all development and crucial to any vision of what the future should be (Barrow 1995c).

As Kathleen Drayton (chapter 2) and other authors have shown, Barrow was born into a family of political activists who were well-educated but who identified with the "masses of the people" and who sought to bring about change in society. A product of a turbulent political epoch in the Caribbean, and influenced by the socialist and humanitarian principles of her family, it is not difficult to understand her adoption of equity as the concept that would inform and guide her. Her commitment both to egalitarian principles and to the goal of self-determination was evident throughout her career, whether seeking to validate indigenous efforts at managing health care or supporting programmes with the ultimate aim of passing on management to "local" communities.

Nita Barrow had a healthy respect for other people's values and morals. This was probably one of the most significant perspectives that guided her work. She was very careful to work along with people and communities, respecting their history and sociocultural situation. She recognized that for programmes to have desired outcomes, it was critical that a conscious effort be made to ensure that the prospective beneficiaries participate in the process of decision-making at all levels. For her, this principle was especially critical in community work at both national and international levels and did much to empower individuals. Her commitment to education at both the formal and informal level was a critical component of her vision to "empower" individuals and communities with knowledge of how to take care – adequately and effectivel – of their own health needs.

These were some of the guiding concepts that underlined her catalytic role in the field of health care at the national, regional, and international levels. Her contributions were innovative and unique. Apart from scoring numerous firsts in her long career, Nita Barrow championed the cause of the underprivileged and pioneered many programmes that aimed to benefit them. Above all, she "always displayed a forthrightness and a particular intolerance of injustice" (Haniff 1988).

Note

1. The traditional Ayurvedic medicine of India is three thousand years old, and aromatic massage is one of its principal aspects. Aromatic herbs and woods are used to make up infused oils with which to massage the body.

Chapter Six

Environmental Management Through Individual Commitment, Community Efforts, and Institutional Support

[Janice Cumberbatch]

It is commitment. We have to have at least one or two or three people committed to make sure that what you have written on the paper goes into practice. We start with the person who says I am going to take one small fragment, see who else is interested, create a network, find allies. I have seen many movements grow because of that philosophy.

– Nita Barrow

Introduction

Sustainable development – humanity living in harmony with nature in order to leave a viable legacy for future generations – is touted as being key to stemming current and potential environmental problems, whether they are manifested as coral reef degradation, inadequate waste disposal practices, desertification or water pollution. At the heart of sustainable development is individual commitment. As Barrow has suggested:

Whether it is the Marshall Islands, where one young woman brought to the world's attention the effect of nuclear testing on women's reproductive systems and their offspring; or the international group DAWN [Development Alternatives for Women of a New Era] which was started in 1985 in Nairobi with one woman who said that women have to get together on issues that affect them; individuals everywhere are realizing that commitment, organization and hard work are the elements which translate lofty idealistic ideas like sustainable development into genuine action. (Barrow 1995e)[1]

This view is also advocated by the Earth Council, a body on which she served, whose philosophy states that people/individuals throughout the world will need to bring about the transition to sustainable, secure, and equitable development.

Individual commitment, expanded into community effort and strengthened by institutional support is critical to the successful implementation of environmental policies and programmes. This chapter examines these three elements: individual commitment, community effort, and institutional support as they reflect Nita Barrow's contribution to the environmental field. It also illustrates how they integrate to ensure the successful achievement of environmental goals.

Individual Commitment

The present generation of mankind is the first one that can irreversibly transform our planet for the worse. It is also the last generation with the capacity to introduce the changes required to avert environmental disaster. (Huntley, Siegfried, Gunter 1989)

The 1972 UN Conference on the Human Environment, which was held in Stockholm, Sweden, is identified as the landmark event which focused the world's attention on the fact that environmental problems were global rather than isolated national concerns. By 1972, there were visible signs of pollution in major industrialized nations, such as the Los Angeles smog and the death of major rivers; there was increasing desertification on the African continent; acid rain was killing and damaging forests and lakes and buildings in Europe; and the over-exploitation of terrestrial and marine resources to deal with debt and poverty crises in the African, Latin American, and Caribbean nations was escalating.

Since the 1972 UN conference, there have been numerous global, regional, and national conferences dealing with every possible aspect of the natural environment. Conventions have been framed, resolutions passed, and policies developed to deal with marine, terrestrial, and atmospheric environmental issues. In summing up the essence of these responses to environmental problems, Naresh Singh (1991), formerly of the Caribbean Environmental Health Institute, succinctly stated that:

> Most, if not all environmental and development speeches appeal for essentially the same set of ingredients changes in the social value system, in attitudes to life and nature, in consumption patterns and waste generation and in the greed for short term gain, and proceed to prescribe educational, institutional and legislative mechanisms to produce the changes.

Essentially, these changes comprise one basic element – they all necessitate the commitment of each individual to personal changes in attitudes and behaviour. The complex nature of environmental problems cause them to appear highly technical, requiring enormously complicated technological solutions. While it is true that the environmental problems will keep scientists well-occupied for decades to come, what is frequently downplayed is the role that each ordinary individual can play in stemming the flow of many of these problems.

Unfortunately, modern societies have become sufficiently far removed from direct contact with natural resources, and, therefore, individuals fail to perceive the critical role that they have to play as managers and stewards of these resources. Nita Barrow was particularly concerned about the interaction between people and the environment:

> There is a difference in our attitudes towards the environment which is a reflection of our present lifestyles. In the past, 95 percent of our people worked in agriculture . . . they had no electricity, they didn't have running water, they didn't have a supermarket, but they did have food, they ate what they grew, they caught fish. There were luxuries they could not afford, little necessities, but they were healthy. I am not saying they didn't suffer from diseases, in fact they are so many of them . . . but there was a philosophy . . . Behaviour was far more environmentally friendly. (Barrow 1995c)

Historically, when economies were directly linked to agricultural production, the importance of natural resources in the social and economic well-being of nations was far clearer. With the growth and expansion of tourism, manufacturing, and information industries, significant proportions of populations became relatively far removed from the actual use of natural resources. The management of these resources is now increasingly seen as the responsibility of central government agencies.

Yet all of us, whether we work in banks, garment factories, or hospitals, rely on nature's resources for some of our most fundamental needs. At the most basic level, there is the need for air, water, and food. At another level, the tourism industry requires healthy beaches, attractive landscapes, and coral reefs. At a more obvious level, farmers, fishers, and people in extractive industries still rely most heavily on natural resources for their livelihoods. It is therefore everyone's responsibility to ensure that vital natural resources are protected and efficiently managed.

It can easily be said that, with respect to individual commitment, Nita Barrow led by example. Her career, described by the United Nations as a profile in service, is testimony to the fact that Barrow practised what she preached when it came to individual commitment. Although employed initially as a nurse, Barrow found time in the course of her career to be actively involved in numerous organizations at a variety of levels, whether on a voluntary basis or in a more formal way. A few examples of these organizations include the Young Women's Christian Association (YWCA), the World Council of Churches (WCC), the Pan American Health Organization (PAHO), the Caribbean Nurses Organization, the Red Cross, Soroptimists International, the International Council for Adult Education (ICAE), the International Women's Tribune Centre (IWTC), the Girl Guides, and the Barbados Youth Council. In addition, she was the patron of and/or advisor to many environmental groups and a member of the Earth Council, as well as a member of the Eminent Persons Group which was constituted for the UN Conference on Sustainable Development in Small Island Developing States. This multifaceted and multilayered involvement grew out of a burning desire to involve herself in critical change. As she stated, "you can only effect change from within" (Barrow 1995e).

In her address to the meeting of the Eminent Persons Group that preceded the meeting of the UN Conference on Small Island Developing States, Barrow openly acknowledged the significant and influential role that people like herself should play in facilitating the changes that governments have to implement to achieve sustainable development:

> Inter-governmental processes are largely constrained by the need to reconcile competing national or group interests, and can often benefit significantly from input and guidance from authoritative independent sources. This is the rationale behind the creation of the present Group of Eminent Persons who, at my invitation, have travelled to Barbados to share with

us the benefit of their combined wisdom and expertise on sustainable development issues as they relate to islands. The product of their deliberations over the next two days will be presented to the Conference at the beginning of its proceedings. The creative ideas which they present will, I am sure, provide an important stimulus and focus for the intergovernmental discussion. (Barrow 1994)

Such was her commitment that it inspired other individuals to commit themselves to the hard work necessary to effect changes. One such person in Barbados was Colin Hudson, an entrepreneur, inventor, and environmentalist par excellence. Speaking of Colin Hudson, Barrow said:

You can't tell him no. When I see him coming through the door, I always say 'tell me what is it now', and it is always something constructive. He has done a lot for himself and for this country. He is a living, breathing example of how these things work. He could have given up, because of lack of support from people and organizations. But he didn't let that stop him. (Barrow 1995e)

Colin Hudson was integrally involved in the conceptualization and implementation of the Village of Hope, which ran parallel to the UN Conference on Sustainable Development in Small Island Developing States. The Village of Hope was a seventeen-day exhibition village, where the people of Barbados, delegates of the conference, and visitors could hear, feel, and see everything involved in a sustainable society. Over three thousand volunteers created an exhibition around twenty-eight themes concerning sustainability on islands.

Inspired by the success of the Village of Hope, Colin Hudson again approached Nita Barrow to propose that a permanent Village of Hope be established. In November 1994, an "Action Committee" was formed under Barrow's patronage and under the chairmanship of local businessman, Dr Basil Springer. Arising out of that initiative, the Future Centre Trust was formed in 1996 with six trustees and an eight-member board. Its declared mission was "To create a permanent stimulus to enhance the quality of life in Barbados and eventually establish Barbados as a role model in the fight to save our planet" ("Introducing the Future Centre Trust" 1996).

The Future Centre Trust currently focuses on outreach through a series of Initiatives of Hope that comprises about 130 tasks ranging from weekly newspaper pages, clean-ups, school activities, and radio spots, to interacting with parallel organizations in other countries, producing advisory leaflets and mobile exhibitions. The centre-piece of its activities is intended to be an exhibition centre that will draw on the experience of the 1992 Village of Hope with twenty-eight "wisdom themes", school exhibits, a job creation centre, a library/reading room, shops selling information and tools for adopting a more sustainable lifestyle, and even a prototype supermarket modelled on the Davis Co-op in California.

The Future Centre Trust is an example of what can result from one person's commitment, creativity, and determination. However, such effort and hard work must eventually evolve into a community of effort if it is to be sustained.

Community Efforts

Community involvement in environmental projects frequently evolves from the commitment of one or two individuals who inspire and bring other persons of like mind on board. As such, community support is vital to the regeneration of energies and strengths of the involved individuals and to the growth and expansion of an idea or project. A community is usually perceived as a group of people living in close geographic proximity to each other. In this case, the concept of community is used to describe an interacting group of people who share a common functional link such as kinship, occupation, interest, place of residence, or religion. Therefore, the members of the Future Centre Trust constitute a community, as much as a group of farmers who, while they may be geographically separated, share and work on critical interests. Indeed, in tackling the global environmental issues, the world's population is a community. Getting the community involved in environmental management is very important because, as Barrow (1995e) said, "A tremendous amount can be achieved when community energy is harnessed and focussed in the right direction."

There are numerous examples of community participation in environmental management across the world. In the Eastern Caribbean, community participation was used to develop a system of protected areas (SPA) on the island of St Lucia. Driven largely by the efforts of the St Lucia National Trust and the Caribbean Natural Resources Institute (CANARI), the SPA was based on a high level of community participation throughout St Lucia, which included the establishment of an active advisory committee comprising national resource management agencies, non-governmental organizations, and the National Youth Council; early consultation with national and local groups, and incorporation of their ideas and advice into the process; and active and continuing public awareness efforts. For example, radio phone-in programmes, public lectures, and community meetings to build recognition and support for the project and to identify resources requiring protection; and twenty public workshops at which a wide range of issues were discussed, including identifying significant local sites and traditions, resolving current or potential conflicts over resource use, and designing and coordinating education programmes (Panos Institute and CANARI 1994).

As a result of these efforts, several local communities began to conduct meetings and field trips to identify and assess significant natural and cultural sites to be included in the plan. To support these efforts, a training workshop was held by the trust and CANARI on "Community Participation in the Planning and Management of St Lucia's System of Protected Areas'" which sought to link local initiatives with national-level activities. This workshop resulted in the preparation of action plans that are currently being implemented through a partnership of communities and agencies. There have also been subsequent workshops and seminars on topics which have been identified by the communities and agencies as critical to the successful implementation of the plans (Panos Institute and CANARI 1994).

All of the ideas, the recommendations, and the results of the research have been compiled into a "Plan for the System of Protected Areas for St Lucia". The plan has been published and serves as a flexible working guide for communities and agencies involved in establishing the SPA. Special provisions are now being included in a proposed amendment to the National Trust Act. These provisions would require local involvement in park planning and management and a transfer of management responsibility to local organizations, thus institutionalizing the participatory process even further (Panos Institute and CANARI 1994).

In Central America, several non-governmental organizations are collaborating with community-based groups on reforestation, tree nurseries, agro-forestry schemes, and seedling distribution. In 1988, in one relatively dry pine forest area in San José de Cusmapa, Nicaragua, the community addressed deforestation and drought problems through consultative project planning with a predominately female cooperative that managed some 1,440 hectares of forests. In other initiatives, 910 acres of pine forest are being managed, charcoal production ovens are being built, technical training and assistance are being provided to local communities, and public awareness of women's integration into forest management is being raised. Over the past five years, the Regional Consultative Council of Women and Forestry in Central America has held two workshops to study how to replicate the Cusmapa experience, especially with regard to female leadership and gender issues in forestry (World Resources Institute 1995).

Across the ocean on the African continent, the Country Women Association of Nigeria (COWAN) seeks to mobilize the strengths of Nigerian women and help them break free from the cage of the traditional economic order through fruitful participation in massive food production, and economic and social development. Identifying self-sufficiency as a central factor in achieving sustainable development, COWAN has developed the following programmes: traditionally responsive savings and credit schemes; health and family planning education and services; training and assistance for agriculture and small-scale technology; and an option life programme for COWAN youth. COWAN states that

> [Our] programmes may not be unique but . . . we have had some significant successes in the execution of the programmes judging from the changes in the lives of our members. We have seen that the issues of sustainable development need not be left to men, but rather women, even at the grassroot level should be involved. In developing countries issues need to be tackled from different angles and from perspectives that are different from that of developed countries. We believe that in Africa, and in other third world countries, sustainable development will be achieved faster and easier if women are involved in the development processes and if some traditional practices are researched and modernized to fit into the processes to provide the vehicle for development. (Country Women Association of Nigeria n.d.)

There are numerous other examples that could be provided of how communities are getting involved in environmental management. This phenomenon of participation is spreading because of the many benefits to be gained. It naturally promotes democracy and equity because it gives community members a greater opportunity to share in the decisions about the use of resources, and therefore a greater share in the benefits gained from their use. This enhances the opportunities to increase the local benefits of resource use because means of production are more likely to be of a smaller scale and owned by resource users themselves.

Community participation is also attractive because priorities are no longer predetermined from the outside by bureaucrats or in board rooms far removed from the everyday concerns of users. Rather, they are determined from within, by those directly affected by such choices. Decentralization of decision making in this way increases the economic and technical efficiency of environmental projects. Users have more clearly defined responsibilities for their decisions and actions, and can provide a wide variety and considerable quantity of local resources (land, skills, technology, labour, capital, knowledge, and infrastructure) to implement the plans. Local responsibility also decreases the need for costly outside enforcement, which governments can ill afford.

As noted by COWAN in the above example, local and traditional knowledge and resource monitoring by community members can provide significant information to planning and development agencies on the characteristics of a resource. This knowledge can be utilized for inventory, management planning and monitoring of the resources. Traditional use of resources can be recognized and integrated into the development of the resource. The cumulative knowledge and experience of a community provide state agencies with a multidisciplinary perspective to deal with the breadth and complexity of resources.

Another benefit of community participation is the fact that it is adaptive and responsive to variations in local, social, and environmental conditions and changes in these conditions. Often it is the failure of such centralized strategies to accommodate the local sociocultural conditions – not the resources conditions – that leads to the failure of the strategies. Furthermore, resource users are constantly aware of the conditions of the resources upon which they depend, and they can be quick to respond and adapt to changes in the conditions of those resources. Local community control, therefore, brings a measure of stability and commitment to management that centralized government cannot duplicate. Government decision making usually operates over a short-term horizon and is often met with resistance on the ground. On the other hand people will show more commitment to decisions they have made themselves based on their own priorities. These priorities should reflect the objectives of long-term sociocultural and resource sustainability, which are clearly in their best interest.

However, to be successful, these local community efforts must be supported and strengthened by national and international policies and mechanisms. In addition to her commitment to these communities in her capacity as patron and advisor, Nita Barrow dedicated much of her time to international bodies such as the Earth Council, where she used her wisdom and influence to create open spaces within policy- and decision-making processes for citizen groups.

Institutional Support

Community participation, environmental education and sustainable development are much-used buzz words. However, more lip service than real effort is put into facilitating meaningful participation in many countries. The staff of non-governmental organizations, community-based organizations, and other development workers would readily admit that the real substantive support required to facilitate community participation is frequently limited or totally lacking.

The Earth Council is one of the international environmental organizations that Nita Barrow served. Its philosophy reflects the supportive role that should be played by institutions – whether at the local, national, or international level to ensure positive outcomes from individual commitment and community efforts. Recognizing that it is people/individuals throughout the world who will bring about the transition to sustainable, secure, and equitable development, the Earth Council (n.d.) has sought to "amplify the voices of those at the grassroots level who are not sufficiently heard or heeded in policy or decision-making" (Earth Council n.d.).

The Earth Council is a non-governmental organization, created in September 1992 as a direct result of the UN Conference on Environment and Development (UNCED) held in Rio de Janeiro in July 1992 (also referred to popularly as the Earth Summit). It is interesting to note that an international women's conference entitled Women for a Healthy Planet had been held in Miami in 1991, prior to the Earth Summit, and Nita Barrow played a role in organizing this important meeting, out of which came a statement known as "Women's Agenda 21". This statement was subsequently presented to Maurice Strong, secretary general of UNCED, and was used extensively in the drafting of Agenda 21, the official declaration issued at the end of the Earth Summit in 1992.

The structure of the Earth Council, its initial activities, and its membership were the products of an extensive process of consultation, involving some ten thousand non-governmental organizations from all regions of the world. From this process twenty-one members were selected, drawn from the political, business, scientific, and various sectors of civil society throughout the world. Among the members of the Earth Council, apart from Nita Barrow, were Maurice Strong (chairman), Justice Elizabeth Evatt (president of the Law Reform Commission), Dr Mahbub ul Haq (special adviser to the administrator of the UN Development Programme), and Jonathan Lash (president of the World Resources Institute). The Earth Council also benefited from the guidance and support of thirteen eminent world leaders who agreed to serve as honorary members. In addition, the council received special advice and support from a broad-based Earth Council Institute Board consisting of individuals and representatives from major environmental and development organizations.

The Earth Council's themes and programmes reflected its commitment to ensuring that communities across the globe obtain the support they require to achieve the goal of sustainable development. These included:

1. promoting greater public awareness dialogue and collaborative action on environment development and related issues;
2. helping concerned groups in civil society gain access to accurate objective information on these issues;
3. amplifying the voices and influence of those who are too often unheard and unheeded in the policy and decision-making processes;
4. evaluating the progress made and supporting the efforts to implement the results of the 1992 Rio process, including the Earth Summit governmental agreements and the various agreements treaties declarations and action plans agreed by the major groups in Rio, for example, the Kari Oca Declaration and non-governmental organization treaties;
5. stimulating action by and interaction between the concerns and agendas of people sectors and communities and helping to link them with the global agenda especially Agenda 21;
6. establishing an ombudsman-type function to facilitate processes of impartial investigation, analyses, consultation and negotiation designed to consider the concerns of the people and help resolve differences which are seen to be unfair or unjust by the stakeholders concerned;
7. catalyzing the movement away from unsustainable patterns of production and consumption towards ways of life that are environmentally secure sustainable and equitable;
8. complementing supporting and contributing to the work and mission of the UN Commission on Sustainable Development. (Earth Council n.d.)

The Earth Council quickly established a reputation as a highly credible institution, deriving recognition and moral standing from the calibre of its members; the qualities of its participants; the transparency of its consultative and decision-making processes; and the consistency, integrity, and objectivity of its products and statements.

As a result, the Earth Council has come to occupy a most strategic position, in that it is able through its membership and programmes to gather information from, as well as provide information and advice to, multiple societal and policy levels. These range from local, community-based organizations to international non-governmental organizations; and from national governments to a variety of international agencies, including key donor institutions. Increasingly, the responsibility has fallen to agencies such as the Earth Council to assist in meeting the many institutional challenges that must be dealt with if environmental management initiatives are to be successful – whether locally, regionally, or internationally. Some of these challenges are discussed below.

Policy and Legislation

Environmental policy reform is required at both the formulation and implementation stages. Currently, policy formulation is performed by an isolated elite in the government and to some extent the private sector. However, it would be more meaningful if it arose out of a process of public sensitization, community consultation, and popular participation. Certainly, far more relevant environmental management policy decisions could be taken if the base of information included local and traditional knowledge of resources.

The challenge to government, therefore, is to open the policy-making process to wider public participation. At the same time, non-governmental organizations can and should facilitate this process by assisting the community groups with whom they work in articulating their knowledge and needs in ways that are accessible by government: "The political will is not something that is there sitting down waiting, you create it by showing that the community is aware" (Barrow 1995e).

With respect to implementation, the policy implementation process has traditionally occurred along sectoral lines. Different activities are shared among various ministries in governments, and decision making is linear, with very little intersectoral cooperation. A good illustration of this is wetlands management, where different departments have responsibility for the management of the resources in the ecosystem. For example, the Department of Fisheries has responsibility for the fish, the Department of Forestry is responsible for the trees, the Health Department uses them as garbage disposal sites, and tourism agencies have them earmarked for conversion to marinas and hotels. With minimum cooperation, because of the reality of the territoriality which exists within central government agencies, the result is significant inefficiency in the management of natural resources. Another challenge – this time to natural area managers – is the development of an interdisciplinary approach to management and interagency coordination. Certainly lessons can be learned from the St Lucian example.

A problem closely related to the poor record of policy implementation is the inadequacy of legal systems to respond with appropriate laws and regulations. In a recent analysis and needs assessment of environmental laws of the Commonwealth Caribbean, the Caribbean Law Institute concluded:

> Much of the resource legislation in the Commonwealth Caribbean lacks adequate environmental and institutional focus. Such environmental-related legislation as exists [is often] inherited from the British, and is often fragmented and dispersed over several enactments. Responsibility for administering applicable legislation is likewise distributed among several government departments, unsupported by appropriate institutional arrangements to coordinate and direct relevant initiatives. (Caribbean Law Institute 1992)

Significant legislative reform and development is therefore required. The knowledge amassed by resource users and natural area managers needs to be used to update and expand existing laws and legislation in ways that will enhance the conservation of resources. This information will also be useful in designing more effective legal instruments of regulation and enforcement.

There is also a need for legal instruments that can provide the basis of transfer of management responsibility from central government agencies to community-based and other private organizations, acting on their own or in partnerships, depending on the situation. In this regard, the standardized fisheries acts, which are now in force in the member countries of the Organization of Eastern Caribbean States, are useful because they provide for the creation of local fisheries management authorities. This transfer of management responsibility from government to community-based groups frees up financial and human resources in government agencies, which can then be focused on providing technical assistance; facilitating the actions of the various collaborating partners and coordinating programme implementation; resolving conflict and providing arbitration between the collaborating parties; and providing incentives for collective action and self-regulation.

Research

Natural area management requires extensive research, and this is carried out largely with respect to the collection and mapping of data on the area to be zoned and managed. However, much less popular but equally important is research into alternate strategies of resource management. This would include research and documentation of popular knowledge and management of resources that may be useful in natural area management plans, as well as the analysis and documentation of the process of natural area management being undertaken by different organization throughout the Caribbean. Such research would permit the distilling of lessons to be learned and duplicated elsewhere.

Education and Training

To be successful, the personnel engaging in natural area management need to be adequately trained in various aspects of resource management. In addition, training is required in the following areas:

> training of members of community institutions and resource users to strengthen their skills in group organization, resource management and other areas essential to collaborative management of resources with other private organizations and government agencies; inter-disciplinary approaches to resource management training, i.e., incorporating economics and other social sciences as well as field-based community oriented courses into existing natural science curriculum to better equip natural area managers to cope with . . . their jobs. (Renard 1991)

Financial Management

This is an era where funding for natural resource programmes is increasingly difficult to secure because of increased competition between and within regions. Sourcing a variety of areas for conservation funding is therefore the only solution. Sources include government subventions, international bilateral and multilateral organizations, international foundations and conservation non-governmental organizations, individual donations, user fees, sales, concessions, debt swaps, trust funds, nature tourism, and charges for environmental services.

The role of multilateral, bilateral, and donor agencies needs to be revised so that they can become more responsive to the needs of community-based organizations and to those of the resources. They should be encouraged to put mechanisms and structures in place to accommodate small-scale community-oriented initiatives. They need to recognize that innovative approaches to natural resource management require flexibility and long-term efforts, and revise their current preference for short-term approaches with predetermined outputs and schedules. They must also provide support for institutional building. Project activities are largely irrelevant if they are not accompanied by a concerted effort to strengthen institutions and to build an indigenous capacity to sustain resource management and development actions. Operations of international institutions must recognize and respect the diversity of needs, opportunities, arrangements, and capabilities that exist in the various countries and communities, and must avoid applying external models to these varied situations (Renard 1991).

Management and Administrative Approaches

In the final analysis, the approach to management and administration of a natural area will determine its success or failure. The first challenge therefore is to ensure that clear agreements are worked out, clearly stipulating the roles and responsibilities of the enacting agencies and organizations. A second challenge would be to use an increasingly participatory approach to planning and management, including the early consultation of all stakeholders; the involvement of resource users in research; the design of participatory decision-making mechanisms; and participation in implementation, monitoring, and evaluation. Yet a third challenge is to strengthen and support community-based organizations to better equip them to participate in environmental management. This strengthening will occur through research and documentation of popular resource use and management systems; the definition and provision of legal instruments to transfer management responsibility to community-based organizations; the use of the participatory planning approach; a definition of clear management agreements; and the building and development of community institutions through financing, training, organizational development, networking, and outreach programmes (Renard 1991). The intervention of agencies such as the Earth Council at this multiplicity of levels is crucial, given the scope of work required to redress environmental problems.

Conclusion

Environmental problems are complex. They do not recognize geographic boundaries and they affect all of humanity regardless of class, colour, or creed. Unfortunately, our social systems are based on insularity, isolation, and segregation. This makes the integrated, interdisciplinary approach to environmental management very awkward. However, as Nita Barrow has said, "Everything is not perfect, and what can *you* do about it is the question that needs to be asked, and then what can *we* do about it. I think that those are two crucial questions" (Barrow 1995e).

Environmental stewardship, practised by each individual, is the key to solving environmental problems. No matter how far removed we believe ourselves to be from the actual location of the natural resources, we still rely on them for survival. This individual responsibility must extend into communities of responsibility, and the governmental and institutional mechanisms must be responsive, providing reliable means of achieving goals of sustainability.

> Communication, dialogue – not talking at the people, not addressing people or lecturing them – but a dialogue. Examining the issues which are affecting their lives . . . I see a lot of emphasis being put on communication now, and assessments of what is important about it. But we keep forgetting that the first thing you have to get is two people or more to sit down together and not have expectations. Not coming to tell me how much money . . . but just to talk [about] what are we going to do about wildlife issues? What have you been doing? How do you see it, and how do we mutually see it? For me that's the simplest of things to start with. How are we going to communicate to each other? How do I get you to come and sit down first, with no preconceived ideas about what the outcome will be. No . . . paper, no action plan except the agenda of things we need help with . . . [I]t might be a bridge, it might be a suck well, it might be a simple thing like a pig farm, it may be just stand-pipes, so that people can go out from their dwelling places where they don't have water. How are we going to start? Let's invite XYZ and or representatives to start to talk to us. And then, sitting there, try to find out why things have gone wrong and seek the solutions. (Barrow 1995e)

Education is key. But as Barrow noted, "the only kind of education that works is to get actively involved" (Barrow 1995e).

These are some of the principles and commitments by which Nita Barrow lived her life. Out of them have come many fruits of success. Through her words and activities, she has left a rich legacy, a testimony to a life lived in service for people at home and abroad.

Note

1. DAWN was funded in Bangalore, India, in 1984. It made its first international appearance at the NGO Forum in Nairobi, Kenya, in 1985. See chapter 9, note 3.

PART FOUR

Citizen and State Diplomacy

Chapter Seven

Institutionalized Violence and the Role of Human Sympathy:

The Case of the Eminent Persons Group to South Africa

[Alan Cobley]

Introduction

Since 1945 the world has seen a proliferation of violent political and military conflicts. One survey of the years 1945 to 1990 identified ninety-seven instances of disputes between states during the period in which one hundred or more people had died. In many of these cases, deaths had been counted in the thousands or even the tens of thousands. The recorded instances of violent conflict in the world would be even higher if this survey had included the dozens of political and military conflicts involving rival groups within states. As the incidence of conflict increased in the latter half of the twentieth century, so did the incidence of attempts at international mediation. The ninety-seven instances of international dispute identified in the survey attracted 364 attempts at international mediation. Less than six percent of these attempts were completely successful, and over 70 percent of them failed even to broker a temporary secession of hostilities. (Bercovitch and Langley 1993: 673–74). This relatively low success rate may be a reflection of the fact that, more often than not, efforts at peacemaking and international mediation have been cynical exercises in big power politics and unacknowledged self-interest.

However, there have been some significant changes in the nature of conflict and in the nature of mediation over the last fifteen years, as the priorities imposed on international relations by the East–West divide since 1945 have crumbled. Increasingly, the international community has been called upon to mediate episodes of conflict within, rather than between, states. At times in this post–Cold War world, such civil wars and internecine feuds have been left to fester because they were not seen to affect the international balance of power or the vital interests of other states. But in those cases where international opinion has pressed successfully for intervention, old-style superpower brokerage has tended to give way to multilateral sponsorship of mediation efforts through such organizations as the United Nations, or through "citizen diplomacy". Citizen diplomacy – mediation by private citizens appointed solely to deal with a particular dispute – is often preferred by the disputants themselves to the "professional diplomacy" of foreign ministers and career diplomats, in circumstances where the impartiality of the mediator is seen to be critical. Examples of such citizen-diplomacy have been seen in recent years in Latin America, the Middle East, Bosnia, and Northern Ireland. Yet despite some successes, the concept of citizen diplomacy is not unproblematic. Sometimes, it has been a means by which powerful states have "unofficially" influenced the mediation of internal disputes in other states, and the impartiality of the mediator has been a convenient fiction.[1] As the catalogue of conflicts continues to grow, it is clear that the need for methods of international mediation that are effective and uncompromised by any hidden agenda is becoming more urgent than ever (Boutros-Ghali 1992).

It is against this background of a search for new forms of international mediation and peacemaking in the last two decades of the twentieth century, that the Commonwealth Group of Eminent Persons (EPG) mission to South Africa, undertaken in the early months of 1986, must be seen. In many ways it was a pioneering effort, which sought to build on the growing international climate of multilateralism and on the successes of citizen diplomacy. It is with the pioneering aspects of the mission, and the special contribution of Nita Barrow to it, that this chapter is concerned.

South Africa and the International Community in the Early 1980s

The EPG went to South Africa at a time when apartheid was in deep crisis. Since the implementation of the apartheid policy by the National Party government elected in 1948, there had been three great explosions of political violence. In 1960, the Sharpeville Massacre left 69 people dead and 11,500 were detained without trial under emergency powers. In 1976–77 the Soweto Rising was accompanied by 575 deaths and 2,500 detentions, according to official statistics. The third great explosion occurred in the latter part of 1984 and was still in progress at the time of the EPG's visit. This was "the time of the comrades", who led a revolt in the townships against the apartheid state. One set of observers wrote:

> South Africa had entered a period of unprecedented political violence as the strong upsurge in the popular struggle against apartheid and for equal political rights was met with the massive coercive powers at the disposal of the state. Even at the crudest level of basic body counts the dimensions of political violence during this period were of an order unlike anything similar in our recent history. (Manganyi and du Toit 1990: 1)

According to government figures, between September 1984 and the end of 1987 there were 2,987 politically related deaths and over 45,000 detentions without trial (Manganyi and du Toit 1990: 1; Meredith 1987).

Even without these outbursts of political violence, South Africa under apartheid was an extremely violent society. As William Beinart notes, this can be seen in "a wide range of social phenomena from high rates of family violence to high rates of murder, judicial hanging and road accidents" (Beinart 1992: 464). Indeed, violence has been called "a structural characteristic" of the apartheid system itself (Marks and Anderson 1990: 30). This "structural violence included such things as forced removals, the brutalizing conditions in the mine compounds and migrant workers' hostels, the harassment associated with pass laws, the dismemberment of family life associated with migrant labour, the ruthless exploitation and subordination of women, the denial of access to justice, the needless propagation of hunger and disease, and the dehumanizing conditions resulting from overcrowding, neglected or non-existent infrastructure, and endemic poverty in the squatter camps and townships. It could also be seen in what Marks and Anderson call the "unusual features of the psychiatric profile of South Africa": a high incidence of retarded psychomotor development in black children; a high incidence of organic brain syndromes such as meningitis; unusually high rates of alcohol and drug abuse; and widespread instances of post-traumatic stress syndrome, especially among ex-detainees (Marks and Anderson 1990: 48–49).

It was this structural violence that impressed the members of the EPG even more than the political violence they witnessed when they arrived in South Africa. In their report they wrote:

> None of us was prepared for the full reality of apartheid. As a contrivance of social engineering, it is awesome in its cruelty. It is achieved and sustained only through force, creating, human misery and deprivation and blighting the lives of millions. (Commonwealth Group of Eminent Persons 1986: 23)

Nita Barrow recalled her own profound sense of shock at the conditions she found:

> People could brief you as much as they like verbally. When the reality hits you it's quite a different matter . . . I couldn't imagine anybody being a non-person . . . and you go to South Africa and you see there [they are treated as if] they don't exist. (Barrow 1995a)[2]

Whereas few societies can claim to be totally free of racial discrimination, South Africa was unique in the world in elevating it to a cardinal principle of government policy, and in launching a vast project of social engineering designed to perpetuate white minority rule over the disenfranchised black majority. It was this that made apartheid South Africa a pariah state in the international community, particularly as the process of decolonization gave a voice to increasing numbers of independent black states in Africa and the Caribbean in the 1960s and 1970s. By the end of the 1970s, many countries around the world, as well as multilateral bodies such as the United Nations, had adopted measures designed to register disapproval of apartheid, to isolate the apartheid regime, and so to hasten the end of the apartheid system.

The Commonwealth of Nations founded by Britain, in which many newly independent black states were grouped, saw itself as having a particular interest and role in the South African problem because of South Africa's historic links with the British Empire. Subsequent to the withdrawal of South Africa from the Commonwealth in 1961 as a result of international condemnation of the Sharpeville Massacre, Commonwealth states had taken a lead in efforts to impose sanctions against the regime. Its most high-profile success was the

Gleneagles Agreement of 1977, which severed all official sporting links between South Africa and Commonwealth countries (Cobley 1989; Schreuder 1992). However, during the early 1980s, the unity of the Commonwealth was sorely tried by the attitude of the British prime minister Margaret Thatcher, who stubbornly refused to accept the calls from every other Commonwealth nation for the adoption of comprehensive economic sanctions against South Africa. Because Britain had greater economic links with South Africa than the rest of the Commonwealth put together, Prime Minister Thatcher's view that economic sanctions would be counterproductive was particularly galling to other member states. The growing tension within the organization was compounded by the dramatic upsurge in political violence in South Africa, where the struggle against apartheid was clearly reaching a critical stage. Many member states of the Commonwealth felt that urgent action was needed. The EPG was seen as a way out of this impasse.

According to Archbishop Ted Scott, a member of the EPG, the idea for the mission had originated in the Canadian Foreign Ministry, and was canvassed among other Commonwealth leaders by Canadian prime minister Brian Mulroney (Scott 1995). Thereafter, the moving spirit was the Commonwealth secretary general Shridath Ramphal. As a result of much lobbying behind the scenes, a new Commonwealth Accord on Southern Africa was finally agreed upon at the Meeting of Commonwealth Heads of Government in Nassau, Bahamas in October 1985. The accord called for the dismantling of apartheid, and to that end, the termination of the state of emergency; the freeing of political prisoners, including Nelson Mandela; the suspension of violence on all sides; and the initiation of dialogue "across lines of colour, politics and religion, with a view to establishing a non-racial and representative government". In terms of practical steps, the accord committed member states to implement some limited economic sanctions, and warned vaguely that "some of us would consider other steps" if progress were not made within six months. But the centre of the Commonwealth's strategy was the planned appointment of the EPG "to encourage through all practicable ways the evolution of that necessary process of political dialogue" in South Africa, and "by all practicable means to advance the fulfilment of the objectives of this accord". A committee of seven heads of government (representing Zambia, Australia, the Bahamas, Canada, India, the United Kingdom, and Zimbabwe) was deputed to work with Shridath Ramphal in setting up the group (Commonwealth Group of Eminent Persons 1986: Annexure 1).

The seven members of the EPG were nominated by the Committee of Heads of Government set up under the accord. They were carefully chosen to be as representative as possible of all the regions of the Commonwealth and with an eye to the racial mix, eventually settled as three black, three white, and one brown member. They included Dame Nita Barrow from Barbados, General Olusegun Obasanjo from Nigeria, John Malecela from Tanzania, Archbishop Ted Scott from Canada, Malcom Fraser from Australia, Lord Barber from the United Kingdom, and Sardar Swaran Singh from India. As Shridath Ramphal noted in his introduction to their report, they were a group characterized by "integrity, humanity, compassion, understanding, and a wide experience" – all qualities vital to any effort at international mediation. Both Obasanjo and Fraser, who co-chaired the group, were former heads of government, while Malecela, Barber, and Singh had all been senior Cabinet ministers in their respective countries. The inclusion of Archbishop Scott and Nita Barrow was a recognition of the role of the churches and of many non-governmental organizations in the struggle against apartheid.

Two nominees stand out in this list. The first is Lord Barber. He was a former Conservative chancellor of the exchequer and had been chairman of the Standard Chartered Bank since 1974. His nomination to the group by Mrs Thatcher suggests that she viewed the EPG largely as a diversionary tactic. Perhaps she hoped to ensure by his presence that the group's final report would not call for further economic sanctions whatever the outcome of its mission. If that was her intention, she must have been sadly disappointed when the final report asserted that further sanctions were a necessity. As Barrow recalled, by the end of the group's mission, Lord Barber was "the biggest convert" to the call for sanctions (Barrow 1995a).

The other outstanding nominee was Nita Barrow. At first sight, she was a surprising choice for inclusion in the group, despite the fact she came from a region that had lead the Commonwealth in the anti-apartheid struggle. She had never held political office in the Caribbean and had not had a high profile in the anti-apartheid movement there. In fact, however, her long association with the Young Women's Christian Association (YWCA), including a stint on the World YWCA Executive Committee and as president of the organization from 1975 to 1983, and her time with the World Council of Churches (WCC), both as an executive member, as director of the Christian Medical Commission (CMC) and latterly as president for the Caribbean region, gave her enormous credibility in the struggle against apartheid. This was especially true within

South Africa itself. The YWCA had supported a non-racial affiliate in South Africa since 1951 in the teeth of white hostility and government harassment, while the WCC had risked the wrath of conservative evangelical Christians in South Africa and worldwide during the 1970s to lend financial support to exiled liberation movements in Africa such as the African National Congress (ANC). In fact, Barrow had played a key role in unlocking humanitarian aid from the WCC for the ANC after she had seen first-hand the appalling conditions endured by women and children in the ANC's refugee camps in Zambia and Tanzania while working as director of the CMC. It was she who persuaded the organization to provide funds to improve the situation. Apart from the issue of credibility, innumerable personal contacts she had made through these two organizations over the years gave her unique and unparalleled access to non-governmental networks in South Africa. For these reasons, it quickly became clear that she was an indispensable member of the group. If Obasanjo and Fraser were the figures who gave the EPG authority, it was Nita Barrow who gave it a human face. Her importance to the group was enhanced immeasurably by the fact that she was a woman, because the informal networks in South Africa she helped to access were overwhelmingly female.[3] Furthermore, as this chapter argues, the remarkable breadth of what might be called her "gendered experience" would influence the process of mediation undertaken by the group in critical ways. It is doubtful, however, whether this latter aspect of her contribution to the EPG had been anticipated by those who regarded her nomination as that of the group's "token woman".

The Eminent Persons Group in South Africa

After briefing sessions and preparatory meetings in London, the EPG mission began with a preliminary visit to South Africa and the neighbouring states in the last two weeks of February 1986. This preliminary visit was undertaken by the co-chairs of the group, Obasanjo and Fraser, accompanied by Nita Barrow. Barrow was an essential part of this advanced guard. First, she was the only member of the group with the contacts to bypass official channels and make contacts with ordinary people in the townships via church and other organizations – as she said herself, "I knew so many people there" (Barrow 1995a). Second, because she was already known and trusted by many activists and community leaders in South Africa, she was able to establish the credibility of the EPG in advance of the arrival of the other members. Her role at this stage was critical in allaying fears and breaking down suspicions so that the group could do its work (Scott 1995). The preliminary visit by Obasanjo, Fraser, and Barrow also established the pattern of work subsequently adopted by the full group on its two visits.

The first of the group's full visits was undertaken between the second and thirteenth of March 1986. Each day, a full programme of meetings with interested parties was scheduled. Generally, they began with a working breakfast at 8:30 a.m. This was followed by perhaps two or three meetings in the morning, and a working lunch. In the afternoon, another meeting might be squeezed in, followed perhaps by a swift flight by the group's Lear jet (provided by the Canadian government for the purpose) to another city, where further meetings would be held around dinner. To make maximum use of the time available, a team from the Commonwealth Secretariat would be preparing the next meeting while the previous one was still in progress. Eighteen-hour days were the norm for the duration of the EPG's visits to South Africa.[4]

One of the notable features of the many meetings held was that among the government ministers, representatives of organizations, businessmen, church leaders, and the rest, there were meetings where the interviewees were not identified. On the morning of 10 March, for example, the EPG met a person described in the schedule simply as "A gentleman from the Transkei". Such anonymity was necessary on some occasions to protect anti-apartheid activists who were on the run from the authorities, or people who wished for other reasons to avoid being seen publicly talking to the group. Sometimes, meetings took place late at night for the same reason. These were not included on any formal programme. On occasion, while some members of the group were engaged in a formal meeting, others were elsewhere, operating a parallel informal programme. While such activities are generally not recorded in the EPG's report, it is evident that around the fringes of the formal programme, a number of informal meetings and clandestine visits took place.

Inevitably, the group's activities attracted a great deal of scrutiny from the security police, and members of the group were constantly aware of being watched, and were wary of hotel and meeting rooms being bugged. One lesson of the preliminary visit in February had been that although the government had granted their request to be allowed to meet with whomever they wished without let or hindrance, the group would have to work diligently to shake off the constant police surveillance if they were to achieve anything. As Barrow explained, the group indulged in a great deal of "cloak and dagger" activity – switching hotel rooms, changing meeting venues, avoiding official cars – to ensure that they could operate as freely as possible. Meetings held by the group to discuss their findings were held on open lawns or en route aboard their Lear jet as a means to ensure some measure of privacy. Not surprisingly, the tension took its toll on all of them, and the pauses between each visit were a welcome chance to take stock and recuperate (Barrow 1995a).

Undoubtedly, many of the EPG's conclusions were born out of the formal statement of views they heard from the various parties they interviewed. However, it was the informal level that the mission achieved its greatest insights into the South African problem and, it can be argued, came closest to a successful mediation effort. It was at this level that Barrow's contribution was most powerful.

It has already been noted that Barrow's vast range of contacts provided the EPG with unique access to the ordinary people of the country. Her first action on landing in a new city was always to take out her voluminous address book and head for the nearest telephone. Take just one example of these contacts. In 1976 during the Soweto Rising, eighteen women who were leading figures in the anti-apartheid struggle, some with connections to the South African YWCA, had been detained without trial. The World YWCA in Geneva, under the direction of its general secretary, Elizabeth Palmer, and encouraged strongly by Nita Barrow, had launched a highly successful international campaign to publicize their plight and obtain their release. Although some of these women had never met Nita Barrow, they welcomed her during the visit of the EPG like a long-lost sister.

It should be stressed that what made Barrow's list of contacts special was that it was a *personal*, not a *professional*, network. It was based not only on face-to-face contacts, but also on a staggering volume of personal correspondence, sustained in many cases over decades. This was an astonishing achievement, as Archbishop Scott, no stranger himself to globetrotting with international organizations, has testified, "I don't know of anybody that I have met who has the range of personal contacts which are kept alive . . . A lot of us do it on the formal level, but she does it on the personal level" (Scott 1995).

It is difficult to imagine a more valuable quality for a mediator than a capacity to keep a "personal contacts alive". It might be argued that this attention to the "personal" was a gendered response, and that it came more easily to her, perhaps, than to her male colleagues.

Another invaluable informal contribution which Barrow made to the EPG was her ability, as she herself described it, "to mingle with the crowd". As a rather elderly black woman, she was apparently regarded by the white authorities as an unthreatening presence and found she could easily make herself invisible by exploiting this racial and gender stereotype. This was seen to most effect in the celebrated incident in which she slipped away from the rest of the group to pay a visit to Alexandra Township, after Malcom Fraser and Lord Barber had been refused entry by the police. In a plain skirt and blouse, flat shoes and a head tie she passed easily as "an ordinary native woman" and gained entry to the township without difficulty, although, as she gleefully recounted, the other group members joked that she "must have been the only African woman that was in there with a Gucci scarf tying up [her] head" (Barrow 1995a; Blackman 1995: 134–35).

Barrow's experience as a nurse was an integral part of her "gendered experience" and also proved most valuable to the EPG mission. Nurses were a highly admired group among black women in South Africa, since nursing was one of the few professions open to them under apartheid. As a nurse, Barrow was a figure that black women could both respect and identify with. This was another reason why so many doors were opened to her during the EPG mission. Brigalia Bam, a member of the South African YWCA (also a former executive member of the World YWCA and a former colleague of Barrow's at the WCC) who later became Secretary of the South African Council of Churches, testified that "pride in Nita's profession was specially noted by other women as they met her formally" (Blackman 1995: 129). Another very important impact of her nurse's training on the group's work was her careful observation of body language and human interaction in the many meetings they attended. On her advice, members of the group did not take notes during interviews, in order to put the interviewees at ease, and instead would meet later to write up notes and compare impressions. This allowed the group to pick up nuances of meaning that were often unspoken, but that were critical to understanding and interpreting what they heard.

This technique proved especially important in the one meeting in which the group met State President P.W. Botha. As Barrow recalled, he looked "almost like a person who was spaced out . . . that although he was talking to you, his focus wasn't there":

For two hours – two hours! – he sat and he lectured us, scolded us, kept taking out the Bible and quoting passages . . . I mean reams of garbage, all in the name of the Lord, what God had

> said and what he handed down on Mount Sinai . . . What struck you was that any man who had his position could be so absolutely – tunnel vision – till he allowed no, nothing to percolate. That's how I put it. Not that he didn't hear. Just that he didn't allow anything to percolate that was not his own opinion. And I thought there's very little hope for this country as long as he was there. (Barrow 1995a)

Afterwards, she pointed out to her colleagues how, in the course of the entire meeting, only President Botha, Defence Minister General Malan and Minister for Law and Order Louis le Grange had spoken. The other half dozen ministers in the room had sat looking uncomfortable and not uttered a word. This was a clear indication that the balance of power in the Cabinet favoured the hawks. Barrow also suspected, on the basis of her observation at the meeting, that P.W. Botha was no longer really in control and that the much-feared General Magnus Malan was calling the tune. Such insights were priceless in gauging the attitude of the government as the mission moved towards a conclusion.

One other vital contribution made by Nita Barrow to the EPG, which is worthy of special mention, had its seeds in her experience just prior to the mission. Less than six months before the EPG was appointed, she had been in Nairobi as convener of the non-governmental organizations meeting known as "Forum '85", held in conjunction with the World Conference to review the United Nations Decade of Women. At that forum, Barrow had strongly encouraged the setting up of a Peace Tent by a coalition of women's peace groups led by the Women's International League for Peace and Freedom (WILPF), where women who became locked in heated argument could go to resolve their conflicts. Conflicts had arisen at the forum between Arab and Israeli women, as well as between Iranian and Iraqi women (whose countries were then at war with each other), so the Peace Tent had been called into action. The methodology had been simple. The women who were the leading protagonists in each dispute were identified and sent to the Peace Tent to discuss their differences. This had the incidental benefit that it immediately removed the main sources of disruption from the open sessions. Once in the peace tent, they were each asked three simple questions. How does this issue affect you personally? How does this issue affect your family? How does this affect your country? As Barrow explained, once a basic human sympathy and understanding had been established through the answers to the first two questions, during which the contending women came to understand that they shared many experiences and concerns, the answer to the third seemed less important.

In this way, the organizers of the forum in Nairobi found that no dispute was entirely intractable. Barrow had taken this practical lesson about human sympathy in action with her to South Africa (Barrow 1995).

It is evident that the lessons learned in Nairobi influenced the manner in which Barrow approached the EPG mission in innumerable subtle but profound ways. Above all, perhaps, this influence was seen in her insistence, throughout the group's meetings and deliberations, on clear, reasoned argument. It is noteworthy that when asked to isolate Barrow's particular contribution to the group, Archbishop Scott did not mention any particular opinion she voiced, but instead singled out her capacity to "clarify issues". He also stressed that Barrow had recognized that a commitment to reasoned argument meant it was necessary, as he put it, "to protect your right to grow and change", and to insist on that right for other people. Undogmatic herself, she deplored dogmatic positions adopted by others (Scott 1995). Barrow herself commented that the only interview she had walked out of during the EPG's mission was with Chief Gatsha Buthelezi, after his arrogance and dogmatic remarks had infuriated her:

> Because he sat there – incredibly, he brought a mound of paper next to each of our chairs of every speech he had ever made . . . They're not in my papers because I left them right there. I told them I did not need to take that garbage anywhere so that [it] could stay in South Africa – he didn't listen to a soul. (Barrow 1995a)

Clarity, reasoned argument, lack of dogma, these were all necessary corollaries of human sympathy in action which had contributed to the resolution of conflicts in the Peace Tent at Nairobi.

Johan Degenaar has posited, in a discourse on the concept of violence as it pertained to South Africa in the 1980s, that there are only two ways of countering violence without resorting to counter-violence. These are "the practice of non-violent resistance" and "the act of keeping rationality alive". Rationality, he argues, "keeps integrity intact and teaches a person to become human" (Degenaar 1990). In many ways the EPG mission in 1986 can be seen, above all else, as an attempt to keep rationality alive at a time of escalating violence.

At the end of their visit in March, members of the group felt satisfied that they had consulted "on the widest possible basis" in the time available to them. They had met the State President P.W. Botha, and all the key cabinet ministers; they had interviewed Nelson Mandela in Pollsmoor Prison; they had met leaders of political organizations, community groups, churches, and business associations; and they had held talks with the ANC in exile, and with leaders of the "Front-line States". In the light of their consultations they had come to the conclusion that there was a possibility of a negotiated end to the conflict. As they wrote in their report, "no serious person we met was interested in a fight to the finish; all favoured negotiations and peaceful solutions" (Commonwealth Group of Eminent Persons 1986: 101). However, they wished to do more than merely report back to the Commonwealth Heads of Government on what they had found. They felt that their remit as set out in the Nassau Accord meant that the onus was now on them to suggest possible ways to go forward. This they did by presenting the South African government with a "Possible Negotiating Concept" at the end of the visit. This concept suggested that the governments could help to break the "cycle of violence" by a series of measures designed to establish a climate for negotiations. These measures included the removal of the military from the townships, an end to detention without trial, and the allowance of freedom of association and assembly. It also required the release of political prisoners, including Nelson Mandela, and the unbanning of the ANC and Pan African Congress (PAC). On the part of the ANC and other anti-apartheid groups, the concept required a commitment from them to enter negotiations and suspend violence (Commonwealth Group of Eminent Persons, 1986; 103–4). The next step was up to the contending parties.

As they left South Africa at this stage, members of the group believed their mission had ended. They did not expect the government to accept their "Possible Negotiating Concept" because it had never accepted that the "structural violence" of apartheid was a prime cause of the culture of violence in their country. If the government would not accept responsibility for its part in causing the violence, there was little hope of progress. For her part, Barrow had not anticipated being recalled to another round of meetings, and had just arrived in Barbados when the call came from the South African government inviting the group to return.

In view of their unexpected recall, the second visit of the full group in May 1986 began with great optimism. Over the first four days, briefing sessions were held with all the major parties. At a meeting in Lusaka, the ANC Executive expressed its willingness to participate in negotiations under the terms set out by the EPG. Armed with this assurance, the EPG eagerly awaited the centrepiece of the visit, which was to be a meeting with the Cabinet Constitutional

Committee on the morning of the fifth day. Unfortunately, shortly before the meeting took place, news broke of raids by the South African Defence Force on alleged ANC bases in Lusaka, Harare, and Gaborone. According to their report, members of the group were shocked by this blatant violation of international law and by the casualties caused:

> It was also strongly felt that such wanton action against Commonwealth governments, who were instrumental in setting up the mission on which we were engaged, and especially given its timing, would cast serious doubt on the genuineness of the South African government's attitude towards a negotiated settlement. (Commonwealth Group of Eminent Persons 1986: 117–18)

General Obasanjo and John Malecela were especially outraged at this attack on independent African states, and argued for an immediate pull-out by the EPG in protest. Others in the group felt that they should continue so long as there might be any prospect of progress (Scott 1995). Meanwhile, pending confirmation of the news reports, the planned meeting with the Cabinet Constitutional Committee went ahead. In the event the meeting proved inconclusive. When the final decision to pull out was made that afternoon, it was Nita Barrow once again who clarified the issue for other members of the group. For her, the raids had dramatized the fact that the South African government as a whole was not serious about negotiations. The meeting that day had shown that they were simply covering the same ground. There was simply no point in continuing (Barrow 1995a).

As the group prepared to meet to discuss its final report in London two weeks later, a letter from Foreign Minister Pik Botha confirmed that the South Africa government was still not prepared to accept the terms of the "Possible Negotiating Concept". In their final letter in reply it was clear that the group was exasperated by the failure of the South African government to acknowledge that "suspension of violence" necessarily included the structural violence of apartheid. Until this was recognized, no mediation or meaningful negotiation was possible, and the cycle of violence would continue unabated.[5] In their report the EPG concluded:

> The Nassau Accord asked for the initiation, in the context of a suspension of violence on all sides, a process of dialogue across lines of colour, politics and religion, with a view to establishing a non-racial and representative government. As we have described, there is no such prospect in view. (Commonwealth Group of Eminent Persons 1986: 125)

In retrospect, there seems little doubt that the raids had been an attempt to wipe out the ANC Executive which had been assembled in Lusaka to meet the EPG less than forty-eight hours earlier. This was clear evidence that the inner core of military and security advisors around P.W. Botha were still seeking a hard-line military solution to the spiral of conflict in South Africa, and that they had won the upper hand over the soft-liners in the government, grouped around Foreign Minister Pik Botha and Minister for Constitutional Development and Planning Chris Heunis. It had been these "soft-liners" who had persuaded a reluctant President Botha to allow the EPG to come to South Africa in the first place. There was little question that a window of opportunity had been open during the brief period of the EPG mission, or that it had just as quickly been slammed shut (Adam and Moodley 1993: 40–41).

The EPG Mission in Retrospect

In the immediate aftermath of the EPG mission, there was little doubt in anyone's mind that it had failed. Political violence continued, and even increased in the months following the pull-out of the mission, as a country-wide state of emergency was imposed. In a letter to the Commonwealth secretary general accompanying their report, the EPG acknowledged their failure:

> It is not often that the chance arises to try to serve a whole country, arrest its drift to civil war, and initiate a process that might usher in a new era. We were given such a chance. If we are sad that our efforts to achieve these objectives in South Africa have been unavailing, it is not so much out of a sense of disappointment at the personal level, but acute consciousness and concern at the consequences of our failure for the future of that country. (Commonwealth Group of Eminent Persons 1986: 16–17)

Within the Commonwealth, there were many who felt that the EPG mission had been a sop to Britain and that it had been a waste of precious time and effort. Meanwhile, in South Africa, prospects of a peaceful resolution of the conflict seemed further away than ever as the brief hope of a quick solution brokered by the EPG faded into another phase of protracted struggle (Friedman 1993: 5). It would be another three years before the possibility of negotiation between the contending parties was raised again.

Should the EPG be counted as simply another failed effort at international mediation? In terms of the stated aims of an immediate suspension of violence and the initiation of a meaningful process of dialogue, the answer must be yes. Yet, it is in the nature of peacemaking that the seeds of a final resolution of conflict are often sown in earlier failed attempts. When President F.W. De Klerk initiated a dialogue with the ANC in 1990, it was on precisely the same basis as the EPG had proposed nearly four years earlier. The state of emergency had ended; the military had withdrawn from the townships; political prisoners, including Nelson Mandela, had been released unconditionally; and the ANC and PAC had been unbanned before formal talks began. It is tempting to see the shade of the EPG in all this, although the circumstances were much changed and the balance of pressures much different in 1990 than they had been in 1986.[6]

For their part, both Nita Barrow and Archbishop Scott felt that the EPG mission had made a significant contribution to the struggle against apartheid. Barrow felt that it had brought a sense of hope to those involved in the struggle against apartheid inside the country that "their case was being adequately exposed to the outside world" at a time when South African government propaganda about "reform" of apartheid and the Reagan–Thatcher policy of "constructive engagement" were muddying the waters in the international sphere. Archbishop Scott argued that the unimpeachable credibility of the EPG's report, exposing the spurious nature of the commitment to reform and the underlying intransigence of the South African government, gave powerful ammunition to the lobby arguing for further sanctions, not only in the Commonwealth, where Mrs Thatcher now became more isolated than ever, but also in the United States, where conservative resistance to sanctions began to crumble (Barrow 1995a; Scott 1995).

Apart from these benefits, the EPG mission had a very positive impact on the ANC's international reputation, even in Conservative Britain:

> British officials believed that the South African government deliberately scuttled the EPG mission . . . when ANC acceptance of negotiations was imminent – by attacking purported ANC guerilla bases in Zambia, Zimbabwe and Botswana. The ANC consequently emerged from the EPG episode with considerably enhanced international prestige. Its response to the EPG mission probably contributed to the British decision, signalled by ministerial level meetings with Oliver Tambo [ANC President General], to extend the implicit recognition of the ANC's political importance. (Lodge and Nasson 1992: 185)

Overall, in practical terms, it can be argued that if the EPG mission to South Africa did not bring about the end to apartheid, it did at least make a contribution to the pressure that brought it down.

At a more abstract level, the EPG mission was most notable for the methodology it evolved in the search for a way out of the culture of violence in South Africa, a methodology almost unparalleled in the many efforts at international mediation that had gone before. It is in this regard that Nita Barrow's contribution stands out. Barrow's work with the EPG pioneered a form of international peacemaking in which the promotion of human sympathy between the protagonists, rather than the application of external pressure or skill in political negotiation, was the critical feature. It was more than mere "citizen diplomacy", it was human sympathy in action. In all the contributions she had made to the work of the group, this had been the common thread. It was a form of peacemaking born of a lifetime of gendered experience and depended for its efficacy on her identity as a woman: there was a direct line from her early career as a nurse, through the women's Peace Tent at Nairobi, to her work with the EPG. In the long run, the development of this new methodology of peacemaking may have been the most important achievement of the EPG mission to South Africa, with implications that go far beyond that time and place.

Notes

1. One of the key figures associated with citizen diplomacy has been former President Jimmy Carter of the United States. His "self-consciously amateur style of diplomacy", in which "pure intentions and inspired vision" are the most prized qualities, is well suited to citizen diplomacy. Ironically, this same style had proved disastrous for the United States during the years of his presidency, when his administration staggered from one foreign policy debacle to another (Spencer 1988). On occasion, however, Carter's highly publicized international interventions appear to have been thinly veiled missions for the US State Department, as for example in Haiti.
2. The members of the EPG underwent extensive briefing at Lancaster House in London before departing on their mission. Materials were supplied by the Commonwealth Secretariat and by Ambassador Worrell of the South African Embassy. Copies of much of this briefing material are preserved in the Dame Nita Barrow Papers.
3. Brigalia Bam told Woodie Blackman: "Nita provided the strongest link for the South African women with the rest of the world. She came to us as our heroine, as our greatest female model" (Blackman 1995: 128).

4. Some sense of what these daily programmes were like, and the logistics involved, can be gleaned from itineraries and other material on the EPG's work preserved in Dame Nita's papers.
5. For the full text of this final exchange of letters see the Commonwealth Group of Eminent Persons 1986: 121–24.
6. On the negotiations leading to the end of the apartheid state in South Africa, see Adam and Moodley 1993; Friedman 1993; Ohlson, Stedman with Davies 1994. For radical leftists, criticism of the negotiation process which contrasts markedly with the general chorus of approval in the literature, see Mokonyane 1994.

Chapter Eight

Dame Nita:

A Profile in Service

[Marjorie Thorpe]

> A knight ther was, and that a worthy man,
> That fro the time that he first bigan
> To riden out, he loved chivalrye,
> Trouthe and honour, fredom and curteisye.
> Ful worthy was he in his lordes werre,
> And therto hadde he riden, no man ferre,
> As wel in cristendom and inmhethenesse,
> And evere honoured for his worthynesse.
>
> And everemoore he hadde a soverein pris.
> And though that he were worthy, he was wis,
> And of his port as meeke as is a maide:
> He nevere yet no vileinye ne saide
> In al his lif unto no maner wight.
> He was a verray parfit gentil knight.
>
> – Chaucer, "The Prologue to the Canterbury Tales"

Dame Nita Barrow received her order of knighthood in 1980. Like Chaucer's "parfit knight" whose portrait serves as the epigraph for this chapter, the attributes and achievements which earned her this distinction were the very ones that assured her success as Barbados' ambassador and permanent representative to the United Nations from 1986 to 1990. The term "chivalrye" describes the noble qualities a knight was supposed to have. It includes courage, a sense of honour, and, perhaps most importantly, *a readiness to help the weak and protect women.* In the 1380s, a knight could give expression to these qualities through the causes for which he chose to do battle and by the nature of the challenges he was prepared to undertake. In the 1980s, a dame of St Andrew could demonstrate her command of these same qualities by the integrity and fearlessness with which she sought to uphold the Charter of the United Nations and by the positions that she chose to espouse in the debates of that organization.

In Nita Barrow's mind, the linkage between the charter and the chivalric code appears to have been clearly established. As she herself put it so succinctly, "The Charter [of the United Nations] is, fundamentally, a refuge for those unable to protect themselves, a shield against those who would mislead, would exploit and would abuse the unsuspecting and the powerless" (Barrow 1988a).

Certainly Barrow would have been particularly conscious of this promise of the charter during the ten years preceding her appointment to the United Nations in 1986. In 1975, the United Nations had observed International Women's Year and proclaimed 1976–85 as the UN Decade for Women. The theme of the women's decade – "Equality, Development, Peace" – expressed the aspirations of the world's women for the "peoples of the world"; but it also served to recall to the world community the defining vision of the organization: its mission to establish a new world order in which sexism and racism would be outlawed, and where peace, stability, and security would be the product of increased economic self-sufficiency grounded in what we today describe as people-centred development.

The Equality Debate

During Barrow's tenure of office, the equality question generally emerged in relation to three issues: the role of small states, apartheid, and the advancement of women. The first of these, the role of small states, was the main subject of Barrow's address to the General Assembly in 1987. The discourse centred around three questions:

1. Why should a tiny island like Barbados with few resources enjoy national sovereignty?

2. Can such a small state, having gained its independence contribute anything to the international community?
3. Will such a small state become a burden on the large and powerful states? (Barrow 1987b)

In the preamble to the charter, the forty-six original signatories had declared themselves determined "to reaffirm faith in fundamental human rights, in the dignity and worth of the human person, in the equal rights of men and women *and of nations large and small* . . ." (my emphasis). Article 2 of the charter also states that "[t]he organization is based on the principle of the sovereign equality of all its members". When the United Nations celebrated its fortieth anniversary in 1985, the membership of the world body had already increased to 159 countries, more than three times the initial complement. (By 1997, the organization could boast of 185 member states, with four other states having "observer" status.) More to the point, like Barbados, which was admitted to membership on 9 December 1966, most of the newer member states were former colonies; and like Barbados, several of them were also small developing countries of the South.

To a large extent, it was the economic vulnerability and concomitant dependence of these small states that caused some developed countries to question – privately – the sovereign equality that small states enjoyed within the world body, and perhaps to regret their ability to influence the decisions of the United Nations by virtue of their voting power in the General Assembly and their leadership of several critical committees. As Barrow (1989: 5) observed, "The day to day courtesies which embroider the pursuits of diplomatic folk often obscure the prejudices which govern the behaviour of states."

As the permanent representative of Barbados, Barrow valued highly the opportunity that the United Nations afforded small developing states to debate and influence world policies. Arguing that national sovereignty is the most natural condition of a people's existence, she elaborated the basis for her government's commitment to the principle of sovereign equality and multilateralism with wry irony during the 1987 General Debate. Observing that large and powerful states succumb to the illusion that they can forego multilateral diplomacy, that they can dispense with international cooperation, that they can rely on "balance of power", "spheres of influence" and "alliances" to protect and promote their national interests abroad, she continued, "Small states . . . cannot court self-delusion . . . They must be vigorous exponents of multilateral diplomacy and firm supporters of international organizations" (Barrow 1987b: 6).

In an interview published in the 16–23 November 1987 issue of the *Diplomatic World Bulletin*: "Barbados' Dame Barrow Dedicated to Health & H.R.", Barrow commented on her appointment to the position of ambassador and permanent representative of Barbados to the United Nations in these terms: "I was not looking at my new role from the point of view of a diplomat who has come simply to represent her country's point of view. But, instead, looking at it from the point of view of a person who has seen what the United Nations could do in the field." With more than twenty years of international experience already behind her, Barrow was acutely aware of the benefits that accrue to small states from multilateral organizations and institutions. As she commented on another occasion, "Small states look for their greatest protection to the principles of international law . . . any step which undermines these principles places the future and the safety of small states in serious jeopardy" (Barrow 1988).

But even as she remained alive to the advantages which Barbados and other small states derive from their membership in the United Nations, she was equally alert to the contribution that such states could and do make to that organization, to the added value that their different and differing experiences and perspectives bring to all international bodies. It was this understanding that allowed her to treat so confidently with representatives of the developed world. It was this same understanding that also prompted the following observation during her address to the Institute of International Relations of the University of the West Indies in 1989:

> A superpower is not a superpower in relation to itself; nor is it a superpower in relation to other superpowers. It is only a superpower in relation to smaller powers. We the small states of the world are, to some degree, responsible for the notion and existence of superpowers. We are, through the politics of dependency which we choose to perpetuate and through the adoption of concepts of progress and development alien to our surroundings, our past, our potential. (Barrow 1989: 14)

The sovereign equality of all states was an article of faith for Nita Barrow; but the concept of racial equality inspired some of her most passionate responses. "We are a small nation", she remarked "but our size has in no way impinged upon our capacity to differentiate between human rights and human wrongs" (Barrow 1987b). For Barrow, one of the most pernicious human wrongs was the apartheid system. *Apartheid*, an Afrikaans word meaning separateness, encompassed a system of institutionalized racial segregation, oppression, and exploitation in which the freedom of movement and the political, social, and economic rights of non-whites were sharply curtailed. The following account of efforts by the United Nations to combat South Africa's apartheid system is extracted from a general history of the first forty years of the organization's existence, published in 1986:

> The question of South Africa's racial policies was first raised in the United Nations in 1946, when India complained that the South African government had enacted legislation discriminating against South Africans of Indian origin. The General Assembly expressed the view that the treatment of Indians in South Africa should conform with South Africa's obligations under agreements concluded between that country and India and with the United Nations Charter.

The wider question of racial conflict in South Africa arising from that government's apartheid policies was placed on the General Assembly's agenda in 1952. On that question and on India's original complaint, the South African government maintained that the matter was essentially within its domestic jurisdiction and that, under the charter, the United Nations was barred from considering it.

In fact, the United Nations took a rather different view of the problem. The General Assembly condemned apartheid as a crime against humanity; the Security Council termed it abhorrent to the conscience of mankind; and for the next forty-four years, United Nations bodies, particularly the General Assembly, adopted a wide range of measures aimed at providing political, moral, and material support for the oppressed people of South Africa. These included expressions of support for the liberation movements, calls for the release of political prisoners, sports boycotts, dissemination of information on the evils of apartheid, international meetings on the question, special observances, and voluntary funds to aid apartheid victims (United Nations 1986: 79–91).

In chapter 7, Alan Cobley provides a detailed discussion of Barrow's role as a member of the Eminent Persons Group (EPG) to South Africa set up by the Commonwealth Heads of Government in 1985. Referring to the disappointment with which the EPG regarded the failure of their mission, Blackman (1995: 125) quotes from the letter which accompanied the report of that distinguished group, and which records the shared sadness occasioned by what they described as an "acute consciousness and concern at the consequences of our failure for the future of that country". It is not surprising, then, that Barrow regarded her tenure at the United Nations as a second opportunity afforded her to employ her proven diplomatic skills and her considerable reputation in the service of the oppressed and dispossessed millions of black and coloured South Africans.

Barrow took up her appointment at the United Nations shortly after completing her work with the EPG. Antony Cave (1995: 18), who served as deputy permanent representative to the Barbados Mission throughout Barrow's tenure of office, recalls that "Dame Nita's discoveries and her face-to-face encounters with the imprisoned Nelson Mandela radicalized and riveted her determination to destroy apartheid." The abhorrence with which she regarded that regime was the product of a much older sense of honour, the reflection of a code of conduct that allowed no compromise with acts of injustice, no passive tolerance of abuse, no indifference to the sufferings of the millions rendered weak and powerless by Pretoria's "smug maleficence".

Barrow's first statement as the permanent representative of Barbados to the United Nations concerned the practice of governance by Pretoria. Taking as her theme "the theft of Namibia", she observed:

> The politics of greed and the politics of race have, each in its separate and sinister fashion, brought unspeakable suffering to human life in our time. When conjoined, they have revealed shameful evidence of human potential to be cruel. Namibia is the story of such a sinister alliance. Namibia shows what will result when greed and race become the chief determinants of a country's politics. (Barrow 1986: 1)

Namibia acceded to independence on 21 March 1990, just shortly before Barrow left the United Nations to take up her appointment as the first female governor general of Barbados in June 1990. Nelson Mandela was also released in 1990 after nearly thirty years in prison and, in 1994, became the first democratically elected president of a free, non-racial South Africa. The abolition of apartheid constituted a major political triumph for the peoples of Southern Africa. It marked an even greater moral victory for the peoples of the world. An injustice that had exercised the conscience and energies of member states for more than four decades had finally been resolved to the advantage of several million souls. As Barrow once observed: "That's what the UN gives, a sense of confidence that you are a country. If you look at the human face of it, we get an awful lot done" (1987).

Her vigorous opposition to apartheid and her unflagging commitment to the advancement of women were two distinguishing features of Nita Barrow"s tenure at the United Nations. Yet she was neither a "black" ambassador nor a "female" ambassador: "Her lasting contribution to diplomacy was her exceptional skill in reducing to their appropriate and inevitable human terms the complex issues of disarmament, pollution, debt-reduction and hunger" (Cave 1995: 19).

As president of the World YWCA (1975–83), Nita Barrow is credited with having played a critical role in transforming that organization from an association perceived by many as being dominated by wealthy white women of the North – whose charity determined its priorities – into an institution alert to the implications of Christian equality, and able to respond realistically to the varied and complex challenges of a membership comprising women from ninety countries, both North and South, black and white, rich and poor. She was elected president of the World YWCA at the council meeting in Vancouver in 1975, and re-elected for a second term in 1979. Speaking at the memorial service for Nita Barrow organized by the World council of Churches in Geneva in February 1996, Doreen Boyd, deputy director of the World YWCA, observed:

> Her election was a culmination of years of struggle by previous progressive leadership to promote Third World women as leaders in the YWCA. Nita, highly intelligent with enormous charisma, a deep sense of service and a fighting spirit made it all come together at Vancouver . . . At the end of her term of office a new global awareness of the issues of oppression, poverty, human rights violations, lack of primary health care and the like had been fostered within the movement, as she ensured that the trend for representation of Third World women in top leadership positions continued. (Boyd 1996)

After her time with the World YWCA, Barrow brought her richly deserved reputation for personal integrity and courage to the convenorship of Forum '85, which, as noted elsewhere in this collection, was held in Nairobi in conjunction with the World Conference to Review the Decade for Women in 1985. She also commanded a negotiating capacity honed during her years as a health worker. "Health" she would later observe "is a very political matter. You learn how to woo your government to get things done . . . how you make progress, how you get your plans advanced, how you negotiate. Because you must remember, when you talk health to the government, it is not a profit sector like tourism or trade. So you have to put it in terms of what are the cost benefits" (1987: 5).

The negotiating skills that were the foundation of her success at Nairobi had been further enhanced during those years when she served as president of the International Council of Adult Education, president of the World Council of Churches for the Caribbean region, and president of the World YWCA. Yet she regarded her involvement in Forum '85 as her most challenging undertaking. For one thing, it required overcoming the deep distrust of the Kenyan authorities who saw the forum as being potentially very socially disruptive:

Prior perspectives included the concept that the women who attended the Forum would be combative, disruptive to the host country and bring unwanted ideas to women there. This meant a process of continuous negotiation and continuous discussion in order to have the Forum for all. (*Trinidad and Tobago Review* 1988: 22)

As convenor of Forum '85, Barrow played a leading role in discussions surrounding the formulation of the document entitled, "Forward-looking Strategies for the Advancement of Women to the Year 2000" (FLS), which was issued at the end of the World Conference. Endorsed by the General Assembly in its resolution 40/108 of 13 December 1985, the FLS called, *inter alia*, for the promotion of women to positions of power at every level within all political and legislative bodies in order to achieve parity with men; equal rights under the law; equal employment opportunities; equal pay for work of equal value; equal access to health services; equal access to education and training; and the equal involvement of women, at every stage and level of development. But even as she recognized the positive impact which the FLS could have on the situation of the world's women, she derived particular satisfaction from the way in which 17,500 women of every race, creed and political persuasion came together at the forum, successfully modelling the type of constructive dialoguing without which there can be no lasting progress for human society.

And so you hope in the UN that we can talk to each other as we did in Nairobi, where we had an axiom: you not only had to talk, but you had to listen. And you had to try to understand the position of the other person. I think the Nairobi Conference succeeded in large measure. You had groups of women in the USA and the USSR, women coming from Palestine to talk with women from Israel, and women of Iraq and Iran – despite their political differences. (*Diplomatic World Bulletin* 1987: 12)

Today, when the debate on the reform of the United Nations has grown so intense that the very continued existence of the organization appears to be under threat, one wishes for the commonsense, practical voice of a Nita Barrow who never lost sight of the original purpose of the world body. Charged with outlining an approach to some of the more intractable problems before the organization, she replied,

> I think if I were given a chance, I'd ask the [the representatives of member states] a question. If we could forget our postures of First World, Third World, East, West. And we could begin to think that everybody had an equal right to speak on an issue. What kind of actions do you think we can really do to solve some of the things we've been beating our heads about? (*Diplomatic World Bulletin* 1987: 5)

The Development Debate

Nita Barrow's privileging of the human factor in the activities of the United Nations offers a ready sortie into a discussion of the development debate and her position on some of the issues arising therefrom. The economic and social advancement of developing countries has been a matter of continuing concern to the membership of the United Nations ever since the organization was established in 1945. This is hardly surprising since the preamble to the UN charter includes the stated determination on the part of the signatories "to promote social progress and better standards of life in larger freedom, and for these ends . . . to employ international machinery for the promotion of the economic and social advancement of all peoples". Conscious of this undertaking, in 1961 the General Assembly decided to designate the 1960s as the United Nations Development Decade. This first "Development Decade", described as "the beginning of an ongoing effort to formulate the policies required for coherent and sustained economic and social progress in developing countries" (United Nations 1986: 196), included a call for member states to join forces in a sustained effort to accelerate the advancement of developing countries.

Many developing countries did achieve some increase in their gross domestic product (GDP) during the 1960s; however, these gains were offset by population increases, unfavourable trade patterns, and heavy debt burdens. The International Development Strategy, which the General Assembly adopted on 24 October 1970 as a blueprint for the Second United Nations Development Decade, was also compromised by the amount of debt being carried by developing countries and by the failure of each economically advanced country to transfer each year financial resources to developing countries equal to at least 1 percent of its gross national product (GNP).

According to the strategy, by mid-decade, at least 0.7 percent of GNP should have been transferred in the form of official development assistance (ODA) – low-interest, long-term loans – to developing countries. In fact, the mid-term review of the second decade revealed that the net flow of ODA averaged 0.33 percent of the GNP of the developed countries, less than half the target set by the General Assembly in 1970. During the 1980s, the economies of most of the countries of the South stopped growing, and many of them declined. By the end of the 1980s, the original pattern of financial flows from the North to the South had been dramatically reversed, and the developing world was paying billions more to the rich countries of the North than they were receiving from ODA.

The structural adjustment programmes adopted by developing countries at the insistence of the International Monetary Fund underscored the extent of their economic problems. More significantly, however, they revealed the degree to which the human factor had become incidental in development planning: "[O]ur preoccupation as economists is largely with saving and investment, exports and imports – and, of course, with that most convenient abstraction of all: the gross national product. When we do come to recognize the contributions of human beings as a means of development, we tend to treat them as almost residual elements" (Haq 1990: 4).

The annual *Human Development Report*, first launched in 1990 under the sponsorship of the United Nations Development Programme (UNDP), helped to refocus world attention on the need for people-centred development models. As stated in the "Overview", the report was about people and about how development enlarges their choices:

> It is about more than GNP growth, more than income and wealth and more than producing commodities and accumulating capital. A person's access to income may be one of the choices, but it is not the sum total of human endeavour.
>
> Human development is a process of enlarging people's choices. The most critical of these wide-ranging choices are to live a long and healthy life, to be educated and to have access to resources needed for a decent standard of living. Additional choices include political freedom, guaranteed human rights and personal self-respect. (United Nations 1990: 1)

In fact, the *Human Development Report* expressed a view of the pre-eminence of people in development that had been slowly regaining support over the preceding two decades, in part due to the vigorous advocacy of humanistic international leaders such as Nita Barrow. Repeating a position consistently advanced throughout her varied career, Barrow applauded the new emphasis on human resource development proposed by the UNDP Governing Council in 1989, while observing that

> This will require, as a first priority, that emphasis be placed on satisfying the basic human needs for food, education, health services, housing, and that poverty be eradicated; for only when humankind is freed from a daily struggle to remain alive or just to eke out a meagre existence can attention be turned to loftier goals. (Barrow 1989: 3)

It is of course a tribute to Barrow's larger world vision that she made this plea while representing a country that for many years was well placed in the Human Development Index. But the statement also includes a warning that is particularly relevant today when macro-economic policies, compounded by declining ODA flows, severely constrain the development gains achieved by many Caribbean countries during the 1970s and 1980s: "a focus on management development is all well and good", Barrow observed, "but UNDP must continue to play a major role in ensuring that there is something left to manage in developing countries" (Barrow 1989: 4).

Recognizing that economic growth is the engine of development, Barrow challenged what she described as "a disturbing trend towards the eventual exclusion of several developing countries from grant assistance from UNDP" (Barrow 1989: 4). But Barrow never questioned the axiom that "people are the real wealth of a nation", and she placed great emphasis on the development of national capacity. Consequently, while her concern for the hardships experienced by people caught up in a deteriorating economic situation prompted her to protest any decline in the transfer of external technical and financial resources to the developing world, she would also inform the UNDP Governing Council that "UNDP initiatives would be ill-conceived if they simply attempt to replicate in developing countries management approaches, techniques and structures which are alien to the environment in which they must operate" (Barrow 1989: 4).

In 1992, the United Nations gathered the world community in Rio de Janeiro to discuss the links between environment (more specifically our natural environment) and development. The debate highlighted the ongoing tension between the North and the South on the issue of sustainable development. The Brundtland Commission had defined sustainable development as "development that meets the needs of the present without compromising the ability of future generations to meet their own needs". Mahbub ul Haq, in a gloss on the definition, observes that it begs more questions than it answers:

What are the needs of the present and future generations? Developing countries are not satisfied with their present levels of consumption and have no intention of sustaining poverty. And industrial countries are not entitled forever to an 85 percent of the world's income and to the perpetuation of their present patterns of consumption. In fact, the preservation of the global environment raises serious issues about the distribution of global income and assets in the present. (Haq 1990: 78)

As a spokesperson for the developing world, Nita Barrow was among those who pointed out that environmental degradation was not linked exclusively to the errors and omissions of the developing world, observing that "the problems of acid rain, toxic wastes, nuclear contamination are by and large associated with centres of economic development and industrialization, although their effects are not limited to the more developed nations" (Barrow 1987a). At the same time, she did admit that economic underdevelopment creates conditions that further environmental degradation, a degradation that can, in some cases, be irreversible. Yet her balanced approach in what had become a sharply polarized debate was severely taxed in the summer of 1988 by the spectre of a garbage barge laden with refuse from New York state seeking to negotiate a dumping site in the Caribbean. And, hence, her fearless rebuke to the organization in a statement delivered in 1988:

A situation in which calls for the transfer of wealth and appropriate technology are met with antipathy, while the transfer of wastes is being actively pursued suggests that ours is rapidly becoming a community of contempt. This is a clear challenge to the United Nations Charter. (Barrow 1988: 29)

As Janice Cumberbatch notes in chapter 6, having established herself as a spokesperson on environmental matters at the United Nations, Nita Barrow continued to develop her interests in this area after 1990 in her capacity as governor general of Barbados. In 1992 she attended the Rio conference as one of ten eminent persons invited by Secretary General Maurice Strong to lend their wisdom and experience to the deliberations of that assembly. Two years later, in May 1994, Barbados hosted the First Global Conference on the Sustainable Development of Small Island Developing States (SIDS). Inputted into those discussions were the reflections of a group of international development experts invited by Nita Barrow to share their own understanding of the issues with those participating in the conference, and to propose possible solutions to the development challenges arising from the particular vulnerabilities of this group of countries.

The Group of Eminent Persons opened their statement with the following declarations: "The momentum generated at the Earth Summit is faltering. The failure of the developed countries to honour the commitments made at the United Nations Conference on Environment and Development is undermining the global partnership forged at Rio de Janeiro" (United Nations 1994: 2–3).

Noting that the most encouraging developments have occurred primarily at the level of people and the non-governmental and sectoral organizations through which they act, the preamble continues:

> The industrialized countries have not shown the political will nor have they provided the additional resources required to realize the partnership. Without access to the needed resources and technology, developing countries cannot fulfil their part of the bargain. This calls into serious question the prospects for sustainable development. A way to provide new impetus must be found. (United Nations 1994: 2–3)

Today, it is generally acknowledged that the "Plan of Action" endorsed at the SIDS Conference has not attracted from the international community the level of resources commensurate with the gravity of the problems that need to be addressed. As disappointing as this is, it would hardly have caused Nita Barrow to despair. As she herself had cause to remark in another context: "The Global agenda is not always the United Nations agenda. The latter is an agenda of consensus and compromise, where priorities frequently are brokered and real interests set aside . . . The sincerity of delegations notwithstanding, the agenda is sometimes strained not by what it includes, but by what it is often forced to exclude" (Barrow 1989: 3).

Peace

In his essay "On a Hinge of History", Ivan Head comments:

> This hinge of history on which we endeavour to maintain our balance has posed the clearest of questions: Is the normative model of national conduct and international behaviour to be militaristic? Is power and prestige and preference to be that of unilateral interpretations of law, of equity as a privilege rather than a right? Are human dignity, human decency, human understanding optional qualities, unlikely goals? What weight is to be given social justice, environmental wholesomeness, peaceful resolution of conflict, cultural achievement? (Head 1991: 214)

Nita Barrow's experiencces of apartheid and of the Middle East question had left her with an acute sense of the human dimension of these struggles:

> You're trying to be as fair as possible and make people realize that when we speak of peace in the Middle East, it can't be for some people, it's for all people. The right of existence belongs to all nations. But it also belongs to people, too, so they can function and not live as some do in refugee camps that have gone from being temporary camps to permanent ones in 1987. (*Diplomatic World Bulletin* 1987: 5)

As with the equality and the development debates, then, Barrow saw the resolution to the many and varied sources of conflict and war as being rooted in the fulfilment of the charter's promise to enhance respect for human rights and fundamental freedoms, to promote sustainable economic and social development for wider prosperity, to alleviate distress and to curtail the existence and use of massively destructive weapons. "Peace," she would argue, "cannot be the brokered result of power." Adding, "in today's enlightened world a peace that does not satisfy people's demand for freedom, justice and development will hardly be lasting". And again: "If resources now devoted to the cause of destruction could be diverted to the building of needy nations, those strains and tensions which give rise to conflict would dramatically decline" (Barrow 1987b: 6).

But in the end, as in the beginning, Barrow's vision of the United Nations as an instrument for the advancement and protection of all the world's peoples allowed her to keep faith with the United Nations to the end of her days:

> We would do well to remind ourselves that this is an agency founded as a result of conflict and the context of its operations remains one of conflict. As such, it remains an honest reflection of the human condition. We, all of us, exist in a state of perpetual tension. As individuals we are torn between our need for order and tranquility and our innate abhorrence of fetters and restraint. As political societies, we are torn between demands for sovereignty and the realities of interdependence.
>
> Surrounded by this swirl of contending forces the United Nations becomes something of a moral epicentre. We who gather here year after year must, in my view, seek not to remove such conflict from our midst. We must, more realistically, seek to redirect these natural forces from the avenues of destruction to those of development. This is the fundamental task of the United Nations: to convert the human condition from despair into hope. (Barrow 1988b)

Nita Barrow's unwavering support of policies and strategies that spoke to the dignity of the human person, and her unqualified commitment to the principles of equality, development, and peace rendered her one of the most highly respected members of the international community. She was a valued champion of the women's movement and a tireless advocate of the anti-apartheid movement. Her influence on the development of small-island developing states was significant. The many honours she received attest to the quality of her reputation. Her record of selfless service has enriched and enlarged our lives.

In her study *A Reader's Guide to Geoffrey Chaucer*, the critic Muriel Bowden writes: "There can be nothing idle or accidental in Chaucer's delineation of his knight: that truly 'parfit' and 'gentil' man represents what anyone in the fourteenth century would recognize as a 'good servant of the Lord', always to be met somewhere in the real world, one of the humble in heart but mighty in virtue, not frequently met, alas, but unmistakable when encountered" (Bowden 1965: 23). Ruth Nita Barrow, Dame of St Andrew, was no less virtuous a figure. With her passing, the United Nations – and indeed the entire world community has suffered a great loss.

Part Five

International Leadership, International Service

Chapter Nine

The Challenge of Innovative Leadership of a Traditional Women's Organization:

The World YWCA and Ruth Nita Barrow

[Eudine Barriteau]

Between 1975 and the Nairobi consciousness raising of 1985, the World YWCA faced a decade of crisis and change, which paralleled the momentous changes in women's role in society taking place on a global scale. Finally it demonstrated its resilience and emerged, like the women it represented, 'stronger, bolder, surer'.[1] . . . During this decade 1975–85 the World YWCA proved itself to be a living organism, able to transform itself, freely and fearlessly, in response to historical changes while remaining true to its central purpose.

– Carole Seymour Jones

Maybe you can say the worldwide YWCA was my first introduction to the women's movement because they were ahead of the flag waving as a women's movement . . . Why I say the YWCA was certainly a women's movement because everywhere they went their platform was the advancement of women and girls.

–Nita Barrow, 25 September 1995[2]

A Decade of Women, Crisis, and Change

The decade 1975–1985 redefined women's quest for social change, altered the World YWCA, and further tested the leadership capabilities of Ruth Nita

Barrow. The decade proved to be very significant for the emergence of women's leadership internationally, the practices and mandate of the World YWCA, and the public life of Nita Barrow. This chapter explores the nexus of these three occurrences. I am specifically interested in examining women's leadership in non-governmental organizations (NGOs) and analysing the kind of direction Barrow brought to the YWCA. I discuss the ways in which she dealt with some of the institutional challenges she inherited. Nita Barrow assumed leadership of the World YWCA at a critical juncture in its evolution. She was aware of the constraints posed to the world body by the issues of institutional racism, entrenched class biases, and an external perception of imperial rule. In the 1970s she had to confront an image of the world executive as remote, elderly, and out of touch with the challenges and constituents of the national associations. The dominant perception of the world executive leadership before the decade of change was of "white, wealthy, ladies of leisure, meeting during the day: of white hair and white faces" (Seymour-Jones 1994: 323).

I do not attempt to document the work of the World YWCA or establish its importance to women's lives in industrialized and developing countries. This has been excellently done in several definitive publications (Rice 1947; Boyd 1986; Seymour-Jones 1994). Neither am I interested in endowing Nita Barrow with messianic qualities. She was a remarkable woman who broke new ground in several fields for women, and Caribbean women in particular. My thrust is to begin to isolate those strategies that enabled her to become an agent for change and thus implement or facilitate activities that would transform the policy and practice of the YWCA.

One of the main objectives in analysing Barrow's involvement in the World YWCA is to contribute to creating a new understanding of women's leadership in developing countries. Therefore, I intend to begin the process of isolating the strategies she employed in altering conventional practices, subverting barriers, and forcing change to produce benefits for women and works towards the creation of a more just society. I do not make a case of exceptionalism for Nita Barrow. Rather, I believe she represents a community of women leaders in developing countries whose contributions in the area of leadership is underexplored.

Women's leadership in developing countries certainly existed before the impetus of the Women in Development discourse and discipline "discovered Third World women". Scholars and activists in the South have contributed to the record of women organizing and promoting change in their societies (Reddock 1994; Jayawardena 1986). However, the decade served as an incubator for the rapid growth, expansion, and regeneration of women motivating individuals and organizations to achieve specific goals. The activities of the decade created visibility for women as leaders and made us aware of differing processes of leadership (Statham 1987). It introduced different procedures and interactions that unleashed the leadership potential of new generations of women (Karl 1995: 19).

Through a variety of methodologies and strategies, pioneering women in developing countries have been creating and managing change. Although we have begun the process in the Caribbean of documenting and analysing the contributions of these women (Reddock 1988, 1994; Benbow 1994; Brodber 1986; Martin 1988; Brown 1990) we now have to synthesize what their contributions reveal about women's styles of management, their leadership capabilities, and the strategies used that proved successful.

Overall, there is a paucity of research and analysis on women's leadership in developing countries. Most of the research that exists focuses on women in industrialized countries. These investigations focus primarily on women leaders in the corporate, commercial sectors of the economy, although the body of work on women in leadership in the public spheres of the state, economy, and society is growing (Rosener 1990; Cantor and Barney 1992). In the Caribbean and other areas of the South there remains a lack of information on women and leadership in both the state and non-governmental arenas of civic society.

The United Nations declared the years 1976–85 as the Decade of Women, immediately following the first International Women's Year. With this designation they afforded an international context for examining women's roles and status in society. The United Nations had formally began its mission to graft women issues onto development concerns, assuming then that these constituted separate concerns.

The years of this decade bracketed the birth and growth of an international, politicized women's movement and ushered in the rapid expansion of a range of governmental, parastatal, and non-governmental organizations devoted to advancing women's interests in developing countries (Karl 1995: 121–45). Several new women's organizations were founded. In the Caribbean, the Caribbean Association for Feminist Research and Action (CAFRA) came into being. The international network of feminist scholars and activists, Development Alternatives with Women for a New Era (DAWN), was founded in

Bangalore, India, in August 1984. By 1985, at the NGO Forum convened by Nita Barrow, DAWN had transformed the whole discourse on Women and Development by creating a new analytical frame that gave poor women more leverage within their contextual locations (Jain 1999).[3]

For women's organizations, the significance of the decade was that it began with the first UN conference on women in Mexico City in 1975 and ended with the third conference in Nairobi in 1985. If the primary goal of the first UN decade on development was to promote the idea of development for non-industrialized countries, then the second decade attempted to locate women on this continuum and tried to determine the values that should be assigned to their contributions and the role states and governments should pursue to "bring women into development".

The decade of crisis and change that the World YWCA experienced (Seymour-Jones 1994: 321) was the decade of Nita Barrow's leadership of one of the oldest, continuously functioning women's organization in the world. Nita Barrow became president at the point that the World YWCA engaged in introspection and redefining its mandate to the world's women.

Nita Barrow began and ended the decade in the forefront of international leadership positions. In 1975, she began her tenure as president of the World YWCA. She closed the decade by convening the NGO Forum '85 in Nairobi. When Nita Barrow convened the Nairobi NGO Forum she continued a tradition that began with World YWCA leaders chairing all the women's international NGO meetings from Mexico to Copenhagen and finally Nairobi (Seymour-Jones 1994: 319).[4] Despite the great turbulence that the World YWCA experienced internally, the decade brought immediate recognition for its long history of struggling to create material improvement and psychological tools for women to flourish all over the world (Seymour-Jones 1994: 319; Karl 1995: 25).

Dual Mission, Dual Clientele

From its inception the World YWCA embraced two distinct missions and was intended to serve the needs of two distinct social and economic classes of women in Western society. The vision of the British and American women who founded their respective organizations that would later become the World YWCA revealed these separate missions. The British founders, Miss Emma

Robarts and Mrs Arthur (Mary Jane) Kinnard, envisioned The World Y as "a worldwide Christian movement, of, by and for young women" (Seymour-Jones 1994: 1, 5). Nancy Boyd observes that the American YWCA also began with a dual commitment to personal piety and social service (Boyd 1986: 12). The social standing and economic background of the young women who comprised the collective memberships of the YWCA departed sharply from the social and economic circumstances of the women served by the YWCA. The former were committed to serving "the welfare of young women who are dependent on their own exertions for support" (Boyd 1986: 12).

The YWCA initially ministered to women of the working class of the industrializing cities of Europe and North America during the mid to late nineteenth century. These were the women who euphemistically depended on their own exertions for support. As working women, they were disenfranchised economically and politically. They were drawn into new, urban, industrializing economies without supportive networks of close-knit communities, family and friends. They possessed no skills in negotiating conditions of work and they had no access to social services, which were practically non-existent. They suffered from a lack of adequate housing. They were fair game for "unscrupulous men" eager for recruits for the cities' brothels (Boyd 1986: 12). They comprised a constituency of women who needed survival skills, political representation, social organization, and spiritual upliftment. Motivated by a Christian desire to serve, middle-class, educated women created the YWCA to meet those needs. They also created the YWCA to satisfy their own needs for esteem and self-actualization. The YWCA represented the vision of educated women who had very little outlet for their own talents and creativity. They saw in this new organization an opportunity to help working-class women as well as to lead a life outside that of a dependent, supportive spouse or daughter.

While providing basic and much-needed services and support for working women, the YWCA also existed to provide an outlet for the talent, skills, ambitions, and desires for self-fulfilment of middle- and upper-class women. Their needs may have been higher than that of working-class women when ranked on Maslow's hierarchy of basic needs, but they were no less real. The women who flooded the rapidly expanding, urban centres in search of work would have been understandably more concerned with satisfying basic constraints for food, safety, and shelter. The women who created the YWCA did not have to worry about material conditions of survival. However, the frustrations that both classes of women experienced were equally daunting in a patriarchal society with rigid gender roles defined on the basis of sex.

For the YWCA founders, waged work was socially unacceptable (Seymour-Jones 1994: 4). Ironically, the World YWCA was created by women who for social and ideological reasons could not work, to serve women forced to work. The former group of women comprised educated, dynamic, brilliant women with much to offer their countries. Unfortunately, they existed in societies that were quite unprepared and unwilling to allow public spaces for women's collective contributions outside of rigidly defined traditional roles.

Middle-class Christian women therefore served their needs and the needs of working-class young women as they defined them. The YWCA founders provided accommodation, self-improvement programs, skills training, and a Christian community of women to support the values of Western society. At the same time, the volunteer work of the YWCA women quietly but deliberately subverted the societal practice of confining the contributions of educated, middle-class women to the domestic or private sphere.

This issue of middle-class women and work exposes the interplay of ideological and material relations of gender in nineteenth-century European gender systems. The ideological relations of gender indicate how a society's notion of masculinity and femininity is constructed and maintained. The ways in which masculinity and femininity are constructed reveal the gender ideologies operating in a state and society. Gender ideologies reveal what is appropriate or expected of the socially constituted beings "women" and "men". These ideologies expose how individuals create gender identities. Gender ideologies establish the sexually differentiated, socially constructed boundaries for "males" and "females" (Barriteau 1996b, 1998).

Material relations of gender reveal access to and the allocation of power, status, and resources within a community or society. These relations expose how women and men gain access to or are allocated the material and non-material resources within a state and society. Feminists' analyses of the material relations of gender makes visible the distribution of economic and political power and material resources (Folbre 1994; Barriteau 1996a; Sparr 1994).

Were the YWCA founders aware of or informed by the subversive potential of their act to establish an organization to serve women's needs and train women as leaders? Their actions demonstrate that they were determined to subvert dominating relations of gender that place educated, competent women at a disadvantage to men when women desire to occupy leadership positions in the public sphere. They cleverly manipulated the socially sanctioned vehicles of volunteer leadership and Christian service to carve out leadership roles in the public sphere for women.

Western society does not have a problem with women working and has always counted on women's paid and unpaid labour to maintain economic production and social cohesion. It seems the problem arises with the level at which women enter the labour force. Menial or basic entry level positions are non-threatening and provide useful sources for grunt work.

Women workers are welcome and accommodated in economies as the proverbial hewers of wood and drawers of water. Food and Agriculture Organization statistics on agriculture show that in Africa, women contribute 70 percent of the total labour in hoeing and weeding, 80 percent in transporting and 90 percent of the labour in food processing (Karl 1995: 107). The twentieth-century female factory worker is still with us in Europe, the Caribbean, Asia, the Pacific, Latin America, and Africa, and she represents an exploited majority for working women (Ward 1990; Kelly 1987). Her problems, frustrations, and needs do not interest policy makers (Waring 1990) or the mainstream media. She has to continue to depend on NGOs for representation. Instead the regional and international media are obsessed with the comparatively tiny percentage of women in managerial and other senior positions in the state and economy. They amplify statistics and analyses of these women to suggest that all women are doing better economically and that feminists are engaged in some covert agenda to marginalize men and take over the society (Barriteau 2001).

The industrial revolution relied heavily on women's labour and still does so in contemporary society. The wages women received then and now is less than that paid to men, unless they are employed in the public sector of states committed to equal pay for equal work. At the time the YWCA was founded in the nineteenth century, women were seen as a supplementary labour force, a reserve army of labour. Karl Marx held that nineteenth-century capitalists hired women as a means of depreciating the earning power of men, which is another way of saying that women could be paid less than men (Marx 1967: 372–73; Barriteau 1995: 57). Why then did the work of educated women prove so problematic? These were women who clearly would not have to work for subsistence wages. Their education, economic standing, and social connections guaranteed that any paid work would not be unskilled or at entry-level positions. Was the barrier to educated, middle-class women holding jobs solely because of ideological reasons? Or did the paid work of women in management or policy-making positions indicate a threat to patriarchal economic power? The activities of the World YWCA began a process of exposing and quietly challenging the deeply inequitable beliefs about women and work.

A Living Organism Able to Transform Itself

Nita Barrow's term of leadership coincided with one of the most turbulent periods for the YWCA. The challenges Barrow and the YWCA confronted were both internal and external. Internally, she had to work in an environment historically shaped by entrenched racism and class biases. Externally, the YWCA was rethinking its mandate and seeking to pursue programs reflecting the problems and experiences of women all over the world.

In the second opening quotation to this chapter, Barrow emphasizes that the YWCA had been dealing with the issues of improving the lives of women and girls long before second wave feminism and "ahead of the flag waving as a women's movement" (Barrow 1995d). The YWCA had a long history of serious organizing, strategizing, and planning. It was a mature organization with established structures, strong roots, and well-developed communication channels. Unfortunately, by the late 1960s it was perceived as ossifying into an organization grossly out of touch with the realities of women's lives. The World YWCA was faced with the realization that if the organization was to grow and expand with the new realities confronting women, important changes had to be made in its approaches to programmes, policies surrounding staff and executive, and other matters relating to outmoded ways of reacting to external pressures.

Barrow and other leaders of the World YWCA seemed peeved or annoyed with the attention given to second wave feminists and the women's movement they spawned. Perhaps they were initially taken aback by the sudden rise of the second wave women's movement, which they felt behaved as if it had actually discovered women's lives. In their own words, the Y leaders state they have been improving women's lives since the middle of the nineteenth century and without the fanfare and the media-grabbing attention of feminists in the 1960s and 1970s. Barrow and the other Y leaders were critical and sceptical of the new processes that appeared to discover anew the plight of women. They wondered aloud about the fuss and attention the new women's movement and its organizing principle, feminism, earned for doing what they felt they had being doing all along.

This of course points to a deeper issue – the ambivalence Nita Barrow and other Y leaders felt about feminists and feminism. She states:

I have not considered myself as a feminist leader. I have been a woman who by professional preparation as a nurse (mostly a woman's profession) involved in women's activities such as the YWCA, locally, regionally and internationally have been deeply involved in women's questions – through my church and the World Council of Churches health care emphasis, seen the plight of women particularly in all parts of the world. Naturally therefore issues and the concerns of women everywhere over the decade have been of primary interests. (Nita Barrow 1985b)

Yet Nita Barrow addressed issues that were explicitly feminist:

Women are not expected to be free to choose her [sic] own lifestyle – men can and do. Society male and female condemn her as an unworthy citizen if she steps outside the bounds of what is considered acceptable behaviour. (Barrow 1987a)

Barrow and other Y leaders resented the criticism that the YWCA never challenged institutionalized gender inequalities and unequal power relations; in other words, that the World YWCA was not feminist enough. Carole Seymour-Jones (1994) presents a thorough analysis of this in chapter 15 of her study of the YWCA. She comments that the organization prefers to describe itself as a woman's movement rather than a feminist movement. According to Seymour-Jones (1994: 317), its aim has always been to improve the status of women through established democratic, legal channels, while remaining independent of governments. Barrow commented that there was never any bra burning in the YWCA. Elizabeth Palmer, general secretary of the World YWCA for twenty-five years,[5] said the difference between the World YWCA and other feminist groups was a reflection of words not intent. Athena Tsoudero-Athanassiou, a former president of the World YWCA, added that, "we are doers and avoided philosophy" (Seymour-Jones 1994: 318–20).

Despite the defensive posturing, during the decade of Barrow's leadership the World YWCA was forced to radically overhaul its programmes and policies to make them more responsive to women's needs. Criticism of what had become a tame approach to working with women did not arise only from external sources. Norwegian Helen Bjornoy was very worried that the YWCA was becoming distracted by a focus on celebrating women's culture while the political questions about women's lives went unanswered:

> I think the YWCA has, like all women's work, suffered from the scourge of goodwill. Women's work has become accepted, and thereby disarmed. Women's work has become women's culture instead of women's politics. I think that this is a serious matter for the YWCA. We who have also worked and struggled for equality and human rights, are fed up with an attitude that 'we are all now busy with equality' – without that leading to a single step toward change. And we in the YWCA are too preoccupied with women's songs, women's worship, women's cultural festivals, exhibitions of women's artistic work, etc., etc., All of these are within the framework of what is now accepted for women, for Christians and for the YWCA. And the result is that nobody is concerned about women's politics, that is, those things that bring change . . . Our own struggle has become the means of disarming ourselves. (Bjornoy 1982)

Nita Barrow and the YWCA faced head-on the need to rethink the mission of the organization. Membership was declining although there was a growth in participation. The original "dual mission/dual clientele" was coming back to haunt the YWCA. There was a widening of the gulf between those who served and those who were served. What concerned the leadership was that women were quite willing to use the YWCA as clients, to see it as providing a service and not become involved in the internal structures and processes of the Y. The international upheavals in the political economy of the world in the 1970s and 1980s meant the YWCA could not afford to ignore questions of war and peace, refugees, economic stagnation or decline, the self-defined needs of young women, and a much more politicized way of engaging with the complexities of women's lives.

Nita Barrow's presidency was marked by a focus on the following issues.

- work in Lebanon and its aftermath of continued struggle for peace
- changing situation in China
- end of the liberation struggle in Zimbabwe
- world recession and serious economic dislocation it has brought
- broadening of the women's movement
- broad acceptance within the Y that social change is an imperative that comes to the Y out of the Gospel and is therefore not something the Y can hide from or take as an option (Sovik 1985)

For the first time in its history, the Y was interpreting its Christian mission to serve to also mean active involvement in macroeconomic and political issues. The instruments to do so already existed. Article IV of its constitution states the YWCA "works for international understanding for improved social and economic conditions and for basic human rights for all people" (World YWCA Constitution n.d.).

However, up until the 1970s the YWCA steered clear of overtly political issues. By 1975, it could no longer do so and still maintain its credibility and relevance. Like a living organism, the World YWCA transformed itself for survival. It altered its policies and practices to address the complex, multiple realities of women globally.

In the call to the World Council in 1983, the executive of the World YWCA described the organization as a Christian movement committed to action for social change: "We are women working for peace. We are women committed to the realization of human rights. We are women who care about the stewardship of the earth's environment" (Barrow 1982b).

Peace in the Middle East and the impact of the Middle East crisis on women's lives, particularly Palestinian women, became one of the fundamental issues that absorbed the attention of Nita Barrow and the World Executive as they stepped out of the practice of dealing with sanitized issues.

In 1975 at its council meeting, the World YWCA adopted a statement on Middle East tensions that stated, in part, "The explosive situation in the Middle East is the most serious threat to World Peace today . . . At the heart of the explosive situation is the question of Palestine" (World YWCA 1975).

In 1982, Nita Barrow and other members of the World Executive visited the Middle East, specifically Lebanon and the East and West Banks of Jordan. Their mission was to engage YWCA associations in a preliminary discussion for a World YWCA Middle East Encounter (Barrow 1982).

In August 1984, Barrow spoke on the program of the International NGO meeting on the question of Palestine (Sovik 1985). The World YWCA then became the secretariat of an international coordinating committee of fifteen non-governmental organizations concerned about the Middle East region and its future. Ruth Sovik reports "the World YWCA willingness to undertake this task has without doubt helped to create an absolutely new pattern in NGO–UN relationships" (Sovik 1985).

Nita Barrow and Women's Leadership: Stronger, Surer, Bolder

> Here is a woman not only with a philosophy of internationalism and a world view that takes into account the total welfare of humanity but with a track record of experience to support all of this . . . As woman, black, small-islander, nurse rather than doctor, Third World rather than metropolitan, she is the potential victim of the multiple jeopardy syndrome. But she has longed transformed all these would-be liabilities into the greatest of assets making her a figure commanding worldwide respect and confidence. (Nettleford 1988: 20)[6]

Nita Barrow fitted the prototype of a leader in the World YWCA. She was well-educated, middle class, peripatetic, and possessed solid credentials of public professional service and personal Christian faith. What distinguished her from her predecessors was that she was black, and a very proud West Indian from a small, former British colony in the Caribbean. Although Nita Barrow served as world president for two terms, 1975–79 and 1979–83, her association with the YWCA began in Trinidad in the 1940s (Barrow 1995d). She attended her first World Council meeting in England in 1951 and also represented Jamaica at the council of the world body in Lebanon in that year (Lusan 1996; Blackman 1995: 144). That meeting in Lebanon may have had a lasting impact on her because peace in the Middle East was one of the issues that absorbed her attention and that of the World YWCA during her leadership. By 1955, she was elected to the Executive Committee of the World YWCA and served until 1967.

Dame Nita's rise to the top leadership position of the World YWCA was not serendipity for her or the YWCA. Careful study of Dame Nita's public life does not support the thesis of a happy coming together of fortuitous circumstances. Nita Barrow was often the best candidate for the next path-breaking position. For a black woman from a very small Caribbean colony, that capacity or characteristic should never be misunderstood, nor trivialized as luck. Nita Barrow was already operating at the international level when state-sanctioned segregation was alive and well in the United States (Seymour-Jones 1994). Her status of being constantly a first among equals (World YWCA 1975) came from discipline, ambition, reliability, meticulous preparation, and attention to the job at hand. All of this was accompanied by a simultaneous awareness of the next horizon. Nita Barrow upheld these traits by a demonstrated concern for subordinates and colleagues (Blackman 1995), but most of all by her ability to get the job done. All of these leadership qualities were supported by a vast, well-maintained network of influential friends and colleagues who remained impressed with her record and capabilities.

An interplay of all these factors come together in the appointment of Nita Barrow as the first West Indian matron of the hospital at the Mona campus of the University College Hospital of the West Indies (UCHWI). Lady Foot was instrumental in reorganizing the work of the Jamaica YWCA. She was very keen to see local women take responsibility for formulating new projects and policy. In that capacity she worked very closely with Barrow at the Kingston YWCA. Barrow was employed at the UCHWI and Lady Foot's husband, Governor of Jamaica Sir Hugh Foot recommended Nita Barrow to become matron of the hospital (Lusan 1996). Her appointment in 1954 initially met with the resistance or surprise of several members of the medical establishment (Blackman 1995: 46–47). One in particular, a Professor Gerald Owens, found it necessary to apologize and in the process confirm Nita Barrow's competence:

> I did not welcome you when you were appointed, I feared for the standards of the institution [UCHWI] because you were too young and you had no experience of English teaching hospitals. Now you are leaving I cannot come to tell you goodbye. It may be a promotion for you, but it is a sad loss for the University College Hospital of the West Indies. (Quoted in Blackman 1995: 47)

Nita Barrow was acutely aware of the elitism and class biases that were built into the functioning of the YWCA. She perceived how this focus of the YWCA in serving two classes of women and maintaining a dual mission would eventually result in the stunting of the organization – if not signalling its death:

> Do we suffer from class biases in our membership so that our members are considered to be of a certain class or classes in society even though our programmes may touch a wider range of people in the community? In other words, do all women including the marginalized, whether through education, economics or special groups such as the young, the refugee, the migrant women or other racial group share the planning, the development of policy and the financing of projects which they benefit? Or are we still planning like male policy-makers do, programmes for the people. Do we allow them to become active partners assuming responsibility? Or do we feel because we saw them enter the YWCA as a disadvantaged person that even with their growth and ability 'they are not ready for leadership responsibilities'? Could a negative approach to this be one of the reasons why the young leave us and the more

astute of those for whom we have provided programme opportunities go to other organizations and activities and do not see us as really responsible for their development. They certainly see no relationship to justice because they have not been included in the inner circle. (Barrow 1987b: 5)

Another issue that greatly concerned Barrow was the institutional racism within the organization. As the first black and Third World president, her elevation generated tensions for many national associations and the World Executive. Nita Barrow and many others felt that her election as president should have been followed by the election of Brigalia Bam of South Africa as general secretary. Instead, Erica Brodie, a New Zealander, was selected. Dame Nita spoke out against this:

Brigalia's non-appointment to General Secretary was racism. She was clearly the best candidate but a member of the World Executive said to me in tears, 'I can't go home and tell my board that we've got a black President and a black General Secretary.' 'Why not?' I replied, 'We've always had two white ones.'[7]

Erica Brodie's subsequent resignation before the end of her term of office reawakened dormant tensions. It created the most serious internal challenge Barrow experienced as leader of the World YWCA. Seymour-Jones reports:

Sincere and hardworking, with a wonderful sense of humour, nevertheless Erica Brodie became overwhelmed by her job and found it impossible to delegate to her small staff . . . By the end of 1982 (she) felt her authority was undermined and her integrity was at stake. She handed in her resignation and returned to New Zealand. (Seymour-Jones 1994: 332)

Barrow's acceptance of Brodie's resignation and what others described as Barrow's curt letter to inform national affiliations generated resentment and criticism. Several national associations wrote to Dame Nita, expressing dissatisfaction with the manner in which they were informed of Erica Brodie's departure. They reaffirmed their respect for her work and professionalism and generally raised suspicions as to exactly what had happened.[8]

Before Erica Brodie's departure, Nita Barrow had brought in Ruth Sovik of the United States as associate general secretary to assist with the administrative and managerial difficulties developing at the main office.[9] When Brodie resigned, many national associations, particularly those in the Pacific, intimated that Dame Nita had forced her out of office.[10]

Whether or not Barrow forced the resignation of the general secretary, this issue does illustrate one of the key challenges confronting women in leadership: how to exercise authority and power and not appear to the organization's members as domineering and power hungry. The issue becomes more complex when the organization is run for women by women. Traditionally, women have been either afraid or unaccustomed to exercising power within organizations. Constituencies of women are also more sceptical of decisive leadership by women.

Nita Barrow harboured none of that scepticism about her leadership qualities. She saw herself as an outstanding leader who understood what decisive leadership of a woman's organization required. She was not afraid to make decisions and recognized in the process of leading that she would make mistakes. She saw this as part of the dynamic of leadership:

> I am sure I shall make mistakes but I am not afraid of mistakes . . . who sits in the chair is the most important thing. It is the strength of the movement that will support me in my task. (Quoted in Seymour-Jones 1994: 330).

She demonstrated that she understood her place in the history of the World YWCA and the changes required to make it respond to the issues confronting women in developing countries:

> Elizabeth Palmer was a visionary. She was ahead of her time because she encouraged integrated leadership. She put Third World leaders on the World Executive. Athena (Tsouderos-Athanassiou) was determined and eloquent. When Elizabeth and Athena stopped, *I carried on where they left off.* (Quoted in Jane Seymour-Jones 1994: 371; emphasis mine)

This is how a colleague and close friend comments on Barrow's style of leadership:

> Nita always presented a different point of view. She was very aware when 'feelings' were not right in a meeting. She would notice when people were not engaged and felt it necessary to have a quiet word with that person after the meeting – a one on one engagement. She was willing to change her mind after discussions with that person. She was also willing to help her (the other individual) to see she could not continue in that way. (Lusan 1996)

Nita Barrow valued consensus building as a necessary characteristic of leadership and illustrated this in the following way:

> There was a member, one of my directors of public health who is a very wise old man, an American, and I am saying to him that this student of mine who gets 90 percent in everything

but couldn't get along with anybody. I said to him talk to Helen she is a real leader and he said yes you have to teach her something because however brilliant she is, she is a person walking alone unless she can get other people to walk. (Barrow 1995d)

In addition to consensus building, Nita Barrow valued and prioritized a participatory inclusive style of leadership for programme success, staff loyalty, and promoting justice. She cautioned the World YWCA on the need to remove class biases, ensure the development of the leadership potential of young women, and ensure that migrant women, racial minorities, and other marginalized groups are active partners in planning and assuming responsibility (Barrow 1987b).

The first challenge that the Nita Barrow and Erica Brodie affair raised was the exercise of just and/or compassionate authority, the second was how to get institutions right for women. One of the main objectives of how to get institutions right for women is to ensure accountability. Women leaders are frequently stymied in making decisions on personnel problems for fear their actions to terminate a worker or reassign her or his responsibilities are interpreted as vindictiveness. This situation currently challenges many feminist NGOs.

Anne Marie Goetz advises that a concern with gender justice should be a core value when analyzing institutions and organizations and making proposals for change (Goetz 1995: 2). This is a good guide for leaders faced with difficult choices and it is the one that Nita Barrow seems to have considered. Painful or unpopular leadership decisions should be guided by what is right for the organization's mission and the constituents it serves. A decision should be evaluated on the following basis: Is it just? Does it consider the well-being of its members, and its mission? Does it seek to minimize personal harm to a particular individual without compromising the organizational well-being? Nita Barrow included Ruth Sovik in the executive to assist with the responsibilities of the general secretary. Her acceptance of the resignation of Brodie demonstrated a just concern for the World YWCA's mandate to its national members. Leaders and organizations should not fear acting authoritatively if such activities are governed by a commitment to gender justice. When a decision is made, leaders and organizations should ask the question: is it just? This will work to ensure that they do not reproduce gendered inequalities at the individual, organizational, or community level.

The World YWCA grappled head-on with the question of women's leadership. The organization never experienced the ambivalence of women being in positions of authority that bedeviled many women's NGOs with an explicit feminist agenda. Training in leadership for women and girls constituted an important mission for the World YWCA. It deliberately set out to prepare women and girls for participation in the political and public life of their countries (Karl 1995:25).

Carmen Lusan, retired general secretary of the Jamaica YWCA, reports she was "spotted as a young women with leadership potential by a general secretary" (Lusan 1996). She accepted the YWCA's offer to go and train for a year at the YWCA college in Hampstead, London (Seymour-Jones 1994: 373). The YWCA and its leaders are very proud of the leadership training it offers. "Most of the women now successful in law, government, and teaching in Jamaica began in the Y . . . Our programmes are applicable everywhere. The sense of service, of commitment, never leaves you . . . Wherever you find women giving leadership you find they began in the Y" (quoted in Seymour-Jones 1994: 375). Nita Barrow adds, "YWCA training does not simply provide skills, it stimulates people to think and to work out solutions to their problems with some concrete skills. Traditional attitudes of fatalism and acceptance can be transformed into a new faith in human and specifically women's potential" (quoted in Seymour-Jones 1994: 375).

The literature reflects an obvious contradiction. Second-wave feminists and the organizations they created have characterized organizations such as the World YWCA as "traditional". By that they mean that these "traditional" organizations did not question unequal gender-based relations of power and worked within the status quo. The majority of women's organizations born in the decade of the 1970s politicized women's fundamental inequality in society and stated their intent to work to change this. Second-wave feminists differentiate their agenda from that of earlier feminists by noting that they seek, "to root out the causes of women's oppression, to empower women to participate in decision making at all levels of society, and to transform society through the inclusion of women's participation and perspectives" (Karl 1995: 35).

Yet many of the policies the YWCA implemented provided the basic tools for women to participate at all levels of society. This is not to suggest that this is equivalent to articulating an explicit agenda for transforming unjust gender relations. I believe unjust gender relations must be confronted and exposed. We must also seek creative, just, and workable means for transforming them.

However, it is obvious, that the theoretical distinction imposed on newer "feminist" women's organizations and the older more traditional ones cannot be substantiated. The strategies they use complement each other even if their ideologies and rhetoric differ.

In a study of women leaders in NGOs in Bangladesh, Lisa Pohlmann found that women were uncomfortable with traditional definitions of leadership and thus were uneasy calling themselves leaders (Pohlmann 1995). The comment of one of these women is typical of many women in feminist organizations, "Frankly speaking . . . I cannot say I am really a leader . . . I try to put efforts in what I think is right for women. That drive I have inside of me. I think I would much rather be called an organizer than a leader" (quoted in Pohlmann 1995: 118). Another woman leader adds, "Women have real problems accepting that they are leaders. They're always trying to compensate for it somehow. I think it is lack of social confidence partly, and it comes from wanting to share . . . Most women have that" (quoted in Pohlmann 1995: 118).

Contrast these statements with those of Nita Barrow when she praises the leadership qualities of her predecessors and then states that she continued where they left off. I hypothesize that feminist NGOs that explicitly state they are opposing gender inequities experience a greater degree of ambivalence about women's leadership than the older mainstream women's organizations whose goals centre on improving women's lives.

Feminist NGOs view leadership and authority as essentially androcentric and hierarchical. Yet to lead is to have *and* exercise authority. Authority can be exercised with justice and without domination. We need to rethink some of the concepts we have dismissed as having no meaning for our analytical work and practice. We should redefine ideas and infuse their contents with the new conceptual tools necessary for critical work rather than abandoning them altogether. Kathleen Jones reworks the concept of authority to develop the notion of compassionate authority (Jones 1993). She advances the argument that feminist aversions to the concept should not mean that we abandon or avoid its use or relevance (Jones 1993; Pohlmann 1995: 118). She argues the concept of authority is relevant to feminism because "unless we address directly the question of authority, which is the question of founding a meaningful common life, then we remain silent about the most basic political questions: How do we make sense of public life? How do we act rightfully, and not just act?" (Jones 1993: 7).

As Kathy Ann Ferguson maintains, feminist values of egalitarianism, participation, and connectedness come into conflict with traditional bureaucratic norms of hierarchy, top-down communication, and objectivity (Ferguson 1984). They therefore deliberately challenge traditional hierarchical structures as authoritarian and individualistic. Feminist NGOs seek to implement a variety of management and leadership styles based on inclusivity, consensus, and managerial teams (Pohlmann 1995).

Feminist NGOs actively promote alternative models of leadership. This does not necessarily mean the practice of alternatives or the network of power relations in the organization will not reveal a central dominating figure. The key point is that these organizations actively try to promote alternatives that often create difficulties with how they manage authority (Pohlmann 1995).

Conclusion: The Advancement of Women and Girls

Nita Barrow's stewardship of the World YWCA and the issues the organization grappled with from the 1970s onwards require us to rethink the perception of the YWCA as a traditional organization of elderly women hosting tea parties and cake-icing classes. The organization *has been* racist, imperialist, and operated with a strong bias against leadership from working-class women. Many of these elements probably linger in its organizational culture. However, as a body, the organization has been honest and brave to confront these institutional cancers and attempt to cauterize them. The first step in changing an undesirable situation is to admit to its existence. The second step is to engage in searches for solutions. Centuries-old practices become entrenched and live in the pores of organizations. Seeking to dispel them will not produce change overnight but admitting to their existence and exposing them to the sunlight of justice will helps them to wither away.

Twenty years before the issue of "The Girl Child" and "Women in Power and Decision Making" gained a foothold in the Beijing Platform of Action (United Nations 1996: 109, 145) the YWCA introduced a special programme to develop the leadership potential of young women at the world executive and national levels. The World YWCA has been ahead of many political organizations and administrations in a search for peace for Palestinian women.

The outcome of the intersection of Nita Barrow's leadership with changes in the World YWCA indicates some observations of women's leadership of non-governmental organizations.

1. Women can lead from the front, with authority and still ensure a participatory inclusive style of leadership. Nita Barrow and the World YWCA suffered no ambiguities and ambivalence about women as leaders. Their driving mission was to train women to be leaders, albeit middle-class women initially.
2. The concept of leader does not have to be and is not synonymous with the concept of dictator. When the correspondence, minutes, briefing papers, and other supporting documents of the World Executive and the World Council of the YWCA are examined, it is very clear that all major policies and decisions were subjected to full ventilation, discussion and amendments at several levels. These bodies *always* created and encouraged opportunities for feedback, reflection, and modification. Correspondence and papers frequently captured the constant search for new and better methodologies for a range of programmes and policies. Great attempts were made to ensure organizational democracy by enabling dissenting or opposing positions to be presented. The executives held themselves accountable to the World Council and national bodies, yet recognized and incorporated the authority of the World YWCA president whose office embodied collective authority.
3. Conflict enables the leader and the organization to become innovative. Nita Barrow and the World Executive demonstrated that they expected conflict would exist and were not floored by its occurrences. Instead, they consistently established and tested new structures and procedures to manage it. Many feminist NGOs in the Caribbean naively assume that a shared commitment to noble objectives would automatically guarantee smooth operating procedures. They seem to believe that being dedicated to, and seeking to end dominating relations of gender, sexism, and violence against women, or women's exploitation in the workplace would automatically remove the complications and contradictions of complex personalities that produce friction and organizational trauma.

When confronted with situations that require decisive actions to save the organizations, or repair damaged relations with staff or donors, many feminists leaders become immobilized. They are unable to make a decision or they continuously second-guess an agreed-upon course of action. In other cases, if they need to sever an unproductive work relationship, they create grossly inflated "golden parachutes" to soften the impact of the decision for someone whose decision may have irreparably damaged the organization.

They confuse or conflate the capacity to act with authoritarian leadership. They seem unable to distinguish between the requirements of just leadership and leadership that is punitive or vindictive. Again, the litmus test has to be promoting accountability and gender justice. These conditions raise the question as to whether the ambivalence experienced by women leaders in feminist NGOs arises from an ideological rejection of what they perceive as an androcentric organizational culture rather than a basic discomfort with positions of authority.

Nita Barrow and the YWCA executive understood the relevance of authority and its relation to pursuing organizational justice. They allowed their goals to guide them. They used these goals to sift through what would strengthen the organization and promote gender justice from what was merely organizational politics. The practice may have been challenging, but the policy was assured because "everywhere they went their platform was the advancement of women and girls" (Barrow 1995d).

Notes

1. Words of Dame Nita Barrow quoted in Seymour-Jones 1994; also in Barrow 1985b: 3.
2. Author's interview with Dame Nita, Government House Barbados, 25 September 1995.
3. DAWN was first coordinated by Devaki Jain of Bangalore, India. Jain gave the fifth lecture in the Centre for Gender and Development Studies, Cave Hill, Lecture Series, "Caribbean Women Catalyst for Change", on 17 November 1999. This is dedicated to honouring the memory of Nita Barrow. The coordinator position is rotated every five years and DAWN has been centred in Brazil, Barbados, and now Fiji.
4. In 1975, Mildred Persinger, World YWCA UN representative convened the first women's NGO forum in Mexico City. In 1980, Elizabeth Palmer, retired general secretary of the World YWCA, convened the second women's NGO Forum in Copenhagen.
5. Why did one woman occupy such an important position for a quarter century? This question is posed in the context of the need to develop and expose new women to the dynamics of leadership.

6. Professor Rex Nettleford, commenting on Jamaica's support for Dame Nita's (unsuccessful) candidacy for the presidency of the United Nations in 1988.
7. Dame Nita Barrow, interview by Carole Seymour-Jones, Barbados, October 1993. Quoted in Seymour-Jones 1994: 331.
8. Personal and official correspondence from national associations to Nita Barrow in her capacity as world president, the Dame Nita Barrow Collection of Papers, Centre for Gender and Development Studies, University of the West Indies, Cave Hill.
9. Ruth Sovik was a colleague of Nita Barrow from the World Council of Churches, experienced in administrative and managerial concerns.
10. Personal and official correspondence from national associations to Nita Barrow in her capacity as world president, the Dame Nita Barrow Collection of Papers, Centre for Gender and Development Studies, University of the West Indies, Cave Hill.

Chapter Ten

A Personal Reflection on Nita Barrow and the International Council for Adult Education, 1979–1990

[Budd L. Hall]

Introduction

I am grateful to Dr Eudine Barriteau for creating this book project and for inviting me to write about Nita Barrow and the International Council for Adult Education (ICAE). No one has influenced me more than Nita Barrow. I had the pleasure of working with her from 1979 to 1990 at the ICAE and continued a close friendship with her after both she and I left the ICAE. During the years 1982–90, she served as world president of the International Council for Adult Education while I served as its secretary general.

We First Hear of Nita Barrow

In about 1977 or 1978, Roby Kidd, the Canadian secretary general of the ICAE and a longtime friend of Nita Barrow, mentioned to several of us working with him in the Toronto secretariat, that his friend Nita Barrow had been named world president of the YWCA. Roby had met Nita Barrow while working in

Jamaica in the early 1960s on a plan for strengthening adult education in the region. Nita Barrow (she did not become Dame Nita until 1980) was the principal nursing officer for Jamaica and subsequently the nursing advisor to the Pan American Health Organization. Roby was interested in strengthening the training of nurses through the introduction of adult education theories and techniques. Nita Barrow had been originally trained as a nurse educator at the University of Toronto in 1944–1945. I remember her telling us that when Roby was working in Jamaica, he had been to her office and after talking about the field of adult education, informed her that she was one of the best adult educators he had met. She told us that until that moment, she really hadn't heard of adult education, but the friendship with Roby and his wife Margaret, and their family continued from that time onwards.

Nita Barrow at the time was working with the Christian Medical Commission of the World Council of Churches and, although the Christian Medical Commission was a modest NGO in the face of the large World Health Organization (WHO), her ideas about the role of primary health care gained the ear of the then director general of WHO, who championed her ideas within the world scene. The World Conference on "Health for All by the Year 2000", which took place in Alma-Ata, Russia, was the platform for her ideas to gain global visibility. At this conference, the ICAE representative, Dr Per Stensland, met with Nita Barrow and together they worked the NGO side of the conference very well. Nita Barrow believed that adult education was a necessary component of primary health care. He came back and told us all about Nita Barrow.

The ICAE invited Nita Barrow to join a select group of other world adult education specialists who were going to China in 1979 to look at various aspects of adult education. John Whitehouse (of the International Labour Organization) and Nat Coletta (of the World Bank) were among the group. This group was one of the first of several "Western" specialists invited into China as it began to look at opening up to the rest of the world. Nita Barrow renewed her acquaintance with many aspects of the Chinese health system, such as the "barefoot doctors" and acupuncture treatment. Indeed, she underwent acupuncture treatment on her knee, which was beginning to bother her; this was many years before such treatment was widely accepted by Western medicine.

I was named secretary general of the ICAE in June of 1979 and Dr Robert Gardiner of Ghana was named president. One of the first new networks that we created was one linking adult education and primary health care. Rajesh Tandon of India was named as the network coordinator. Tandon was, along with myself and several others, part of a much younger generation of adult educators who, with Roby Kidd's support, were thrust into ICAE leadership positions in 1979. We had many ideas about working in global actions in new ways. We were convinced that we needed to construct networks of equals helping equals around the world to transform relations of power. Learning was a key to our ideas. It is also fair to say that we were young (I say that looking back) and somewhat critical of generations that had gone before us. I note this because it is important to say that we were not automatically predisposed to taking friends – even of our founding secretary general, Roby Kidd – for granted. In our newer and younger circles, everyone had to prove themselves.

As part of the early work of the primary health care network, we organized a conference in Geneva at WHO headquarters to see how adult education might better link itself to the goals of health for all and primary health care needs. Rajesh Tandon (who in 1998 was world chairperson of CIVICUS, a major global civil society networking organization), Francisco Vio Grossi (who in 1998 was Chilean ambassador to Guatemala) and Ted Jackson (who in 1998 was president of a successful Canadian consulting company) part of the "new team" in the ICAE in attendance at the WHO meeting. I was unable to attend. We had invited Nita Barrow to attend because of her link with the World Council of Churches and the YWCA.

While other results of that meeting are lost in time, the major result was a wave of enthusiastic remarks that came from our young team. They sent letters, phoned, and reported in person that "Nita Barrow is fantastic". She had radical ideas about wresting power from the medical establishment for health, about the role of women in health and elsewhere, about the power of developing countries working together, about the role of music and art in education, and about the excitement of truly participatory education in our societies. The fact that she was some thirty years older than any of them never entered into the conversations. The "Nita Era" of the ICAE had been born.

President Nita Barrow, 1982–1990

Although I had not yet met Nita, I knew that the combination of her qualities was precisely what we needed in the ICAE at the time. We needed someone with an international reputation, with experience in the world of non-governmental organizations, and someone who would support a progressive vision of adult education and allow a younger and energetic generation of leadership to try their hands. In 1980, I heard that she was to be in Toronto and invited her to visit our office. I told her that the ICAE was looking for a new president and that the nominating committee had suggested her name. I told her that we had lots of ideas, lots of energy and would work hard, but that we needed someone with "respectability and courage" who would have faith in us to serve as our president. Would she be interested? I have no idea what went through her head, but to my great excitement she said yes.

At the National Adult Education Research and Training Institute of Marly-le-roi (near Paris) in 1982, Nita Barrow was elected by the World Assembly. That first meeting was a wonderful example of what was to come. All of the younger activists were brought together with the more established adult education associations. Murals were being painted on the walls of community centres in Marly-le-roi. The corridors at night were filled with groups singing. The women's working group composed the highlight song of the conference, a spirited anthem by Arlene Mantle entitled, "Women Hold Up More Than Half the World". This was Dr Gardiner's last meeting as ICAE president and he had brought great dignity and distinction to our organization. I remember after a particularly eloquent speech by Dr Gardiner leaning over to Nita Barrow to say, "This will be a hard act to follow", to which she replied, "Just watch me." Once the gavel had changed hands, Nita addressed the audience, opening her remarks by looking around at her all-male executive committee and saying, "By the time I finish my term, I will not be so lonely." Her predictions were to prove true.

Nita Barrow brought much to the ICAE. One of the first areas she supported was the strengthening of the women's programme. Margaret Gayfer had drawn attention to the role of women in adult education with a remarkable report that was published in 1981 by the ICAE. But it was Linda Yanz who, as coordinator of the Toronto-based Participatory Research Group, brought a background in women's organizing to the methods of the ICAE. Yanz began to build a network of women activists working in the adult education movement *and related* community-based, university and labour organizations around the world. Nita Barrow gave Linda Yanz and her colleagues her overt political support and encouraged the ICAE executive to put women's issues on the agenda for the council. To the ICAE executive committee, Barrow brought a style of leadership that balanced an openness to new ideas, with a firm yet democratic hand in meetings where she made sure that everyone who wished to speak could do so. She also made sure that overly domineering figures in the executive committee were kept in their place. She used firmness and humour with great aplomb. If there were tensions or conflicts, she dealt with them at once. She was fearless in the face of inappropriate authority.

In 1983, the ICAE executive committee was invited to hold its annual meeting in Iraq. Iraq was still technically at war with Iran. The ICAE had been anxious to hold a meeting in the Arabic-speaking region and because the host of the 1983 meeting was the Arab League Educational Cultural and Scientific Organization (ALECSO), it was agreed to meet there. A first surprise was to find that, for security purposes, the meeting was switched at the last moment to a new conference facility located behind carefully monitored, fenced perimeters. Upon arriving at the conference headquarters for the first plenary session, we found that because Iraq was still at war, the minister of education and all of the senior officials were dressed in military dress. It was quite a sight to see Nita seated next to the minister of education, she in a flowing colourful African-inspired dress and the minister, our host, in khaki green.

The first thing that she did, on noticing that many of the host officials were smoking was to announce that "This conference will be held under WHO rules, which means that no cigarette smoking will be allowed in the conference rooms. If you wish to smoke, please do so outside the meeting rooms." With this straightforward request, she cleared the smoke and established her authority for the meeting to be held for the entire week.

The next act of the meeting was the approval of the agenda for the conference. Iraq was quite justly proud of its literacy campaign, which had been recognized by international bodies for good results. But when they prepared for us to learn about their work, all of the speakers featured were men. Nita Barrow, upon seeing this, turned to the minister of education seated beside her and said, "I know that you have many women leaders in your fine national literacy campaign. We would like to see them featured on the programme first thing in the morning." She then gathered all of us together and told us, "If they do not have a woman speak to us about literacy by the morning, I am leaving Baghdad and going to the press. You can make up your own mind what you do, but I will leave and I will go to the press."

The next morning was filled with tension as we took our seats in the conference hall. As secretary general, I was beside myself with nervousness. One by one, our hosts, still in uniform, streamed into the conference hall. The minister of education came in at last and we awaited his announcement. He began speaking in Arabic and then the translations began to stream into our earphones. Audible sighs went up and not a little applause as it was announced that we would be having several presentations on the national literacy work and that all of the presenters were the women, who in fact were at the very heart of their success. And moreover, the minister of education appeared to be absolutely charmed by Nita Barrow.

The Right to Learn Declaration

The Fourth UNESCO International Conference on Adult Education took place in Paris, at UNESCO headquarters, in 1985. Paul Bertelsen, the legendary adult educator from Denmark who was working at UNESCO in Paris, was the conference secretary. Paul Belanger, who in 1998 was the director of the UNESCO Institute for Education in Hamburg, Germany, was at the time the vice president of the ICAE for North America. Belanger and myself developed a well-orchestrated plan for influencing the outcome of the 1985 proceedings. These UNESCO adult education events, coming as they do only once every twelve years, are extremely important to the adult education movement. This was the first time that an NGO leader was invited to speak to the plenary of this event, which was mostly the place of government delegations often led by government ministers. The speech that Nita Barrow delivered with authority and passion was received so well by the assembled delegates, that a movement began to turn her speech into a declaration for the conference. This declaration, which later became known as the "Right to Learn Declaration", remains one of the most important normative statements about adult education and is one of Nita's strongest contributions to the professional field of adult education

The Eminent Persons Group and the Nairobi Women's Conference of 1985

Working with Nita Barrow often meant involvement in the many other events of her life. One of her remarkable gifts was her willingness to mix together all her friends, colleagues, and relatives in all that she was doing. She never made us feel out of place or unwelcome. We were together with her in Buenos Aires, Argentina, in 1985 when she was named a member of the Group of Eminent Persons, the critical Commonwealth delegation that went to South Africa during the final days of the apartheid government. She told us of her meeting with Nelson Mandela while he was still in prison. She also told us about covering her head with a headscarf to be driven into Alexandra Township to speak directly with the residents, something that was in direct opposition to the orders of the South African government of the day. Her car was stopped as it went through security posts going into the township, but Nita Barrow said nothing and passed as just one more resident returning home from work in the city. Some sources claim that Nita's rational, eloquent, and politically astute conversation with De Klerk about the importance of releasing Nelson Mandela from prison was a turning point in the return to democracy there.

For the ICAE, Nita's involvement as chair of the NGO Forum for the UN Women's Conference in Nairobi in 1985 was a highlight as well. Lynda Yanz, the ICAE Women's Programme coordinator used the occasion to bring many of the women from the adult education movement into contact with women from literally every other sector of world development. Yanz and others from the ICAE network worked to provide a support team for Nita Barrow and to organize many of the practical aspects of those exciting days. There were many stories from Nairobi to be told; but one that seems to capture her generosity so well was told to me by Linda Yanz. Nita Barrow was housed in an apartment on the edge of the University of Nairobi campus. Despite the furious pace and pressure of this most powerful of women's conferences, where she was in demand from the world's press corps, the official delegations, nervous Kenyan government officials, and her own crew of volunteers and organizers, she found time to invite these same volunteers and helpers to a fish dinner that she cooked herself in her Nairobi apartment.

The United Nations

In 1986, the Government of Barbados named Nita Barrow ambassador plenipotentiary and permanent representative to the United Nations in New York. During this term in office, the ICAE played a very active role in her campaign for president of the UN General Assembly. The Canadian government and many others were heavily involved in putting Nita's name forward, but no one worked harder on her campaign than the adult education movement. We produced an informative piece about her life and accomplishments and published it in many languages. All the adult education associations throughout the world contacted their governments to lobby for her. Our campaign became so visible that the eventual winner of the campaign, the Argentine foreign minister Dante Caputo raised an official protest that the ICAE was playing an unfair advocacy role. Barrow's response was characteristically clear and fair, "The ICAE," she said, "is free to support any candidate they wish." And although she lost the vote by a close call, I think that to this day, those close to the United Nations know that she was that organizations most brilliant "president that never was".

Barrow's location at UN headquarters in New York was a boon to the ICAE as well. The ICAE had called for the creation of a UN International Year for Literacy in 1982 at a conference held in Udaipur, India. The recommendation was furthered in 1985 at the Fourth International Conference on Adult Education. The recommendation was then forwarded to the Economic and Social Council of the United Nations for action prior to an ultimate decision by the UN General Assembly itself. Nita Barrow (of Barbados) and Stephen Lewis (the Canadian ambassador) made a strong team of advocates who tirelessly roamed the corridors in New York. They worked in support of the motion put forward by the government of Mongolia who had decided to champion this action as one of their priority actions at the United Nations. It was with great excitement, that in late 1988, the UN General Assembly issued the declaration that 1990 would be named as the UN International Year of Literacy.

The People's Launch of the UN International Year of Literacy

Barrow's last official act as president of the ICAE was presiding over the "People's Launch" of the UN Year of Literacy that took place in January 1990 in Bangkok, Thailand. This launch was combined with the World Assembly of the ICAE and brought literacy learners from around the world to a celebration of learning that was a tribute to the great organizing skill of the Thai adult and non-formal education community. Nita Barrow signed a literacy book that was sent around the world during International Literacy Year from literacy class to literacy class in literally all continents of our globe. Nita's friend, Pat Rodney, also a resident of Barbados, had gone to Toronto to work with the ICAE secretariat with special responsibilities for International Year of Literacy. While in Bangkok, Nita Barrow also launched the International Task Force on Literacy, an NGO coalition working on the issues, and still had time to enjoy some shopping in Bangkok with her beloved sister Sybil and a friend. The ICAE created in Nita's name a new award and announced it to her on the occasion of her stepping down after her second term. The Dame Nita Barrow Award is given each year by the ICAE to the adult education association throughout the world that has done the most to support the learning needs of women.

Adult Educator of the Decade: Hamburg, 1997

At the Fifth International Conference on Adult Education organized by UNESCO and other cooperating bodies in July 1997, it was decided to recognize two adult educators who had died during the years 1985 through 1997. Paulo Freire, the inspirational adult educator from Brazil was one of those so honoured. The other was Nita Barrow. And what was touching was that both Nita and Paulo had worked together in Geneva, Switzerland, in the 1970s working for the World Council of Churches. Video footage of Nita Barrow speaking on adult education was shown to the 1,600 delegates assembled on the evening of 17 July in the Congress Hall in Hamburg. Accounts of her life were recalled and it was my privilege to be able to offer this poem on that evening. I offer it here to readers as an appropriate close of this chapter.

The Countless Stars of a Caribbean Night

Her Excellency Dame Ruth Nita Barrow
Governor-General of Barbados
Ambassador to the United Nations
Dame Nita

Nita
Bajun woman
Caribbean woman
World woman
Nurse
Nurse Tutor
Educator
Adult Educator
Learner, so very much learner

Nita
Sister
Auntie
World Leader
Friend
Cooker of fine fish dinners
Dancer to the music everywhere
Honest confidante of Prime Ministers and Presidents
You even knew Fergie!

Nita
Gardener
Painter
Filling kitchens, living rooms, churches, conference halls,
The United Nations General Assembly and
Our children's birthday parties with fun!

Nita
You had the greatest capacity for friendship of anyone we ever knew.
We remember your very special black book of names and addresses
Held together with rubber bands and containing names of thousands of us
From literally every country in the world.

We remember listening in hushed silence as you told us your
Conversations with Nelson Mandela when he was still in prison

You said that he was ready to lead a new South Africa and
That he was fit, well dressed and wore brightly polished shoes

And we remember when you came to your first meeting as
President of our International Council for Adult Education.
You told us as you looked around the table at our nearly all male
Executive Committee,
"By the time I leave, I will not feel so lonely"
And you were not!

Nita
You are the countless stars of a Caribbean night
Stars
Of strength and dedication,
Of joy and of hope
Stars
Thrown across our universe
Stars
Falling into our lives
Stars
Here tonight
Stars
In our hearts
Nita

CHAPTER ELEVEN

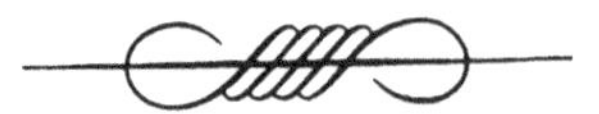

A Selective Curriculum Vitae of The Honourable Dame Nita Barrow, 1916–1995

[JENIPHIER R. CARNEGIE]

Education

1928–1934	Attended St Michael's Girls' School
1935–1940	Basic nursing education, Barbados General Hospital
1940	Registered Nurse
1942	Midwifery preparation, Port of Spain General Hospital, Trinidad
1942	Registered Midwife
1943–1944	Public Health Diploma, School of Nursing, University of Toronto
1944–1945	Nursing Education Diploma, School of Nursing, University of Toronto
1951–1952	Sister Tutor's Diploma, Royal College of Nursing, Edinburgh University
1963–1963	BSc, Teacher's College, Columbia University

Positions Held

1940–1941	Staff Nurse/Charge Nurse, Barbados General Hospital
1945–1950	Nursing Instructor, West Indian School of Public Health, Jamaica
1949–1952	Founder President, Jamaica Nurses Association
1951–1958	Member and Chairman, Kingston Board of the YWCA
1952–1954	Sister Tutor, Kingston Hospital School of Nursing, Jamaica
1952–1970	Chairman, Regional (West Indian) Committee of YWCA
1954–1956	Matron, University College Hospital, Jamaica
1955–1967	Member, World YWCA Executive Committee, Geneva
1956–1962	Principal Nursing Officer, Jamaica
1963–1967	Vice President, World YWCA
1967–1971	Nursing Advisor, Pan American Health Organization, Commonwealth Caribbean
1970	Member, team that established the Advanced Nursing Education programme at the University of the West Indies, Mona, Jamaica
1971–1975	Associate Director, Christian Medical Commission of the World Council of Churches
1972–1980	Member of the Editorial Board of *Contact* (journal published by the Christian Medical Commission of the World Council of Churches)
1975–1983	President, World YWCA
1980	Convenor, Health Network – Mid-Decade Forum of UN Decade for Women, Copenhagen
1981–1995	Health consultant to the World Health Organization and other health-related agencies
1982–1984	Member of the Advisory Board, Barbados Youth Council
1983	Co-chairperson, Scientific Seminar, Moscow
1983	Co-chairperson, International Seminars in Adult Education, People's Republic of China
1983	Gamaliel Chair Lecturer, University of Wisconsin at Milwaukee
1983	Member of the Board of Trustees, Caribbean Resources Development Foundation

1983–1985	Convenor, Non-Governmental Forum for the World Conference to Review the UN Decade for Women, Copenhagen
1983–1989	Chairperson, Executive Committee of ICAE Annual Meetings in Canada, USSR, China, Iraq, Zimbabwe, Argentina, Thailand
1983–1991	President, World Council of Churches (one of seven presidents)
1986–1990	Director, Global Fund for Women, USA
1986–1990	Member, Board of the International Peace Academy, USA
1986–1990	Member of the Board of Directors, Foundation for International Training, Canada
1986–1990	Permanent Representative of Barbados to the United Nations
1987–1990	Member of the International Jury for the Africa Prize for Leadership, USA
1988–1990	International Advisor, Synergos Institute, USA
1988–1990	Member of the International Jury for the Liberty Medal, Philadelphia, USA
1989–1990	Member of the West Indian Commission
1989–1990	President, International Council on Adult Education
1990–1995	Governor General of Barbados
1992	Co-chair of ECO-ED (World Congress for Education and Communication on Environment and Development) sponsored by UNESCO, International Chamber of Commerce and the United Nations Environmental Programme
1993–1995	Co-chair of Friends of the United Nations Fiftieth Anniversary Celebrations
1993–1995	Member of Earth Council, Costa Rica
1994	Convenor of the Eminent Persons Group of the First United Nations Global Conference on the Sustainable Development of Small Island Developing States, Barbados
1994–1995	Co-chair of Secretary General's International Group of Advisers on We the People: 50 Communities Award

1994–1995	Member of Secretary-General's International Advisory Group for UN50
1994–1995	Member of the Latin American and Caribbean Commission on Social Development preparing for the Social Summit, Copenhagen, March 1995

Memberships

1943	YWCA of Trinidad
1966	Caribbean Nurses Association
1968	Business and Professional Women's Club of Guyana
1992–1995	Academic Environment and Development, University of Geneva

Conferences Attended

1951	World YWCA Meeting, Beirut, Lebanon, Member of Delegation
1975	World Council of Churches Assembly, Nairobi
1977	World Population Conference, Bucharest, Member of Delegation
1978	Primary Health Care Conference, WHO/UNICEF, Alma-Alta, USSR, Leader of WHO Medical Commission Delegation
1980	Mid-Decade Conference of Decade for Women, Copenhagen, Coordinator of Health Workshops
1982	ICAE Assembly, Paris
1982	Quadrennial meeting of International Council of Nurses
1982	Quadrennial meeting of the World YWCA
1983	World Council of Churches Assembly, Vancouver
1985	Forum '85 and the World Conference to Review the Decade for Women, Nairobi, Conference Convenor
1985	ICAE Assembly, Buenos Aires
1989	Participated in first New York Convocation for Peace
1990	ICAE Assembly, Bangkok
1991	World Council of Churches Assembly, Canberra

1991–1995	Participated in the International Advisory Committee, Leadership for the Environment and Development Programme, sponsored by the Rockefeller Foundation
1992	United Nations Conference on Environment and Development (UNCED) in Rio de Janeiro, one of ten eminent persons invited by Secretary General Maurice Strong

Peace Efforts

1982	Led delegation of World YWCA Women to Middle East on mission for peace for all the countries of the Middle East
1986	Member of the Commonwealth Group of Eminent Persons to negotiate the end of apartheid
1986	Member of the International Advisory Committee, Global Cooperation for a Better World
1986	Patron of the Million Minutes for Peace in the International Year of Peace
1987	Attended Day of Prayer for Peace at invitation of His Holiness Pope John Paul II at Assisi, Italy
1988	Participated in Japanese Peace Bell site of Ceremony Celebrating International Day of Peace dedicated to children

Honours and Awards

1943–1945	Rockefeller Fellowship, School of Nursing, University of Toronto
1951–1952	Colonial Development Scholarship, Edinburgh University/Royal College of Nursing
1962–1963	Pan American Health Organization/World Health Organization Fellowship, Teacher's College, Columbia University
1975	Honorary Doctor of Laws, University of the West Indies
1980	Dame Grand Cross of the Order of St Michael and St George

1980	Fellow of the Royal College of Nursing
1982	Honorary Doctor of Science, McMaster University
1984	Spirit of Caribbean Award, Caribbean Resource Foundation
1985	West Indian of the Year, *Bajan* Magazine
1986	Caribbean Council of Churches Award for Peace
1986	Caribbean Prize for Peace through the Struggle for Justice, Caribbean Council of Churches
1986	Most Outstanding Citizen of the Year Award, Kiwanis Club of Barbados
1987	CARICOM Women's Award
1987	Honorary Doctor of Humane Letters, Morris Brown University, Atlanta, Georgia
1987	Honorary Doctor of Laws, University of Toronto
1987	Honoured by the International Women's Anthropology Conference and the Latin American and Caribbean Studies Program of Hunter College, New York
1988	Award for Contribution to Development of Women, Medger Evers College, City University of New York
1988	Honorary Doctor of Humanities, Mount St Vincent University
1988	Honorary Doctor of Laws, University of Manitoba
1988	Liberty Medal, Brooklyn College
1989	Christiane Reimann Prize, International Council of Nurses, Geneva
1989	Honorary Doctor of Humane Letters, Spelman College, Atlanta, Georgia
1989	R. Louise McManus Award, Columbia University
1990	Dame of St Andrew in the Order of Barbados
1990	Honorary Doctor of Laws, York University, Ontario
1990	Honoured by the St Michael School Alumni Association, Barbados
1991	Honorary Doctor of Laws, Queen's University, Ontario
1991	Honorary Doctor of Laws, Smith College
1993	Women First Award, YWCA of the USA, 135th Anniversary

1994	Honorary Doctor of Laws, Adelphi University
1994	Honorary Doctor of Letters, Wilfrid Laurier University, Waterloo, Ontario
1994	Order of the Caribbean Community
1995	Honorary Chairperson of the Inaugural Meeting of the Inter-American Development Bank Advisory Council on Women in Development

Selected Writings

1974	*Report of Consultant in Nursing Services*, University Hospital, Mona, Jamaica, 20 September–20 October 1974. Doc. no. 74/P3/AMR/630, WCC, Geneva.
1976	"Breast Feeding: A Myth or a Must?" *Contact* 35 (Oct. 1976): 1–5.
1978	"The Role of the Nurse in the Delivery of Health Care". *The Changing Roles and Education for Health Care Personnel Worldwide in View of the Increase of Basic Health Services.* Papers from a consultation sponsored by the Society for Health and Human Values, Bellagio, Italy, May 1977. Philadelphia: Society for Health and Human Values.
1979	"Women of the 'Third World' and Health". Paper presented to the Communications Commission of Evangelical Missions, Hamburg, 1979, by Director of Christian Medical Commission of the World Council of Churches.
1980	"Nursing: The Art, Science and Vocation in Evolution". *Contact* 59 (Dec. 1980): 1–13.
1981	"Knowledge Belongs to Everyone: The Challenge for Adult Education and Primary Health Care". *Convergence* 14, no. 2 (1981): 45–52. Edited transcript of a Special Lecture on Adult Education and Primary Health Care delivered by Dame Nita Barrow at University of Nairobi in Oct. 1979.
1982	"The Role of NGOs in Primary Health Care". *Convergence* 15, no. 2 (1982): 92–93.

1982	"Women in the Front Line of Health Care". *Convergence* 15, no. 2 (1982): 82–84 [Excerpt from paper prepared for the Sixth Commonwealth Health Ministers' Meeting in Tanzania in 1980].
1983	"Social Action and Development: A Liberating Power". *Convergence* 16, no. 1 (1983): 46–50.
1985	"Reflections on the Women's Decade 1976–85". *Women's Education Des Femmes* 4, no. 2 (Winter 1985): 16–20.
1986	"The Role of the Nurse in the Changing Caribbean". Keynote Address delivered to Opening Session of the Sixth Biennial Conference of the Caribbean Nurses' Organization, University of the West Indies, Kingston, Jamaica, 24 July 1968. Jamaican Nurse 25, nos. 1, 2 & 3 (Aug. 1986): 15–16.
1986	"We Are Different Women: Stronger, Bolder, Surer". From the Statement at the Opening of the NGO Forum '85 held during the Women's Decade Conference in Nairobi. *Convergence* 19, no. 2 (1986): 7.
1990	"Listening to the Voices of the Marginalized: International Literacy Year: An Interview with Dame Nita Barrow". Interview with Karen Yarmol-Franko. *Convergence* 23, no. 1 (1990): 9–13.
1992	"The Coming of Age of Adult Education: An Interview with Dame Nita Barrow". Interview with Karen Yarmol-Franko. *Convergence* 24, no. 4 (1992): 48–56.
1994	Foreword to *In a Class of Their Own*, by David Wigg (Washington, DC: World Bank).

Sources

Blackman, Francis. 1995. *Dame Nita: Caribbean Woman, World Citizen.* Kingston, Jamaica: Ian Randle Publishers.

The Dame Nita Barrow Collection. Centre for Gender and Development Studies, University of the West Indies, Cave Hill, Barbados.

References

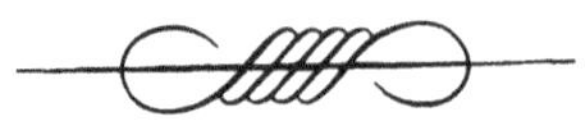

Compiled by

[Jo-Ann Granger and Jeniphier Carnegie]

I. Primary Sources

A. Manuscripts (at Archive)

Baksh-Sooden, Rawwida. 1991. Letter submitted to *Trinidad Guardian*, 17 May. Centre for Gender and Development Studies, University of the West Indies, Cave Hill, Barbados.

Barrow, Nita. 1973. Speech to Methodist Conference, Montserrat, 4 June. The Dame Nita Barrow Collection. Centre for Gender and Development Studies, University of the West Indies, Cave Hill, Barbados.

_______. 1982a. "Report on My Visit to the Middle East, April 27–May 8, 1982". The Dame Nita Barrow Collection. Centre for Gender and Development Studies, University of the West Indies, Cave Hill, Barbados.

_______. 1982b. "Call to World Council 1983". Draft II. The Dame Nita Barrow Collection. Centre for Gender and Development Studies, University of the West Indies, Cave Hill, Barbados.

_______. 1983. Speech, Mills College. November. The Dame Nita Barrow Collection. Centre for Gender and Development Studies, University of the West Indies, Cave Hill, Barbados.

_______. 1984. Speech to Ecumenical Assembly, Purdue University, 24–25 July. The Dame Nita Barrow Collection. Centre for Gender and Development Studies, University of the West Indies, Cave Hill, Barbados.

_______. 1985a. Speech to the UN Committee on the Elimination of All Forms of Discrimination Against Women. The Dame Nita Barrow Collection. Centre for Gender and Development Studies, University of the West Indies, Cave Hill, Barbados.

________. 1985b. Address delivered by Dame Nita Barrow to the Opening Plenary Forum, Kenyatta International Conference Centre, 10 July, Nairobi, Kenya. The Dame Nita Barrow Collection. Centre for Gender and Development Studies, University of the West Indies, Cave Hill, Barbados.

________. 1985c. "Where Are We Now: Women in 1985. Where Have We Come From During the Decade". Speech given to "Woman '85", Jamaica Pegasus Hotel, October.

________. 1985d. "Western Feminism and Third World Women". Keynote Address, Symposium on Western and Third World Feminism, Tufts University, November. The Dame Nita Barrow Collection. Centre for Gender and Development Studies, University of the West Indies, Cave Hill, Barbados.

________. 1987a. Handwritten notes, 328 Cliff Avenue, Pelham, New York, 1 April. The Dame Nita Barrow Collection. Centre for Gender and Development Studies, University of the West Indies, Cave Hill, Barbados.

________. 1987b. "Development with Justice: Development as if People Matter". Paper presented at the World YWCA Council Meeting, Phoenix, Arizona, 25 August–5 September. The Dame Nita Barrow Collection. Centre for Gender and Development Studies, University of the West Indies, Cave Hill, Barbados.

________. 1993. Speech to the Women's Coalition of St Croix, 25 March. The Dame Nita Barrow Collection. Centre for Gender and Development Studies, University of the West Indies, Cave Hill, Barbados.

________. 1994. Address of Her Excellency Dame Nita Barrow, GCMG, DA, Governor General of Barbados, at the Opening Meeting of the Eminent Persons Group on the Sustainable Development of Small Island Developing States, Barbados, 21 April. The Dame Nita Barrow Collection. Centre for Gender and Development Studies, University of the West Indies, Cave Hill, Barbados.

________. 1995a. Interview by Alan Cobley, 3 May. Government House, Barbados. Tape recording. The Dame Nita Barrow Collection. Centre for Gender and Development Studies, University of the West Indies, Cave Hill, Barbados.

________. 1995b. Interview by Margaret Gill, 10 August. Government House, Barbados. Tape recording. The Dame Nita Barrow Collection. Centre for Gender and Development Studies, University of the West Indies, Cave Hill, Barbados.

________. 1995c. Interview by Sheila Stuart, August. Government House, Barbados. Tape recording. The Dame Nita Barrow Collection. Centre for Gender and Development Studies, University of the West Indies, Cave Hill, Barbados.

________. 1995d. Interview by Eudine Barriteau, 25 September. Barbados. Tape recording and transcript. The Dame Nita Barrow Collection. Centre for Gender and Development Studies, University of the West Indies, Cave Hill, Barbados.

________. 1995e. Interview by Janice Cumberbatch, 6 September. Government House, Barbados. Tape recording. The Dame Nita Barrow Collection. Centre for Gender and Development Studies, University of the West Indies, Cave Hill, Barbados.

———. 1995f. Interview 1 by Kathleen Drayton, Barbados. Tape recording and notes. The Dame Nita Barrow Collection. Centre for Gender and Development Studies, University of the West Indies, Cave Hill, Barbados.

———. 1995g. Interview 2 by Kathleen Drayton, Barbados. Tape recording and notes. The Dame Nita Barrow Collection. Centre for Gender and Development Studies, University of the West Indies, Cave Hill, Barbados.

———. N.d.a. Handwritten notes on nursing. The Dame Nita Barrow Collection. Centre for Gender and Development Studies, University of the West Indies, Cave Hill, Barbados.

———. N.d.b. Notebook. The Dame Nita Barrow Collection. Centre for Gender and Development Studies, University of the West Indies, Cave Hill, Barbados.

———. N.d.c. Personal papers. The Dame Nita Barrow Collection. Centre for Gender and Development Studies, University of the West Indies, Cave Hill, Barbados.

———. N.d.d. "Western and Third World Feminism". The Dame Nita Barrow Collection. Centre for Gender and Development Studies, University of the West Indies, Cave Hill, Barbados.

Bjornoy, Helen, to Nita Barrow. September 1982. "Evaluation on Atlanta Consultation". The Dame Nita Barrow Collection. Centre for Gender and Development Studies, University of the West Indies, Cave Hill, Barbados.

Christian Medical Commission. *c.* 1980. "Summary of CMC Activities, July 1979–April 1980". The Dame Nita Barrow Collection. Centre for Gender and Development Studies, University of the West Indies, Cave Hill, Barbados.

Hall, Budd. 1997. "The Countless Stars of a Caribbean Night". Poem read at the Tribute Night in Memory of Dame Nita Barrow, 17 July 1997, Fifth UNESCO International Conference on Adult Education, Hamburg, Germany. The Dame Nita Barrow Collection. Centre for Gender and Development Studies, University of the West Indies, Cave Hill, Barbados.

Jacobs, Carol. 1996. Interview by Sheila Stuart, Rockley, Barbados. January. Tape recording. The Dame Nita Barrow Collection. Centre for Gender and Development Studies, University of the West Indies, Cave Hill, Barbados.

Kilburn, Susan. 1985. Toronto YWCA, to Nita Barrow, 3 July. The Dame Nita Barrow Collection. Centre for Gender and Development Studies, University of the West Indies, Cave Hill, Barbados.

Lusan, Carmen. 1996. Retired Caribbean Area Secretary, YWCA. Interview by Eudine Barriteau, 5 January. Barbados. Tape recording and transcript. The Dame Nita Barrow Collection. Centre for Gender and Development Studies, University of the West Indies, Cave Hill, Barbados.

Public Record Office. 1939. "Memo by Gerald Clauson, 7 July". CO852/250/15606 pt. 2. London.

Scott, Ted. 1995. Retired Primate of the Anglican Church of Canada. Interview by Alan Cobley, 7 May. Government House, Barbados. Tape Recording. The Dame Nita Barrow Collection. Centre for Gender and Development Studies, University of the West Indies, Cave Hill, Barbados.

Sovik, Ruth. 1985. "General Secretary's Report: World YWCA Executive Committee Meeting, June 22–

July 2, 1985". The Dame Nita Barrow Collection. Centre for Gender and Development Studies, University of the West Indies, Cave Hill, Barbados.

YWCA. N.d.a. "Caribbean Area Assessment Project". Mimeo. The Dame Nita Barrow Collection. Centre for Gender and Development Studies, University of the West Indies, Cave Hill, Barbados.

________. N.d.b. "Constitution of the World Young Women Christian Association". Draft. The Dame Nita Barrow Collection. Centre for Gender and Development Studies, University of the West Indies, Cave Hill, Barbados.

YWCA of Canada. 1985a. National Board of Directors. "Resolution #7 Amendment #1, Middle East". The Dame Nita Barrow Collection. Centre for Gender and Development Studies, University of the West Indies, Cave Hill, Barbados.

________. 1985b. "Resolution #7 Original Motion, Middle East". The Dame Nita Barrow Collection. Centre for Gender and Development Studies, University of the West Indies, Cave Hill, Barbados.

YWCA World Council. 1975. "West Indian for New World YWCA President". Statement of the World YWCA Council meeting, University of British Columbia, Vancouver, British Colombia, Canada, July. The Dame Nita Barrow Collection. Centre for Gender and Development Studies, University of the West Indies, Cave Hill, Barbados.

B. Official

Barbados. 1986a. *Address by Dame Nita Barrow to Committee of Experts to Monitor the UN Convention on the Elimination of All Forms of Discrimination Against Women (CEDAW).* New York: Permanent Mission of Barbados to the United Nations.

________. 1986b. *Statement by Her Excellency Dame Nita Barrow to the Fourteenth Special Session of the United Nations General Assembly (Question of Namibia) Wednesday 17 September.* New York: Permanent Mission of Barbados to the United Nations.

________. 1987a. *Statement by Her Excellency Dame Ruth Nita Barrow to the United Nations in the Debate on Item 82(e), the Environment.* New York: Permanent Mission of Barbados to the United Nations

________. 1987b. *Statement Delivered During the General Debate of the Forty-Second General Assembly of the United Nations.* New York: Permanent Mission of Barbados to the United Nations.

________. 1988a. *Statement Delivered in the General Debate of the Forty-Third Session of the General Assembly*. Barbados: Permanent Mission of Barbados to the United Nations.

________. 1988b. *Statement Delivered at the Resumed Session of the General Assembly of the United Nations on Item 136, Report of the Secretary General on the Decision of the Government of the United States to Close the Offices of the Permanent Observer Mission of the Palestine Liberation Organization to the United Nations, March 21, 1988*. New York: Permanent Mission of Barbados to the United Nations.

________. 1989. *Statement by Her Excellency Dame R.. Nita Barrow to the Thirty-Sixth Session of the Governing Council of the United Nations Development Programme, June 13*. New York: Permanent Mission of Barbados to the United Nations.

Barbados. N.d.a. *Barbados Development Plan, 1960–1965*. Barbados: Government Printing Office.

________. N.d.b. *Barbados Development Plan, 1973–77*. Barbados: Government Printing Office.

________. N.d.c. *A Ten Year Development Plan For Barbados: Sketch Plan For Development, 1946–1956*. Barbados: *Advocate*.

________. N.d.d. *Dame Nita Barrow: A Profile in Service*. New York: Permanent Mission of Barbados to the United Nations.

Earth Council. N.d. *Philosophy, Structure and Programme*. San Jose, Costa Rica: Earth Council.

Pan American Health Organization. 1968. "Report of the Seminar on Nursing Education, Georgetown, Guyana, 17–30 April 1968". *Reports on Nursing*, no. 8. Washington, DC: PAHO.

________. 1972. "Nursing Education: Report of Seminar on Nursing Education, Port of Spain, Trinidad, 6th to 17th September, 1971". *Reports on Nursing*, no. 15. Washington, DC: PAHO.

________. 1980. *Health For All by the Year 2000: Strategies*. Official Document, no. 173. Washington, DC: PAHO.

________. 1983. *Women in Health and Development*. Scientific Publication, no. 448. Washington DC: PAHO.

Panos Institute and CANARI. 1994. *Community and the Environment: Lessons From the Caribbean – Community Participation in St Lucia*. Washington, DC: Panos Institute.

United Kingdom. Colonial Office. 1945. West India Royal Commission, 1938–39. *West India Royal Commission Report*. London: HMSO.

________. Colonial Office. 1947. *Development and Welfare in the West Indies, 1945–1946*. London: HMSO.

________. Colonial Office. 1950. *Development and Welfare in the West Indies, 1947–1949*. London: HMSO.

________. Colonial Office. 1951. *Development and Welfare in the West Indies, 1950*. London: HMSO.

_______. Colonial Office. 1952. *Development and Welfare in the West Indies, 1951.* London: HMSO.

United Nations. 1986. *Everyone's United Nations.* New York: United Nations.

_______. 1990. *Human Development Report.* New York: Oxford University Press.

_______. 1994. *Statement by the Group of Eminent Persons on the Sustainable Development of Small Island Developing States, Bridgetown, Barbados 21–22 April, 1994.* New York: United Nations.

_______. 1996. Department of Public Information. *The Beijing Declaration and the Platform of Action, Fourth World Conference on Women, Beijing, China, 4–5 September 1995.* New York: United Nations Department of Public Information.

United States Agency for International Development (USAID). 1978. *Report on the Status of Women in Development.* Washington DC: USAID.

West Indian Commission. 1992. *Time for Action: The Report of the West Indian Commission.* Christ Church, Barbados: The West Indian Commission.

World Bank. 1979. *Recognizing the "Invisible" Woman in Development.* Washington, DC: World Bank.

_______. 1989. *Women in Development: Issues for Economic and Sector Analysis.* Policy, Planning and Research Working Paper, 269. Washington, DC: World Bank.

_______. 1990. *Women in Development: A Progress Report on the World Bank Initiative.* Washington, DC: World Bank.

World Commission on Environment and Development. 1987. *Our Common Future.* Oxford: Oxford University Press.

World Health Organization. 1994. *Progress in Human Reproduction Research*, no. 30. Washington, DC: WHO.

World Resources Institute. 1995. *International Perspectives on Sustainability.* Washington, DC: World Resources Institute.

II. Secondary Sources

A. Books

Adam, Heribert, and Kogila Moodley. 1993. *The Negotiated Revolution: Society and Politics in Post-Apartheid South Africa.* Johannesburg: Jonathan Ball.

Adams, W. M. 1990. *Green Development: Environment and Sustainability in the Third World.* London: Routledge.

Angelou, Maya. 1994. *Wouldn't Take Nothing for My Journey Now.* New York: Bantam Books.

Antrobus, Peggy. 1990. *Women, Health and Development.* Trinidad and Tobago: PAHO/WHO.

Baly, Monica E. 1995. *Nursing and Social Change.* 3d ed. London: Routledge.

Barriteau, Eudine. 2001. *The Political Economy of Gender in the Twentieth Century Caribbean.* London and New York: Macmillan and St Martin's.

Barrow, Nita. 1989. *Some Issues on the Global Agenda of the 1990s.* Distinguished Lecturer Series. St Augustine, Trinidad: Institute of International Relations, University of the West Indies.

Beckles, Hilary. 1988. *Afro-Caribbean Women and Resistance to Slavery in Barbados.* London: Karnak House.

________. 1989. *Natural Rebels: A Social History of Enslaved Black Women in Barbados.* London: Zed Books.

________. 1990. *A History of Barbados: From Amerindian Settlement to Nation-State.* Cambridge: Cambridge University Press.

Benbow, Colin H. 1994. *Gladys Morrell and the Women's Movement in Bermuda.* Bermuda: Writer's Machine.

Blackman, Francis. 1995. *Dame Nita: Caribbean Woman, World Citizen.* Kingston, Jamaica: Ian Randle.

Bolland, O. Nigel. 1955. *On the March: Labour Rebellions in the British Caribbean, 1934–39.* Kingston, Jamaica: Ian Randle.

Boserup, E. 1970. *Woman's Role in Economic Development.* New York: St Martin's and George Allen and Unwin.

Boutros-Ghali, Boutros. 1992. *An Agenda for Peace: Preventive Diplomacy, Peacemaking and Peace-Keeping. Report of the Secretary-General Pursuant to the Statement Adopted by the Summit Meeting of the Security Council on 3 January 1992.* New York: United Nations.

Bowden, Muriel. 1965. *A Reader's Guide to Geoffrey Chaucer.* London: Thomas V. Hudson.

Boyd, Nancy. 1986. *Emissaries: The Overseas Work of the American YWCA 1895–1970.* New York: Women's Press.

Brasileiro, Ana Maria, ed. 1996. *Women's Leadership in a Changing World: Reflecting on Experience in Latin America and the Caribbean.* New York: UNIFEM.

Browne, G. Orde. 1939. *Labour Conditions in the British West Indies.* London: HMSO.

Cantor, Dorothy W., Toni Barney, with Jane Stoess. 1992. *Women in Public Power: The Secrets of Leadership.* Boston: Houghton Mifflin.

Caribbean Law Institute. 1992. *Environmental Laws of the Commonwealth Caribbean: An Analysis and Needs Assessment.* Cave Hill, Barbados: Caribbean Law Institute, University of the West Indies.

Charlton, Sue Ellen M. 1984. *Women in Third World Development.* Boulder: Westview Press.

Cole, Joyce. 1982. *Women and Education in the Caribbean.* Cave Hill, Barbados: Institute of Social and Economic Research (Eastern Caribbean), University of the West Indies.

Commission on Health Research for Development. 1990. *Health Research: Essential Link to Equity in Development*. Oxford: Oxford University Press.

Commonwealth Group of Eminent Persons. 1986. *Mission to South Africa: The Commonwealth Report*. Harmondsworth: Penguin.

Constantine, S. 1984. *The Making of British Colonial Development Policy, 1914–1940*. London: Macmillan.

Dawes, R. T., ed. 1985. *Chaucer: The Prologue to the Canterbury Tales*. London: Harrap.

Fanon, Frantz. 1970. *Toward the African Revolution*. London: Pelican.

Ferguson, Kathy Ann. 1984. *The Feminist Case Against Bureaucracy*. Philadelphia: Temple University Press.

Folbre, Nancy. 1994. *Who Pays For the Kids?: Economics and the Structures of Constraint*. London: Routledge.

Friedman, Steven, ed. 1993. *The Long Journey: South Africa's Quest for a Negotiated Settlement*. Johannesburg: Ravan Press.

Gill, Margaret, and Joycelin Massiah. 1986. *Women Work and Development*. Cave Hill, Barbados: Institute of Social and Economic Research (Eastern Caribbean), University of the West Indies.

Golding, John. 1994. *Ascent to Mona: As Illustrated by a Short History of the Jamaican Medical Care: With an Account of the Beginning of the Faculty of Medicine University of the West Indies*. Kingston, Jamaica: Canoe Press.

Haniff, Nesha Z. 1988. *Blaze a Fire: Significant Contributions of Caribbean Women*. Toronto: Sister Vision.

Haq, Mahbub ul. 1990. *Reflections on Human Development*. New York: Oxford University Press.

Head, Ivan L. 1991. *On a Hinge of History*. Toronto, Ontario: University of Toronto Press.

Henry, Mervyn U. 1987. *Health Situation Analysis, Barbados*. Barbados: PAHO.

Hoyos, F. A. 1972. *Builders of Barbados*. London: Macmillan Educational.

________. 1978. *Barbados: A History From the Amerindians to Independence*. London: Macmillan Caribbean.

Huntley, Eric. 1993. *Two Lives: Florence Nightingale and Mary Seacole*. London: Bogle-L'Ouverture Press.

Huntley, Brian J., Roy Siegfried and Clem Sunter, eds. 1989. *South African Environments into the Twenty-first Century*. Tafelberg: Human and Rousseau.

Jain, Devaki. "Nuancing Globalisation, or Mainstreaming the Downstream, or Reforming Reform, As You Like It. Caribbean Women: Catalysts for Change". Lecture delivered at The University of the West Indies, Cave Hill, Barbados, 12 November 1999. The Centre for Gender and Development Studies, University of the West Indies, Cave Hill, Barbados.

Jayawardena, Kumari. 1986. *Feminism and Naturalism in the Third World*. London: Zed Books.

Jones, Kathleen B. 1993. *Compassionate Authority: Democracy and the Representation of Women*. London: Routledge.

Karl, Marilee. 1995. *Women and Empowerment: Participation and Decision Making*. London: Zed Books.

Kelly, Deirdre. 1987. *Hard Work Hard Choices: A Survey of Women in St Lucia's Export Oriented Electronic Factories*. Occasional Paper, no. 20. Cave Hill, Barbados: Institute of Social and Economic Research (Eastern Caribbean), University of the West Indies.

Leo-Rhynie, Elsa, Barbara Bailey, and Christine Barrow, eds. 1997. *Gender, A Caribbean Multi-Disciplinary Perspective*. Kingston, Jamaica: Ian Randle.

Lewis, W. Arthur. 1939. *Labour in the West Indies: The Birth of a Workers' Movement*. London: Victor Gollancz.

Lodge, Tom, and Bill Nasson. 1992. *All, Here, and Now: Black Politics in South Africa in the 1980s*. London: Hurst.

Macmillan, W. M. 1935. *Warning From the West Indies: A Tract for Africa and the Empire*. London: Faber.

Manganyi, N. Chabani, and Andre du Toit, eds. 1990. *Political Violence and the Struggle in South Africa*. London: Macmillan.

Manley, Michael. 1974. *The Politics of Change: A Jamaican Testament*. London: Andre Deutsch.

Manning, N., and C. Ungerson. 1990. *Social Policy Review, 1989–90*. Essex: Longman.

Marchand, Marianne H., and Jane L. Parpart, eds. 1995. *Feminism Postmodernism Development*. London: Routledge.

Martin, Tony. 1988. *Amy Ashwood Garvey: Pan-Africanist, Feminist and Wife No. 1*. Dover, Mass.: Majority Press.

Marx, Karl. 1967. *Capital: A Critique of Political Economy*. Vol. 1, *The Process of Capitalist Production*, edited by Frederick Engels. New York: International Publishers.

McGlen, Nancy E., and Meredith Reid Sarkees. 1993. *Women in Foreign Policy: The Insiders*. London: Routledge.

Meredith, Martin. 1987. *South Africa: Time of Agony, Time of Destiny: The Upsurge of Popular Protest*. London: Verso.

Mernissi, F. 1975. *Beyond the Veil: Male and Female Dynamics in Modern Muslim Society*. Cambridge, Mass.: Schenkman. Rev. ed. 1987, Bloomington: Indiana University Press.

Mohammed, Patricia, and Catherine Shepherd. 1988. *Gender in Caribbean Development*. Barbados: Women and Development Studies, University of the West Indies.

Mohanty, C., A. Russo, and L. Torres, eds. 1991. *Third World Women and the Politics of Feminism*. Bloomington: Indiana University Press.

Mokonyane, Dan. 1994. *The Big Sellout by the Communist Party of South Africa and the African National Congress: Recent Developments in South Africa and the Eclipse of the Revolutionary Perspective*. London: Nakong Ya Rena.

Momsen, Janet. 1991. *Women and Development in the Third World.* London: Routledge.

________, ed. 1993. *Women and Change in the Caribbean: A Pan-Caribbean Perspective.* Kingston, Jamaica: Ian Randle.

Mordecai, Pamela. 1989. *Journey Poem.* Kingston, Jamaica: Sandberry Press.

Moser, C. O. N. 1993. *Gender Planning and Development.* London: Routledge.

Munroe, Trevor. 1972. *The Politics of Constitutional Decolonisation: Jamaica, 1944–1962.* Kingston, Jamaica: Institute of Social and Economic Studies, University of the West Indies.

Nzomo, M. 1992. *Women in Politics.* Association of African Women for Research and Development Working Paper, 2. Nairobi: AAWORD.

Ohlson, Thomas, Stephen John Stedman, and Robert Davies. 1994. *The News Is Not Yet Born: Conflict Resolution in Southern Africa.* Washington, DC: Brookings Institution.

Overholt, C., M. Anderson, and J. Austin, eds. 1985. *Gender Roles in Development Projects.* West Hartford, CT: Kumarian Press.

Parpart, Jane. 1989. *Women and Development in Africa.* Lanham, Maryland: University Press of America.

Poovey, Mary. 1988. *Uneven Developments: The Ideological Work of Gender in Mid-Victorian England.* Chicago: University of Chicago Press.

Post, Ken. 1981. *Strike the Iron: A Colony at War: Jamaica 1939–45*, 2 vols. New Jersey: Humanities Press.

Reddock, Rhoda. 1988. *Elma Francois: The NWCSA and the Worker's Struggle for Change in the Caribbean.* London: New Beacon Books.

________. 1994. *Women, Labour and Politics in Trinidad and Tobago: A History.* Kingston, Jamaica: Ian Randle.

Rice, Anna. 1947. *A History of the World's Young Women's Christian Association.* New York: Woman's Press.

Sen, G., and C. Grown. 1987. *Development, Crises, and Alternative Visions: Third World Women's Perspectives.* New York: Monthly Review Press.

Seymour-Jones, Carole. 1994. *Journey of Faith: The History of the World YWCA, 1945–1994.* London: Allison and Busby.

Shepherd, Verene, Bridget Brereton and Barbara Bailey, eds. 1995. *Engendering Caribbean History: Caribbean Women in Historical Perspective.* Kingston: Ian Randle.

Smith, M. G. 1984. *Culture, Race and Class in the Commonwealth Caribbean.* Kingston, Jamaica: Department of Extra-Mural Studies, University of the West Indies.

Sparr, Pamela. 1994. *Mortgaging Women's Lives: Feminist Critiques of Structural Adjustment.* London: Zed Books.

Spencer, Donald S. 1988. *The Carter Implosion: Jimmy Carter and the Amateur Style of Diplomacy.* New York: Praeger Publishers.

Swaby, Gertrude. N.d. *The Profession of Nursing: A Brief Historical Survey With Special Reference to Jamaica and the Caribbean.* Kingston: Stephenson's.

Tinker, I., ed. 1990. *Persistent Inequalities: Women and World Development*. Oxford: Oxford University Press.

Tinker, I., and M. Bramsen. 1976. *Women and World Development*. Washington, DC: Overseas Development Council.

Turshen, Meredeth. 1989. *The Politics of Public Health*. London: Zed Books.

Walters, Ena. 1995. *Nursing: A History From the Late Eighteenth–Late Twentieth Century Barbados*. N.p.: Ena Walters.

Ward, Kathryn, ed. 1990. *Women Workers and Global Restructuring*. Ithaca, New York: Cornell University International Relations Press.

Waring, Marilyn. 1990. *If Women Counted: A New Feminist Economics*. San Francisco: Harper.

Wieringa, Saskia, ed. 1995. *Subversive Women: Women's Movements in Africa, Asia, Latin America and the Caribbean*. New Delhi: Kali for Women.

B. Articles, Chapters in Books

"Barbados' Dame Barrow Dedicated to Health and H.R". 1987. *Diplomatic World Bulletin*, 16–23 November, 1.

"The Dame Moves Out Front". 1988. *Trinidad and Tobago Review*. March: 22.

Aksayan, Secil. 1994. "Education of Nurses for Primary Health Care". *World Health Forum: International Journal of Health Development* 15, no. 2: 150–52.

Anglin-Brown, Blossom. 1994. "Regional Cooperation in Health Care: The Example of the University of the West Indies". *Courier*, no. 147 (September–October): 92–94.

Baksh-Sooden, Rawwida. 1994. "Women Must Take a Stand on Hijab Issue". *Sunday Express* (Trinidad), 18 September, 42–43.

Barriteau, Eudine. 1995. "Socialist Feminist Theory and Caribbean Women: Transcending Dualisms". *Social and Economic Studies* 44, nos. 2–3: 25–63.

________. 1996. "A Feminist Perspective on Structural Adjustment Policies in the Caribbean". *National Women's Studies Association Journal* 8, no. 1 (Spring): 142–56.

________. 1998. "Theorizing Gender Systems and the Project of Modernity in the Twentieth-Century Caribbean". *Feminist Review*, no. 59 (Summer): 186–210.

Barrow, Nita. 1968. "The Role of the Nurse in the Changing Caribbean". *Jamaican Nurse* 25, nos. 1, 2 and 3 (August): 15–16.

Beckley, S. 1989. "Women As Agents/Recipients of Development Assistance: The Sierra Leone Case". In *Women As Agents and Beneficiaries of Development Assistance*. Occasional Paper Series, 4. Dakar, Senegal: Association of African Women for Research and Development.

Beinart, William. 1992. "Political and Collective Violence in Southern African Studies". *Journal of Southern African Studies* 18, no. 3: 455–86.

Beneria, L., and G. Sen. 1981. "Accumulation, Reproduction and Women's Role in Economic Development: Boserup Revisted". *SIGNS* 7: 279–98.

Bercovitch, Jacob, and Jeffrey Langley. 1992. "The Nature of the Dispute and the Effectiveness of International Mediation". *Journal of Conflict Resolution* 37, no. 4: 670–91.

Bolland, O. Nigel. 1988. "The Labour Movement and the Genesis of Modern Politics in Belize". In *Labour in the Caribbean*, edited by Malcolm Cross and Gad Heuman, 258–84. London: Macmillan.

Brasileiro, Ana Maria, and Karen Judd. 1996. "Introduction: Can Women Change the World?" In *Women's Leadership in a Changing World: Reflecting on Experience in Latin America and the Caribbean*, edited by Ana Maria Brasileiro, 3–16. New York: UNIFEM.

Brathwaite, Kamau. 1996. "A Great River and Another Tributary . . . ". *Barbados Advocate*. 5 January.

Brodber, Erna. 1986. "The Pioneering Miss Bailey: Erna Brodber Talks to Amy Bailey". *Jamaica Journal* 19, no. 2: 9–14.

Brown, Wayne. 1990. "Diaries of Edna Manley: Simply a Woman of Character". *Caribbean Affairs* 31, no. 1: 135–45.

Cave, Anthony. 1995. "Dame Nita: Towering and Tireless". *Daily Nation* (Barbados), 28 December, 18.

Chowdhry, Geeta. 1995. "Engendering Development? Women in Development (WID) in International Development Regimes". In *Feminism Postmodernism Development*, edited by Marianne H. Marchand and Jane L. Parpart, 26–41. London: Routledge.

Cobley, Alan. 1989. "Apartheid, Sanctions and Sport". *Bulletin of Eastern Caribbean Affairs* 15, nos. 2–3: 23–29.

Cumberbatch, Janice. 1994. "CANARI Assists Sustainability of the Caribbean". *Caribbean Contact*, May, 19.

Cumper, Gloria. 1990. "Neglecting Legal Status in Health Planning: Nurse Practitioners in Jamaica". *Health Policy and Planning, a Journal on Health and Development* 1, no. 1: 30–36.

de Monterrossa, Esperanza, Ilta Lange, and Roseni Rosangela Chompre. 1990. "Political Changes for Nursing in Latin America: The Next Century". In *Nursing Leadership Global Strategies: International Nursing Development for the Twenty-first Century*, edited by Claire M. Fagin, 221–27. New York: National League For Nursing.

Degenaar, Johan. 1990. "The Concept of Violence". In *Political Violence and the Struggle in South Africa*, edited by N. Chabani Manganyi and Andre du Toit, 70–86. London: Macmillan.

French, Joan. 1995. "Women and Colonial Policy in Jamaica After the 1938 Uprising". In *Subversive Women: Women's Movements in Africa, Asia, Latin America and the Caribbean*, edited by Saskia Wieringa, 121–46. New Delhi: Kali for Women.

Future Centre Trust. 1996."Introducing the Future Centre Trust". *Newsletter of Friends of the Future Centre Trust* 1 (June): 1.

Goetz, Ann Marie. 1991. "Feminism and the Limits of the Claim to Know: Contradictions in the Feminist Approach to Women in Development". In *Gender and International Relations*, edited by R. Grant and K. Newland, 477–96. Bloomington: Indiana University Press.

_______. 1995. "Institutionalising Women's Interests and Gender-Sensitive Accountability". *IDS Bulletin* 26, no. 3 (July): 1–10.

Hart, Richard. 1993. "The Labour Rebellions of the 1930s". In *Caribbean Freedom: Economy and Society From Emancipation to Present: A Student Reader*, edited by Hilary Beckles and Verene Shepherd, 370–75. Kingston, Jamaica: Ian Randle.

Henry-Wilson, Maxine. 1989. "The Status of the Jamaican Woman, 1962 to the Present". In *Jamaica in Independence: Essays on the Early Years*, edited by Rex Nettleford, 229–53. Kingston, Jamaica: Heinemann Caribbean.

Johnson, Howard. 1977. "The West Indies and the Conversion of the British Official Classes to the Development Idea". *Journal of Commonwealth and Comparative Politics* 15, no. 1: 55–83.

_______. 1978. "The Political Uses of Commissions of Enquiry (1): The Imperial-West Indies Contexts – The Forster and Moyne Commissions". *Social and Economic Studies* 27, no. 3: 256–83.

Mack, Raymond W. 1967. "Race, Class and Power in Barbados". In *The Democratic Revolution in the West Indies*, edited by Wendell Bell, 140–64. Cambridge, Mass.: Schenkman.

Mair, Lucille. 1988. "Foreword". In *Gender in Caribbean Development*, edited by Patricia Mohammed and Catherine Shepherd. Cave Hill, Barbados: Women and Development Studies, University of the West Indies.

Marks, Shula, and Neil Anderson. 1990. "The Epidemiology and Culture of Violence". In *Political Violence and the Struggle in South Africa*, edited by N. Chabani Manganyi and Andre du Toit, 29–69. London: Macmillan.

Maslow, A. 1943. "A Theory of Human Motivation". *Psychological Review* 50: 370–96.

Massiah, Joycelin. 1993. "Living with Dignity: Barbadian Women in the Work Force". In *Emancipation IV, Series of Lectures to Commemorate the 150th Anniversary of Emancipation*, edited by Woodville Marshall, 1–28. Mona, Jamaica: Canoe Press.

Mayers, Janice. 1995. "Access to Secondary Education for Girls in Barbados, 1907–43: A Preliminary Analysis". In *Engendering History: Caribbean Women in Historical Perspective*, edited by Verene Shepherd, Bridget Brereton, and Barbara Bailey, 258–78. Kingston, Jamaica: Ian Randle.

Mbilinyi, M. 1989. "I'd Have Been a Man: Politics and the Labour Process in Producing Personal Narratives". In *Interpreting Women's Lives: Feminist Theory and Personal Narratives*, edited by the Personal Narratives Group. Bloomington: Indiana University Press.

Momsen, Janet. 1988. "Gender Roles in Caribbean Agricultural Labour". In *Labour in the Caribbean*, edited by Malcolm Cross and Gad Heuman, 141–58. London: Macmillan.

Moser, C. O. N. 1989. "Gender Planning in the Third World: Meeting Practical and Strategic Gender Needs". *World Development* 17, no. 11: 1799–1825. Reprinted in R. Grant and K. Newland, eds. 1991. *Gender and International Relations*. Bloomington: Indiana University Press.

Nettleford, Rex. 1988. "The Dame Nita Affair: Of Commonsense and Cousinhood". *Money Index*, March, 19–20.

Nzomo, M. 1993. "Political and Legal Empowerment of Women in Post-Election Kenya". In *Empowering Kenyan Women*, edited by M. Nzomo. Nairobi: National Commission on the Status of Women Publication.

Papanek, H. 1977. "Development Planning for Women". *SIGNS* 3, no. 1: 14–21.

Parpart, Jane. 1993. "Who Is the 'Other'? A Post Modern Feminist Critique of Women and Development Theory and Practice". *Development and Change* 24, no. 3: 439–64.

Pohlmann, Lisa. 1995. "Ambivalence About Leadership in Women's Organizations: A Look at Bangladesh". *IDS Bulletin* 26, no. 3 (July): 117–24.

Post, Ken. 1969. "The Politics of Protest in Jamaica, 1938: Some Problems of Analysis and Conceptualisation". *Social and Economic Studies* 18, no. 4: 374–90.

Potter, Phillip. 1995. "Dame Nita: Shining Example". *Daily Nation* (Barbados), 20 December, 19.

Rai, Shirin M. 1995. "Women and Public Power: Women in the Indian Parliament". *IDS Bulletin* 26, no. 3 (July): 110–16.

Rathgeber, E. M. 1990. "WID, WAD, GAD: Trends in Research and Practice". *Journal of Developing Areas* 24, no. 4: 489–502.

Reddock, Rhoda. 1993. "Transformation in Needle Trades: Women in Government and Textiles Production in Early Twentieth Century Trinidad". In *Women and Change in the Caribbean: A Pan-Caribbean Perspective*, edited by Janet Momsen, 249–62. Kingston, Jamaica: Ian Randle.

Renard, Yves. 1991. "Institutional Challenges for Community-Based Management in the Caribbean". *Nature and Resources* 27, no. 4: 4–9.

Richardson, Bonham. 1992. "Depression Riots and the Calling of the 1897 West India Royal Commission". *NWIG* 66, no. 3: 169–71.

Rosener, Judy B. 1990. "Ways Women Lead". *Harvard Business Review*, November–December, 119–25.

Schreuder, Deryck. 1992. "The Commonwealth and Peacemaking in South Africa". In *Peace, Politics and Violence in the New South Africa*, edited by Norman Etherington, 73–101. London: Hans Zell.

Slutkin, Gary. 1993. "Can AIDS Prevention Move to Sufficient Scale?" *Network Family Health International* 13, no. 4 (May): 16–17.

St Pierre, Maurice. 1978. "The 1938 Jamaica Disturbance: A Portrait of Mass Reaction Against Colonialism". *Social and Economic Studies* 27, no. 2: 171–96.

Statham, Anne. 1987. "The Gender Model Revisited: Differences in the Management Styles of Men and Women". *Sex Roles* 16, nos. 7 & 8: 409–29.

Stewart, Sheelagh, and Jill Taylor. 1995. "Women Organizing Women: Doing it Backwards and in High Heels". *IDS Bulletin* 26, no. 3 (July): 79–85.

Stolberg, Claus. 1989. "British Colonial Policy and the Great Depression: The Case of Jamaica". *Journal of Caribbean History* 23, no. 2: 142–63.

Vassell, Linette. 1995. "Women of the Masses: Daphne Campbell and 'Left' Politics in Jamaica in the 1950s". In *Engendering History: Caribbean Women in Historical Perspective*, edited by Verene Shepherd, Bridget Brereton, and Barbara Bailey, 318–36. Kingston, Jamaica: Ian Randle.

Ward, Peter. 1987. "Reproduction of Social Inequality: Access to Health Services in Mexico City". *Health Policy and Planning* 2, no. 1: 44–57.

Theses, Unpublished Papers

Barriteau, Eudine. 1994. "Gender and Development Planning in the Post Colonial Caribbean: Female Entrepreneurs and the Barbadian State". Ph.D. dissertation, Howard University.

________. 1996. "Theorizing Gender Systems and the Project of Modernity in the Post Colonial Caribbean". Paper presented at the South to South Research Programme in History (SEPHIS) and the Indian Council of Historical Research Workshop, New Delhi, 5–8 February.

Country Women Association of Nigeria (COWAN). N.d. *Integrated Approach to Sustainable Development and Population Policy: A Community Point of View*. Nigeria: COWAN.

Cumberbatch, Janice. 1994. "Institutional Arrangements for Natural Area Management". A paper presented at the CEPAT Regional Course on Development and Management of Parks and Beaches, Dover Convention Centre, Barbados, 28 November–9 December.

Mair, Lucille. 1974. "A Historical Study of Women in Jamaica, 1655–1844". Ph.D. dissertation, University of the West Indies, Mona, Jamaica.

Mohammed, Patricia. 1994. "A Social History of Post-Migrant Indians in Trinidad from 1917–1947: A Gender Perspective". Ph.D. dissertation, Institute of Social Studies, The Hague.

Reddock, Rhoda. 1984. "Women, Labour and Struggle in Twentieth Century Trinidad and Tobago, 1898–1906". Ph.D. dissertation, The Hague, 1984.

Richards, Glen. 1987. "The Maddened Rabble: Labour Protest in St. Kitts, 1896–1935". Paper for the Society for Caribbean Studies, Hoddesdon.

Singh, Naresh. 1991. "Sustainable Development: Its Meaning for the Caribbean". Paper presented to the Association of Caribbean Economists, Santo Domingo, 16–20 July.

Vassell, Linette. 1993. "The Jamaica Federation of Women and Politics, 1944–50". Paper presented at the Twenty-fifth Conference of Caribbean Historians, University of the West Indies, Mona, Jamaica.

Contributors

Eudine Barriteau is Senior Lecturer and Director of the Centre for Gender and Development Studies, University of the West Indies, Cave Hill, Barbados. She is the author of *The Political Economy of Gender in the Twentieth Century Caribbean* (London: Macmillan; New York: St Martins, 2001). Her most recent publications include "Theorizing Gender Systems and the Project of Modernity in the Twentieth-Century Caribbean" (*Feminist Review*, no. 59 [1998]), and "Liberal Ideology and Contradictions in Caribbean Gender Systems" in *Gender Portraits: Essays on Gender Ideologies and Identities*, edited by Christine Barrow. She has published several articles on feminist theorizing and is currently coordinating three research projects that collectively examine Caribbean political economy and social change from the perspective of gender. She is the inaugural Dame Nita Barrow Women in Development Fellow, Ontario Institute for Studies in Education, University of Toronto (1997). (The University of Toronto established the fellowship to honour the memory of Nita Barrow, who pursued training there in 1943.) She founded the Women's Forum of Barbados in 1988.

Alan Cobley is Senior Lecturer in History and Dean of the Faculty of Humanities, University of the West Indies, Cave Hill, Barbados. His research interests are in the social and cultural history of South Africa, the comparative history of southern Africa and the Caribbean, and African and diasporic history. The author of many publications, Dr Cobley's most recent books are *The Rules of the Game: Struggles in Black Recreation and Social Welfare Policy in South Africa* and, co-edited with Glenford Howe, *The Caribbean AIDS Epidemic.*

Hilary McD. Beckles is Pro Vice Chancellor, Board for Undergraduate Studies and Professor of History at the University of the West Indies, Cave Hill, Barbados. He has a major research interest in gender in Caribbean slavery and has published several books and articles on the subject, including *Natural Rebels: A Social History of Enslaved Black Women in Barbados.*

Jeniphier Carnegie is a reference librarian at the Main Library, University of the West Indies, Cave Hill, Barbados. She has a Bachelor of Arts (Hons) degree in English from the University of the West Indies and a Bachelor of Library Science from the University of British Columbia, Vancouver. She has interests in the bibliography of creative West Indian literature and in gender studies. She has published *Critics on West Indian Literature: A Select Bibliography, 1979*, and the "Selected Bibliography of Criticism and Related Works" in *Out of the Kumbla: Women and Caribbean Literature*, edited by Carole Boyce Davies and Elaine Fido. Other bibliographic contributions include an annual listing in the *Journal of West Indian Literature* and "Selected Bibliography on the Works of Professor Elsa Goveia, Dr Walter Rodney and Dr Eric Williams" in the *Bulletin of Eastern Caribbean Affairs* (1982).

Janice Cumberbatch is currently reading for the Master of Philosophy/Doctor of Philosophy degree in Sociology at the University of the West Indies. She obtained a master's degree in Environmental Studies, York University, Toronto, Canada (1992) after successfully completing a Bachelor of Science degree in Applied Sociology at the University of the West Indies, Cave Hill, Barbados. She was a recipient of the Kellogg International Leadership Programme 1995–98. The scholarship is used to develop the leadership skills of the participants/fellows. She is a member of the Barbados National Trust and the Barbados Museum and Historical Society. She is also the secretary of the Barbados Association for Mentally Retarded Children. Her primary interest is in the area of the environment. She has written and published papers on environmental and social issues in the Commonwealth Caribbean.

Kathleen Drayton was educated at the Bishop Anstey High School in Trinidad from 1938 to 1949, and in 1950 proceeded to the University College of the West Indies, Mona, Jamaica, on a Trinidad Scholarship (Cipriani Memorial Scholarship). She was among the first group of Arts graduates in 1953 and then among the first group of students awarded Diplomas in Education from the University College of the West Indies in 1954. She taught in Edinburgh, Ghana, and Guyana before her appointment in 1972 to the Faculty of Arts, University of the West Indies, Cave Hill, Barbados. She was a member of the steering committee that set up the Women and Development Studies at the University of the West Indies and became the first Cave Hill Women and Development Studies Coordinator. She has published several articles in a variety of journals on education, gender and culture. She was Senior Lecturer in Education and Regional Coordinator of Women and Development Studies when she retired in September 1991. Her research interest is in the history of education for boys and girls in Barbados. She serves on a number of boards and committees in Barbados and also devotes time to the Barbados Association of Retired Persons, which she founded with eight others in 1995.

Margaret Gill is presently pursuing her Master of Philosophy/Doctor of Philosophy degree at the University of the West Indies, Cave Hill, Barbados, where she received her Master of Arts degree in 1996, and her Bachelor of Science degree in 1978. In 1983–84 she was the recipient of the Tinker Fellowship to the University of Florida, Gainesville, and the 1982–83 Inter-American Foundation Fellowship to the same university. She has received several other honours. She devotes her time to a number of organizations, including the Barbados Association of Literary Artists; Voices: Barbados Writers Collective; the Caribbean Association of Feminist Research and Action (CAFRA), for which she is the Barbados national representative; the University of the West Indies Women and Development Studies Group; and the Women's Forum of Barbados, of which she is a founding member. She has published several poems as well as academic work. Her current research interests are in nationhood and identity in Barbados and Bermuda, industrial relations in Barbados, and women and the informatics sector in Barbados.

Jo-Ann Granger is a librarian at the University of the West Indies, Cave Hill, Barbados, where her duties include cataloguing and the management of the main library's VTLS system. Her interests include computer applications for library services and functions. She is currently working on a bibliography on gender in the Commonwealth Caribbean.

Budd Hall is Chair, Department of Adult Education, Community Development and Counselling Psychology, Ontario Institute for Studies in Education (OISE), University of Toronto, and coordinator of the Dame Nita Barrow Distinguished Lecture Series at the University of Toronto, Dame Nita's alma mater.

Sheila Stuart is a sociologist with an interest in women and development issues. She worked for ten years with the Women and Development Unit (WAND), which is part of the outreach programme of the School of Continuing Studies, University of the West Indies. WAND works with women's groups and organizations throughout the Caribbean, although most of its programmes are concentrated within the Eastern Caribbean. In 1994, Ms Stuart was seconded from WAND to work with the Institute of Social and Economic Research (Eastern Caribbean), University of the West Indies, Cave Hill, Barbados, on a research project on women's reproductive health in the Caribbean. The aim of the project was to identify the factors that lead to the formation of attitudes and values in young people and later influence their reproductive behaviour and, therefore, health outcomes.

Marjorie Thorpe is a consultant with the College of Science, Technology and Applied Arts of Trinidad and Tobago, with responsibility for establishing the division of Liberal Arts and Human Services. She has held several posts in the Faculty of Arts and General Studies at the University of the West Indies, St

Augustine, Trinidad and Tobago. Dr Thorpe collaborated with colleagues in establishing Women and Development Studies at the University of the West Indies, and she served as the first coordinator of the programme at the St Augustine campus. She has also had many apppointments within the United Nations and UN organizations. Dr Thorpe's publications include articles, conference papers, and addresses on issues related to women in literature, gender and development, and sustainable human development.